DUTY

DUTY

The True Story of

W/O Norman Cyril Jackson VC

by

David Jackson

www.bombercommandbooks.co.uk

First published 2025 by Aviation Books Ltd., Merthyr Tydfil, CF47 8RY, United Kingdom.

Copyright © 2025 David Jackson

The right of David Jackson to be identified as Author of this work is asserted by him in accordance with the Copyright, Designs and Patents Act 1988.

All rights reserved. No part of this publication may be reproduced, stored in a retrieval system, transmitted in any form or by any means, electronic, mechanical or photocopied, recorded or otherwise, without the written permission of the copyright owners.

The information in this book has been researched, compiled and written by its author, who has made every effort to ensure the accuracy of the information contained in it. The author will not be liable for any damage caused, or alleged to be caused, by any information contained in this book. E. and O.E. The author has made all reasonable efforts to contact copyright-holders for permission and apologises for any omissions or errors in the form of credits given. Corrections may be made to future printings.

Please contact the publishers by email: aviationbooksuk@gmail.com with any concerns.

Cover design: Topics - The Creative Partnership www.topicsdesign.co.uk

A CIP catalogue reference for this book is available from the British Library.

ISBN 9781915335555

Norman Cyril Jackson

Contents

Foreword by Lord Ashcroft KCMG PC 10
Introduction 12
Part One: Formative Years 19
Childhood 20
Joining Up 32
Sunderlands in Scotland 37
Flight Engineer 47
'For Freedom' 54
Part Two: Operations 73
Operation 1: Leverkusen, 22nd / 23rd August 1943 81
Operation 2: Nuremberg, 27th / 28th August 1943 86
Operation 3: Münchengladbach / Rheydt, 30th / 31st August 1943 90
Operation 4: Berlin, 3rd / 4th September 1943 93
Operation 5: Ludwigshafen-Mannheim, 5th / 6th September 1943 98
Operation 6: Hagen, 1st / 2nd October 1943 102
Operation 7: Munich, 2nd / 3rd October 1943 105
Operation 8: Stuttgart, 7th / 8th October 1943 108
Operation 9: Leipzig, 20th / 21st October 1943 111
Operation 10: Modane, 10th / 11th November 1943 115
Operation 11: Berlin, 18th / 19th November 1943 118
Operation 12: Berlin, 22nd / 23rd November 1943 124
Operation 13: Berlin, 26th / 27th November 1943 128
Operation 14: Berlin, 2nd / 3rd December 1943 132
Operation 15: Berlin, 20th January 1944 144

Operation 16: Magdeburg, 21st / 22nd January 1944 147
Operation 17: Berlin, 27th / 28th January 1944 150
Operation 18: Berlin, 29th January 1944 153
Operation 19: Berlin, 30th January 1944 156
Operation 20: Berlin, 15th /16th February 1944 159
Operation 21: Leipzig, 19th / 20th February 1944 163
Operation 22: Stuttgart, 20th / 21st February 1944 167
Operation 23: Stuttgart, 1st / 2nd March 1944 170
Operation 24: Clermont-Ferrand, 16th /17th March 1944 174
Operation 25: Frankfurt, 18th /19th March 1944 177
Operation 26: Stettin Bay, Swinemunde, 18th / 19th April 1944 198
Operation 27: La Chapelle, 20th / 21st April 1944 202
Operation 28: Brunswick, 22nd / 23rd April 1944 204
Operation 29: Munich, 24th / 25th April 1944 207
Operation 30: Schweinfurt, 26th April 1944 211
Part Three: 'The Most Conspicuous Bravery' 219
"Terror Flieger!" 231
Part Four: Aftermath 245
Return of a Modest Hero 246
ME669: After the Attack 251
Following On 255
End Note 258
Morality of the Bombing Campaign 260
Appendix 1: Operations Record of F/Sgt. Norman Cyril Jackson 272
Appendix 2: Citation for W/O Norman Cyril Jackson, VC 273
Appendix 3: Citation for F/Sgt. Frank Higgins 274
Appendix 4: POW Questionnaire – Norman Jackson 276

Appendix 5: POW Questionnaire – Maurice Toft 279
Appendix 6: POW Questionnaire – Frank Higgins 282
Appendix 7: POW Questionnaire - Ernest Sandelands..................... 285
Appendix 8: POW Questionnaire – Walter Smith 288
Appendix 9: 'Johnny' Johnson's Letters Home............................. 289
Appendix 10: Letter to Cliff Johnson from Ernest Sandelands. 315
Appendix 11: Air Ministry Letter to Johnny's Father. 321
Appendix 12: Letter from Miff to Johnny's Father. 323
Appendix 13: 1943 Christmas Card from Miff................................ 325
About The Author 327

Foreword by Lord Ashcroft KCMG PC

Lord Ashcroft's account in the Sunday Telegraph was closest to the truth.

As the humble custodian of more than 200 Victoria Crosses amassed over a period of almost 40 years, I am sometimes asked which is my favourite medal group. I feel uncomfortable answering the question directly because it is a bit like a parent being asked to identify his, or her, favourite child. The truth is that I treasure each and every one of my medal groups: they are special because they are the tangible mementoes of an individual's service and bravery. Furthermore, behind each VC medal group lies a wonderful story of courage in the presence of the enemy.

However, as a military historian and medal collector, I am willing to say that I consider the actions of Flight Sergeant – later Warrant Officer – Norman Cyril Jackson in the skies above Germany more than 80 years ago to be arguably the greatest single act of gallantry in the entire history of the medal. I don't say this lightly given the extraordinary examples of valour displayed by VC recipients over a period of more than 170 years and dating back to the early days of the Crimean War.

I was therefore delighted to learn relatively recently that David Jackson, one of Norman Jackson's seven children, had written a biography of his late father. I was even more privileged when David, who had kindly once helped me research a newspaper article on his father, asked me to write the Foreword to his book.

There is no need for a 'spoiler alert' in this Foreword because it would be wrong of me to reveal exactly what the then 25-year-old Flight Sergeant Jackson did when his Lancaster aircraft was hit and caught fire after being attacked by a German nightfighter while on a bombing raid to Schweinfurt, Germany, in April 1944. Those brave actions, which took place at some 200 miles per hour and at around 20,000 feet, are well documented in this book.

What I will say, however, is that David Jackson has researched his father's life and military career with great determination, devotion and attention to detail. The result is a hugely affectionate biography of a man who was much more than simply a courageous airman: he was a conscientious worker, a dedicated husband and a much-loved father.

Anyone wanting to pay their wider respects to the men of Bomber Command should visit the Bomber Command Memorial in Green Park, central London, which was unveiled by Queen Elizabeth II in 2012. The memorial is a fitting tribute to the Bomber Command crews who lost their lives during the Second World War. The average age of the aircrew was just 22 and the youngest were only 18. Some three out of every five airmen became casualties and statistics tell their own chilling story: 55,573 men were killed, 8,403 were wounded and 9,838 were captured and held as Prisoners of War.

This splendid biography of Warrant Officer Norman Jackson VC also helps preserve the memory of the men of Bomber Command. I congratulate David Jackson on a labour of love and for taking such care to detail the life of a quite exceptional man whose bravery must never – and will never – be forgotten.

Lord Ashcroft KCMG PC is an international businessman, philanthropist, author and pollster. For more information on his work, visit lordashcroft.com. Follow him on X/Facebook @LordAshcroft.

Introduction

This is a story of a time in our history that should never be forgotten. A time when the world in which we live faced an evil that threatened to change the world and destroy freedom. It is a story of young men who came together to serve their nation in its quest to preserve the freedom of the world.

This book does not glorify war, it is about duty. The story is of course primarily about my father, Norman Cyril Jackson, but it is also about the other young men that he served alongside, and their courage. They were mostly, like my father, not regular members of the Royal Air Force but came together as volunteers. They were carpenters, engineers, school teachers, plumbers, bank clerks, managers, just ordinary people. Facing danger night after night as aircrew in Bomber Command, knowing full well that their chances of survival were the lowest among any of the armed services, underlines the outstanding courage of these men. None of them, including their comrades who paid the ultimate price, received recognition at the end of the war for their service and sacrifice.

I have felt from a very young age that an accurate account of my father's action should be written and published, to put the record straight on an act of gallantry that would for most people be beyond comprehension. It is dedicated not only to him, but the members of Bomber Command aircrew, all volunteers, along with the ground crew, all of whom were such an important part of his young life, and following the end of the war, Bomber Command was almost forgotten, intentionally, by the government of the day, despite their courageous service to this nation during its hour of need and in helping to bring humanity back from the edge of destruction.

This book tells the story of my father's early life through to his leaving the Royal Air Force in 1946. It does so factually, with events as they happened, and details the operations that he flew as a member of 106 Squadron including his thirtieth operation in April 1944 which led to him being awarded the Victoria Cross. It also includes details of the day-to-day work of 106 Squadron including the constant training and the life of the airmen who were almost always on duty. In doing so, it provides the context for my father's time on the squadron until his abrupt relocation to Germany.

Much has been written in books, newspapers, magazines, and on the internet over the years about my father's actions on the night of 26/27th April 1944. Without exception these accounts either contain inaccuracies or are not the full story. The citation for the award of Norman's Victoria Cross itself carries inaccuracies that, at the time it was published in The London Gazette in 1945, the crew wanted changed to represent what they had said when being interviewed regarding the action.

My father told them it was of no concern to him, as all he wanted to do was move forward with his life; what happened in the past, should stay in the past. He had been hospitalised for ten long months because of this action and, as had his crewmates, spent time in a prisoner of war camp. The war in Europe was now over, Germany had been defeated, and people wanted to forget the horrors and move on. He stressed that he had only been doing his job and his duty. Tens of thousands of their fellow Bomber Command aircrew members had paid the ultimate price, and it seemed plainly wrong to him that all this attention was being focused on him. As far as he was concerned, acts of so-called heroism had happened every day during the war, and he was genuinely embarrassed by all the attention.

According to Squadron records the story of my father's heroism was revealed when the surviving members of the crew were debriefed as normal when returning from captivity, and all gave the same account. The records disclose that in his own debrief Norman said absolutely nothing about the incident. Whilst he might have wanted the whole matter forgotten, others took a very different view.

His crewmates were concerned that the official citation seemed to be a complete distortion of what they had said when interviewed. The only part of the citation that was taken from their reports was the statement that his parachute deployed accidentally in the cockpit. That had certainly been the perception of those who witnessed that part of the incident but it had been dark in the cockpit so they had been unaware that the deployment of the parachute was as all part of Norman's plan. The rest of the citation detailed little of what followed, other than the events following their evacuation of the aircraft. Ernest Sandelands, wireless operator in Norman's crew, recorded the whole incident in his diary which the author was shown by Ernest's son, Roy Sandelands[1]

The closest any of the reports on this action came to the actual truth was a full-page article in the Sunday Telegraph on Remembrance Sunday, 14th November 2021, written by Lord Michael Ashcroft, who is the owner of the largest collection of The Victoria Cross, the article was titled, *'Was this the bravest VC of them all?'*

As I grew up, I attended most of the Victoria Cross and George Cross functions with my parents at Buckingham Palace, Windsor Castle, Clarence House, and others. At these functions I met several, if not all, of the surviving recipients of the Victoria Cross. They all told me that they felt that my father's valiant act was the most incredible, greatest and most remarkable they knew of, and that he was the most deserving recipient of all of them. This was, I thought, an incredible statement for them to make. Without exception these men were all very humble. I had read about their exploits in books, and was completely in awe of them, yet when I was in a room with them, studying them as they moved from guest to guest, I realised that they, just like my father, were *'...all trying to do exactly the same thing, to look and be accepted as ordinary men, something of course that they are not.'*[2]

I had the pleasure of accompanying my parents Norman and Alma to Sir Arthur 'Bomber' Harris's 90th birthday celebrations in London. My father carried out his usual routine of refusing to put his medals on until he was well inside the building or even at the table. Sir Arthur Harris was at this time quite frail and in a wheelchair. When my father introduced me to him, Sir Arthur took my hand, looked me in the eye,

---

[1] Roy and the author first met in 2005 during the filming by a Canadian company for the Heroes with Wings series which was made for Channel Five.

[2] This comment was made by the then Prince of Wales, His Royal Highness, Prince Charles (now King Charles III).

pointed a finger at my father and said with emphasis, *"SPECIAL"*. I have never been quite sure if Sir Arthur was referring to my father's actions that led to him being awarded the Victoria Cross, or the fact that he was a member of aircrew in Bomber Command. One can only imagine how proud I felt at that moment and have done ever since.

Some books that I have read which include my father's story state that his action left him deeply religious. This impression came about after the war when being interviewed, he was asked whether God played a part with Bomber Command aircrew before an operation. He replied that no one prayed harder than he did, which was taken to show him to be deeply religious. Whilst my father had a faith he was not an avid church goer, and to label him as deeply religious would be an affront to those who are devout believers. He has also been described as suffering flashbacks to his action during the war, leading to deep depression; this I can also categorically deny. My father never dwelt on the past and was one of the humblest, most modest, and level-headed human beings I have ever encountered He had a wonderful sense of humour and would constantly be giving advice to his children saying, for example, that the three most important things in life are health, a sense of humour, and a little bit of initiative, in that order. He also urged us, *"If you cannot do someone a good service, do not do them a bad one."*

Air Chief Marshal Sir Arthur Harris, C-in-C Bomber Command

This account is related as my father told it to me and corroborated by the two members of his crew that I met when I was around twelve years of age, and as young boys generally are, interested in all things military. What you are about to read is the story of my father's early life, operational service, and the truth regarding his actions. I have always believed that the citation was not accurate, and there had been much more to the incident. It was only on questioning my father on many occasions, as children do, that the sequence of events became clear. Though I never used his given name to his face, for the rest of this book I use it for reasons of objectivity.

I am grateful to Simon Hepworth and Steve Smith of Aviation Books Ltd. for allowing me to use much information from Chris Ward's excellent 106 Squadron Profile. Simon and Steve also edited this book and provided much additional information from their extensive archive. Thanks also to Andy Jones, of Topics – The Creative Partnership, for his excellent cover for the book. I am also very grateful to the people who knew my father through his early years to adulthood, for access to their information and records, especially Barry Raymond who supplied the letters and many of the photos included in this book.

Above all, I must thank my partner Penelope for her forbearance, tolerance, patience and support over the past three years whilst this book has taken shape. I could not have completed the task without her.

David Jackson
May 2025

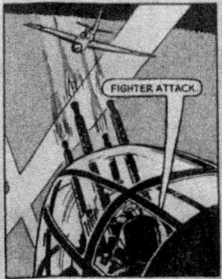

Norman's story became the stuff of legend for a new generation of youth.

Part One: Formative Years

Childhood

Norman Cyril Jackson was born on the 8th April 1919 in Ealing, West London. His mother was in a relationship with a soldier, falling pregnant during his leave in the Summer of 1918, and they planned to get married on his next leave from the Western Front.

The Germans had mounted a major offensive in March 1918, known as the 'Ludendorff Offensive' after General Erich Ludendorff who planned it. They had gained a temporary advantage following Russia's capitulation and withdrawal from the war, which freed up almost 50 German divisions for service on the Western Front. The Germans were desperate to take advantage of their increase in strength before the Americans, who had entered the war in April 1917, could ship soldiers across the Atlantic and reinforce the Allies' resources. The ground gained by the German forces in this offensive was only held in the short term. The Allied troops were boosted by the eventual influx of American soldiers in July 1918, and they mounted a counter offensive the following month.

Returning to the front from his leave in time for this counter offensive, Norman's father was killed in action, probably not knowing that his wife-to-be back in England was expecting their child. Norman's mother did not know of her partner's demise until a few months after his death, only learning of it after she checked with his regiment as she had not heard from him for some time. Single mothers were common at that time due to the loss of their husbands at the front, and being a widowed single mother carried with it respect. Sadly a single unmarried mother was something quite different, and social pressures at the time encouraged adoption, which was what happened to Norman.

There was a shame and stigma associated with illegitimacy, but no legal status or formal adoption process existed until 1927. Before that any adoptions were arranged informally, often facilitated by the church, and were more akin to guardianship or fostering. These did not entail a formal change of name for the child, who would usually use the guardians' or foster parents' surname. This process, being totally

Birth certificate of Norman Cyril Jackson. No name is given for his father, who had been killed in action the previous year.

informal, could also leave open the door for the birth mother to take back the child if circumstances changed and she subsequently married. Whilst Norman's mother did get married, she did not, for whatever reason, take back Norman, something for which he never forgave her. In 1945 with all the publicity around him, she tried to get in touch, but Norman would have nothing to do with his birth mother.

Norman was adopted by a Mr and Mrs Edwin Gunter who lived at 19 Camac Road, Twickenham, Middlesex, and this is

Norman's adoptive parents, Edwin and Mrs. Gunter.

where he lived until joining the Royal Air Force in 1939. Taking their surname, he spent his childhood and teenage years known as Norman Cyril Gunter. Mr and Mrs Gunter had another adopted boy, Geoffrey Oliver Hartley, who was three years older than Norman, and they grew up together as brothers.

Edwin Gunter had served in the army during the First World War and was quite a good boxer, intent on passing his skills in the activity on to the boys as they grew. As Geoffrey was taller than Norman, Edwin would place one of his boxing gloves over Geoffrey's neck so that it would hang just below his chin, and then, to make it fair, had Geoffrey place one hand in his pocket. The glove was a target for Norman, who was to try and hit it, whilst Geoffrey had to try and stop Norman from hitting the glove. Edwin told Norman, "Always have a target to go for on your opponent, no matter how big they are. Concentrate on hitting that, move around until you believe you can hit it and then throw your punch. Do not waste your energy by just throwing punches, always concentrate on the target." He also taught them the importance of having a fit body and showed them a range of exercises that they could work on. Geoffrey, who eventually attained an impressive height of 6' 2", outstripped Norman's 5' 9".

Edwin worked as a paper hanger. He was apparently a very good one, never being out of work. He worked hard for his family and felt a powerful sense of responsibility to look after his family, keep a roof over their heads and food on the table. He passed this sense of responsibility on to Norman. 19 Camac Road was a first floor flat, with two bedrooms, a kitchen, living room, bathroom and inside lavatory. The latter was a luxury not enjoyed at that time by every property. The staircase to the flat was at the rear of the property and was accessed through the back garden.

Twickenham is a town in the southwest of London, through which the River Thames runs. A well-known feature in the river is the Eel Pie Island and Hotel, sitting in the middle of the river and reached by Twickenham Bridge. The island and hotel were famous for the Rolling Stones and other well-known bands playing there regularly in the 1960s.

Norman's childhood home was the first floor flat at this house in Camac Road, Twickenham.

The riverside at Twickenham and the footbridge to Eel Pie Island, photographed c. 1955.

In the first half of the nineteenth century the Thames was a working highway and, as leisure time and activities gradually increased, people would visit the hotel on the island, arriving by pleasure steamers for picnics and parties. Boats were built and hired out locally for people to row or sail on the river. Hammerton's was a local boatyard which took over from the well-known Charlie Shores in 1926. Several of the 'little ships' that crossed the English Channel in May 1940 to take part in the Dunkirk evacuation of the troops were from Twickenham and most likely built by Hammerton's.

Around 1970 the author's mother introduced him to a widow named Rosie then in her mid-seventies, who had lived in Camac Road since childhood and who still lived there. Rosie was one of the real 'characters' that most towns had in those days. She knew everyone, seemed to know everything that was going on, and did not suffer fools gladly. She had known Norman and Geoffrey from when they were just babies to fully grown men. "I remember them as if it was just yesterday," she told the author, "I can tell you that you would be hard pushed to find two finer boys."

As the boys grew older, they shared the second bedroom, which served as their sleeping room, gymnasium, boxing ring and study. According to Rosie, both Norman and Geoffrey were known locally as polite, well-mannered boys, always willing to help with any jobs or errands that needed doing for anybody without any expectation of reward. They were both strong characters who knew their own minds but still showed a great deal of compassion for others.

One Christmas the boys received bicycles as presents. Norman, being four years of age, and not at that stage as tall as he may have been, was given what was known locally at the time as the smallest bicycle in Twickenham. He was always trying to take it apart to see how it all worked and could apparently repair his own punctures at the age of five. He and Geoffrey would spend some of their weekends playing along the banks of the River Thames, swimming, fishing and exploring.

They befriended an elderly gentlemen named Ted, who was always around the banks of the Thames. One day the boys asked Ted how old he was, who replied that he was not sure, but knew he had been around ten years of age at the time of the Charge of The Light Brigade. As that event took place in 1856 and it was now around 1925, this would have made him about 79 years of age. Ted had a small boat which he moored on the Thames alongside Twickenham swimming baths. The boat appeared to be almost as old as Ted and had been repaired many times over the years using bits of wood, rope and tar. With Mr and Mrs Gunter's permission, Ted used to take the boys fishing in his boat, rowing down the river towards his favourite spot at Teddington. The boys, using old tin cans, had to bail out water from the bottom of the boat as the Thames leaked in. The three of them went on this boat trip quite regularly at weekends during the summer months, until Ted decided that the boat was no longer safe to venture out onto the water, and it was best that the fishing expeditions stopped. The boys were disappointed but understood and were always grateful to Ted for these wonderful times. The following winter Ted was found dead in his bed in his ground floor room where he lived alone. When the boys were told they were understandably very upset and wished that they could have spent more time with their old friend.

Norman and Geoffrey were both educated at Archdeacon Cambridge School in Twickenham, which they attended from the age of five. When asked about his schooling, Norman always said that he received a varied but good education, with maths, English, and sports being amongst his favourite subjects. As the years passed, the boys grew in height and strength, regularly exercising and practicing their boxing in their bedroom. One place they would walk in at weekends was the Fulwell Park area, which was little more than a mile or so from Twickenham.

Like a lot of other local people, they knew some boys who called themselves the Butts Farm Gang, after the estate on which they lived. This was in the town of Hanworth, close to one side of the Fulwell Park area. This gang used to bully the local boys and, whenever they saw Norman and Geoffrey, the intimidation would normally start with shouting abuse such as, "There go the two with no real parents", or "There are the bastard brothers." Norman and Geoffrey ignored them as best they could, but sometimes the intimidation was only stopped by the involvement of adults who happened to be nearby.

One Saturday afternoon when they were walking through Fulwell Park, they met a couple of their friends from school and started chatting. The friends mentioned that the Butts Farm Gang were in the area and that they were doing their best in trying to avoid them. They finished their conversation and then started to walk off. As they left their friends, Geoffrey suddenly ran off and, saying he would be back in a couple of minutes, disappeared through some bushes. After a minute or so, the Butts Farm bullies turned up and, seeing that Norman was on his own, started shouting the same old abuse. They added that he was in their area, which meant that there would be consequences.

By this time, Norman's two friends were about 50 yards away and later admitted that they felt too scared of the gang to get involved. Outnumbered five to one it seemed that Norman's only option was to run, which he no intention of doing. He told the gang that he was free to go wherever he wanted, that this was not their territory, so they may as well get on with their so-called 'consequences'. The supposed tough guys circled Norman, threatening and insulting him in an attempt to frighten him. Then their leader, who wore a very heavy ring on one of the fingers on his right hand and was the most abusive, attacked Norman, punching and kicking, and was joined by the other four. Norman concentrated on staying on his feet but he did get caught on the left side of his face by a glancing blow from the hand with the ring on the finger. Managing to keep upright, Norman remembered what he had been taught by his adoptive father, focused on the target of the area around the ringleader's chin, and caught him with a good punch on his jaw. The thug went straight down, just as Geoffrey leapt out of the bushes, ran over to the melee and waded in throwing punches left, right and centre at the remaining bullies.

Geoffrey and Norman stood back-to-back, throwing punches as they had learnt in the boxing ring, and almost immediately another two of the gang were knocked to the floor. The Butts Farm Gang, including their leader who had regained his feet, backed off and withdrew, shouting obscenities as they staggered away.

Norman looked at Geoffrey and asked, "How long before you ran off did you see the gang?" "Oh, only a minute or so," said Geoffrey, "Just when we were talking to our school friends. I thought if they saw you on your own, they would come over and start a fight. You see, they are just cowards and only feel superior in a group. I thought I would hide in the bushes until the fight started and then come to the rescue. I knew you would not run, and so the fight was a sure thing. They needed teaching a lesson once and for all. I also knew that you would go for the leader first, just as Dad had taught us. The others were nothing without him, just loud-mouthed cowards, all of them, just cowards."

Norman was just eleven years of age and Geoffrey had just turned fourteen, whilst against the Butts Farm Gang who were aged around fifteen and sixteen. Norman had a nasty cut on his left cheek and a bit of swelling around his face. When they arrived home Edwin asked what had happened to cause the injury, so the boys told the story of the fight with the gang. Edwin told them, "With five of them you should not have got hit. That's only two and a half each, you should have done better!" Geoffrey pointed out that when his brother was hit it was five to one. Edwin thought for a moment and said, "That's a fair point, well done lads, I hope they learned a lesson not to mess with my boys".

Norman carried that scar on his left cheek for the rest of his life, and on his entry papers into the Royal Air Force, the applicant description states height: 5ft 9 inches, Hair: dark brown, Eyes: hazel, Marks, Scars etc: left cheek.

The following Monday the story of the fight spread throughout the school, disseminated by their two friends who had been present. The gang were well known to a lot of the pupils and Norman and Geoffrey became the subject of considerable hero worship, which both Norman and Geoffrey found quite difficult to deal with. Unexpectedly, they were called into the headmaster's office and given a lecture that violence is never the answer. To send a message to the other pupils, the two lads were given one hour's detention for two nights a week for the coming four weeks. That evening the boys had to inform their parents of the detention as they would be later than normal in coming home. The following day Edwin called into see the headmaster to complain about the treatment of his boys. The headmaster explained that as far as he was concerned Geoffrey had instigated and encouraged the fight by leaving Norman on his own.

Edwin pointed out that on several previous occasions the gang had confronted the boys and intimidated them, but any violence on the side of the gang had been stopped by nearby adults. On these occasions both boys were together, and if Geoffrey had not left his brother with the intention of dealing with the bullies once and for all, the gang would still have tried to attack them. He added that if it had not been then, it would certainly have happened on another occasion, and that bullies have to be confronted at some time. Edwin said that he thought the headmaster was acting outside his authority, as the incident happened away from school premises and out of school hours. In this instance both boys were the parents' responsibility and not the school's. He insisted that the detention was cancelled immediately. The headmaster said that, on reflection, he had not thought it through properly, had acted too harshly and incorrectly, and agreed to cancel the detention.

A couple of weekends later, when they were at Fulwell Park again, Norman and Geoffrey came across the Butts Farm Gang. The gang stopped, turned, and went off in another direction. "Just bullies and cowards," Geoffrey said, "All bullies are just cowards."
Geoffrey and Norman left Archdeacon Cambridge School at the age of fourteen, Geoffrey first in 1930 and Norman following on in 1933. At that time it was quite common to finish schooling and start work at that age. Geoffrey secured an apprenticeship as a builder, while Norman was offered and accepted an apprenticeship with a local engineering company as a fitter turner. A fitter turner is a highly skilled craftsperson

generally involved in the setting up of machinery to enable the manufacture of engineering products. Norman learned how to understand detailed technical specifications, and use specialised tools to construct, manufacture and assemble industrial components, along with the installation and maintenance of plant, machinery, construction and commissioning work. This proved to be a perfect grounding for his Royal Air Force career as an aircraft engineer and then flight engineer. The work for both lads was hard, with ten-hour days being quite common.

During their teenage years Norman and Geoffrey would play football at the weekends for a local team in Marble Hill Park Richmond and, during the summer months, cricket on Twickenham Green. They were both fitness fanatics and would undertake cross country runs, compete against each other with push-ups in their bedroom at home, and carry out set after set of a stamina-building exercise shown to them by Edwin. This involved standing with both feet on a dining chair, climbing down and back up again as fast as they could, repeating the movement as many times as possible within a set period of time, usually between 30 seconds and a minute. Little did Norman know then that this same exercise would come up during his medical for aircrew several years later.

Norman had quite a following of young girls who would gather to watch him play football and cricket, attracted by what they considered to be his Hollywood good looks and dark brown, almost black, wavy hair. At that tender age, though, Norman showed little interest, and although polite to the girls, went happily on his way after the matches in the company of Geoffrey.

Geoffrey was finding life mundane, working as a builder with the same routine every day and he craved excitement and challenge. At the age of 20 he joined the Coldstream Guards on December 1st, 1936, and after training served with the Guards in various parts of the world. During the Second World War, and still serving with the Coldstream Guards, he was captured in Italy and incarcerated in Italian prisoner of war camp PG 53 near the town of Macerata. His official records state that while trying to escape he was shot in the leg by the Fascists and on recapture received no treatment for his wound. Shortly afterwards, in early

October 1943 he was transferred to Stalag VIIA, a POW camp in Moosburg, Southern Bavaria. This was just before the Italians changed sides and joined the Allied powers on October 13th, 1943. The Italians then declared war on their former Axis partner, Germany. At Stalag VIIA Geoffrey received what he described as satisfactory treatment from a German doctor and his wounds healed. The camp was liberated on 30th April 1945 by the American 14th Armoured Division.

Following the war, Geoffrey met and married a German girl. After a spell in England, he was finding life a bit dull and, once again wanting excitement, travelled with his wife to Malaya where he joined the police force. He found plenty of excitement as, during the Malayan troubles, he was awarded the George Medal for Gallantry. On February 12th, 1951, Geoffrey was in a Land Rover escorting a radio van which was transporting, as well as the crew, a woman and three children. As the convoy passed through high banks near Kuantan, the leading vehicle came under heavy fire. Geoffrey, armed with a Bren gun, ran back to the radio van to protect the woman and children. After a continuous exchange of fire with the bandits, his ammunition ran out, and so he ran the gauntlet of fire back to the leading vehicle, where the ammunition was, in order to reload. Then, single-handed, he moved towards the party of five bandits who were advancing on the vehicles, all of them firing continuously in the direction of Geoffrey and the radio van. He brought one bandit down, then wounded another and the rest fled. Thanks to his courage there were no injuries to the woman or three children in the radio van.

After leaving Malaya Geoffrey went on to Kenya, to serve in the Nairobi police force. This was during the *Mau Mau* uprising of 1952 to 1956, and it was here that he was called to an incident at a farmhouse that was being attacked by the Mau Mau. He was first on the scene and could see the attack unfolding before his eyes. Knowing that government troops were on their way but may not arrive in time, he worked his way around the rebels and up to the farmhouse armed only with a side arm. Possibly this was with the thought of trying to delay the inevitable until the troops arrived. As he was standing in front of the farmhouse, the terrorists moved up and stood in front of him. They were armed with rifles, handguns, and their preferred weapon, pangas or as we know them, machetes.

All Geoffrey could do to delay them was to try to reason with the rebels. According to the farm owners, who were inside the farmhouse behind barricaded windows, he ordered them to stop by holding his hands up and then lowering them to the ground laying his weapon there. He then, stood up and pointed at them to do the same, shouting intimidating commands. Even though he was in police uniform which would normally have demanded a level of respect, he must have known this would not happen, but it did buy more time.

Just then, whilst the rebels were talking amongst themselves and no doubt discussing their next move, the government vehicles arrived with Kikuyu loyalists aboard. An internecine war raged between the rebels and the loyalist Kikuyu, and indeed many of the Mau Mau rebels were from the Kikuyu tribe themselves. The Kikuyu loyalists were brutal in their treatment of any Mau Mau rebels they encountered, and the Mau Mau were aware of this and so any reasoning was now out of the question. As the Kikuyu government troops ran into the farm compound and opened fire on the Mau Mau rebels who were standing in front of Geoffrey, the Mau Mau attacked Geoffrey with their pangas whilst opening fire on him and the advancing Kikuyu. Geoffrey was killed but those rebels that survived the onslaught retreated into the bush and the farm owners were saved. The farm owners said they owed their lives to Geoffrey, who gave his life by delaying the Mau Mau rebels long enough for the Kikuyu loyalist troops to arrive.

Joining Up

While travelling to work on his bicycle, in late 1938, Norman, who was then aged 19, often passed an attractive fair-haired young woman walking through the streets of Twickenham. Deciding that she was in some way special he thought he would like to get to know her. Though he waved and said, "Good morning", she would turn away as if to ignore him. Norman persisted with the greeting whenever he saw her, but always with the same result. It was at a local event in Twickenham in early 1939 that he finally got to meet this young lady.

Alma Lilian Peake, aged 17.

Her name was Alma Lilian Peake, and on that occasion, she was in the company of her lifelong friend, Nelly Hall. Alma admitted to Nelly[3] that she did rather like him, as he seemed polite and was undoubtedly very good looking and charming. Nelly told her, "You are not alone, most of the local girls like Norman." Having broken the ice, Alma no longer ignored his morning greeting, and on seeing her he would get off his bicycle and walk along with her as far as he could before they had to go their separate ways. Norman would chat to her and tell amusing stories. His tactics evidently successful, as they were married in 1942.

---

[3] Nelly Hall never married and was known to all of Norman and Alma's children as 'Auntie Nelly', she was a great character with a wonderful sense of humour. She remained a large part of their lives until her death in 2021 at the grand old age of 99 years. Years afterwards, the author recalls collecting Nelly for a family function. He asked her, in passing, if she had ever had a boyfriend, to which Nelly replied, "Yes, there was a chap I used to go dancing with, called Johnny Diamond, if I remember right as it was many years ago. He wasn't very good at dancing though, as he had a problem with his feet, the author asked, what was wrong with his feet, Nelly replied I can't quite remember but i think one of them was on the wrong way round!"

On 3rd September 1939 the war started. At the time Norman was in what could have been a reserved occupation, as it was important to the war effort. However, he had decided that he wished to join the armed services as soon as possible. He deliberated for a while on joining the Royal Navy but decided his skills as an engineer would be best suited in the Royal Air Force which was now needing a rapid expansion. He signed up in the latter service and on 20th October 1939 presented himself to RAF Uxbridge for enlistment as a Volunteer Reservist. There were other Reservists from different parts of the country who were presenting themselves for duty at the same time, all looking and feeling apprehensive as to what was before them. They were shown to the barracks, about 20 to a room but with plenty of space. The metal beds were quite unusual and like nothing Norman had seen before. They would slide out from the head end to the foot, and the mattresses were in three parts known as biscuits. This meant that the beds could be stored away when not being used, clearing the floor of the barrack room for other use during the day. Norman quickly learnt the importance of neatness in service life. There was a place for everything, and everything had to be in its place. This sense of discipline, and the routine of the barracks, were explained to the new recruits by the staff NCOs in no uncertain terms. The shower blocks had the luxury of inside lavatories and hot and cold running water, something that most of the recruits had not experienced before.

After being shown the barracks, the recruits were formally sworn in, where each became legally bound by the Royal Air Force Act and swore one's allegiance to the Crown. Each airman was given their service number, along with an identity card and name tag, which they always had to have with them. Norman's number was 905192. There followed a roll call of surnames, initials and religion. The sergeant called out the name "Jackson, N.C," which was met with silence, as no one of that name seemed to be present. In a tone that signified annoyance, the Sergeant called out again, "Jackson, N.C!" at which point, suddenly it dawned on Norman that he had signed up in that name, as it was on his birth certificate, rather than 'Gunter' which he had used all of his life up until that moment. He called, "Present, Sir!" to the sergeant, who naturally demanded an explanation over the delay in answering to his name, a matter which the NCO did not think should have been

The first page of Norman's RAF Service Record. The later award of his VC is noted rather unobtrusively in the 'Particulars of Medals, etc.' box, bottom left, but someone has been sufficiently impressed to note it in large letters next to his name.

particularly taxing. The sergeant accepted Norman's reasons with a surprising degree of understanding and added wryly, "I suspect that the name of Jackson, N.C. will become rather well known in the Royal Air Force[4].' It did take some time for Norman to get used to his revised surname and it did sometimes take an instant for him to realise that when he heard the name being called, it was his attention that was required.

---

[4] In 1945 when Norman's award of the Victoria Cross became known, the first telegram of congratulations he received was from this sergeant.

The recruits received a short and intensive course of training in the handling of arms, general discipline, and hygiene, before proceeding to specialist schools for training in their respective trades. On 15th December 1939 after a period of 55 days at the Royal Air Force depot at Uxbridge, the group's basic training was finished, and the airmen went to Uxbridge railway station for transportation to their relevant postings. On such occasions local youngsters, showing enterprise, turned up at RAF Uxbridge with barrows made from orange boxes and pram wheels, on which they offered to wheel the airmen's kit bags to the railway station, in the expectation of at least sixpence as a tip. Norman was transferred to 5 Wing, RAF Halton, to start training as a ground engineer. He was designated Fitter IIE with the rank of Aircraftman Second Class (AC2). AC2s, the lowest rank in the Royal Air Force, were commonly known as 'Erks'[5]. According to Royal Air Force documents Norman's first recorded character assessment was 'Very Good', and his proficiency 'Outstanding'.

RAF Halton was a well-established station with a swimming pool, school buildings, gymnasium, workshops and a station church. At six o'clock each morning, the lads would take turns to visit the cookhouse and collect a bucket of tea and box of biscuits for the barrack room. The tea was commonly known as 'gunfire' due to its strength and colour[6].

The barrack room at Halton housed around 30 men; on getting up every morning their first job was to make the beds. All blankets and sheets were neatly folded to make what was known as a 'neat sandwich'. This was usually followed by either rifle drill or physical training before breakfast. After breakfast, they would march in ranks to their relevant workshops, sometimes accompanied by their own band.

---

[5] 'Erk' is said to derive from the Cockney pronunciation of 'Aircraftman'; it was used almost affectionately and was not resented by the Erks themselves, who tended to prefer it to the official term, 'Other Ranks'.
Source: https://tailendcharlietedchurch.wordpress.com/halifax-bomber/ground-crew/

[6] This habit was hard to break. The author recalls that every morning, at around 7 a.m., Norman bringing his children a cup of tea with the words, "Time to get up, here's a cup of gunfire to get you started."

The workshops hosted lectures on metallurgy, heat treatment and basic fitting amongst much else. Then the men progressed to the dismantling of engines, first a De-Havilland Gypsy Moth engine, then the larger and much more complex Rolls Royce Kestrel and Merlin engines. In addition, they tackled a Pegasus radial engine. After dismantling whichever engine they were working on, they then had to reassemble it.

There were courses on carpentry and pipework along with blacksmithing. Engine runs were carried out on the airfield. As well as all the workshop training, they were all required to clean the bathrooms and polish every floor within the barrack rooms. They played a lot of sport, which was encouraged to keep fitness levels up, these activities including swimming, athletics and cross country running. Norman was still extremely keen on physical fitness and in addition to the organised training would daily carry out his routine of chair-climbing, as many times and as quickly as he could much to the amusement of the other lads in the barracks, who would count and time him doubtless encouraging him enthusiastically.

Sunderlands in Scotland

After a period of just over three months Norman left RAF Halton on 29th March 1940, and was posted to 4 Wing at RAF Hednesford, southeast of Stafford. RAF Hednesford was home to No. 6 School of Technical Training. The men arrived at RAF Hednesford by train at a station called Moors Gorse, from where, carrying their kit bags, they marched up Marquis Drive, which had a long steep incline all the way up to the camp and was known to the RAF boys as 'Kit Bag Hill'.

As Norman started climbing the hill with his kit bag over his right shoulder, he heard the sergeant who was with them call out to a man named Tomkins to pick up the pace as he was struggling to keep up. Tomkins was of a light frame with little upper body strength, and with the weight of his kit bag, which he carried in front of him, he could not maintain the pace. The sergeant called to Norman, "Jackson, you are one of the fittest amongst us, see if you can give Tomkins a helping hand up to the camp!" Norman, who was at the front of the pack, with his kit bag over his right shoulder, walked back down the hill to help poor Tomkins. He took hold of one end of Tomkins' kit bag in his left hand and together they carried it all the way up to the camp. When they arrived, the other airmen had formed a line to applaud their arrival.

The accommodation consisted of over 200 wooden huts at its peak; the more fortunate inhabitants were billeted in one of the sixteen huts near the northwestern end of the camp. Here the huts were linked to the shower and ablution blocks by covered or completely enclosed walkways. This made nighttime visits to the lavatories less unpleasant than for those in the other blocks of accommodation, who had to brave adverse weather when caught short.

Three large aircraft hangars housed the instructional aircraft, and there was a large steel-framed workshop building of some 70,000 square feet where practical training was to be carried out on workbenches. There was no active airfield, but some instructional aircraft were flown in and landed on the camp's sports field.

Norman was given two days leave on 24th October and was due back at RAF Hednesford no later than 2300 hours on the 26th. He thought that, even though the timings would be tight, he would take a chance and travel by train to Twickenham to see his parents and Alma. On the morning of 26th October, he was at Twickenham railway station for the return journey, but the train was delayed and then cancelled so he decided to hitchhike. However, on finding that there was a train later that day, he decided to chance it and wait, but this was cancelled as well. The next train that would get him back to Hednesford would be in two days' time. He returned to his parents' house and stayed the night. First thing next morning, when the post office opened, he sent a telegram to the Officer Commanding, RAF Hednesford, explaining what had happened, but he knew full well that he would be disciplined on his return.

Norman's relationship with Alma had continued to blossom, to the point that Norman chose to make the most of his unexpected extra time with her, regardless of the consequences when he returned to base. They were walking in the late afternoon, along the banks of the Thames past the oldest pub in Twickenham, The White Swan, which dated from the 1700s. Norman stopped at a bench, sat Alma down, went down on one knee and asked Alma to be his wife, Alma gladly accepted but said he would have to get permission from her father.

Norman waited for Mr. Peake to get home in the early evening, asked to speak to him in private and was led into the dining room. He asked for Alma's hand in marriage, Mr. Peake gave his blessing, and they became engaged. Norman had at that time no ring to offer Alma, but Mr. Peake said he had some good quality copper wire that may suffice for the time being and went off in search of it. Norman asked for a wooden spoon and checked the size of the handle against Alma's engagement finger, finding that it was very similar. Mr. Peake returned with a large reel of the copper wire and handed it to Norman, who wound the copper wire several times around the handle of the wooden spoon. He slipped it off the handle, and cut another length off the copper wire, which he wound around the ring, over and under, in order to keep it all together and make it robust. When he had finished, he placed the newly formed ring on Alma's engagement finger. It fitted perfectly.

Norman told Alma, that it would have to do for the time being, but he will purchase a proper engagement ring just as soon as possible". Alma said that would not be necessary as she absolutely loved this one, he had made it specially, so she kept it till she had the wedding ring to outrank it.

Norman returned to RAF Hednesford at 1700 hours on 28th October, by which time he had been absent without leave for a period of 42 hours. He was placed in detention and then marched before his commanding officer and told that absence without leave was never acceptable unless you had been killed, which may, just may, be considered as 'reasons beyond your control.' He was sentenced to detention for 120 hours, which was five days. Though it had been unintentional, Norman acknowledged that he was in the wrong and accepted the punishment without argument; secretly he thought it was a small price to pay as he had now become engaged to Alma.

Norman's Service Record also notes the forfeiture of five days for his absence without leave, and subsequent period of detention.

A 210 Squadron Sunderland being moored at the maintenance base, Oban.

A 210 Squadron Sunderland on convoy protection duty.

From RAF Hednesford Norman was posted to No. 3 Flying Training School at Oban, on the west coast of Scotland. This was a base for flying boat training, where Norman was to become proficient as a ground engineer on the massive Short Sunderland flying boats.

The base itself was on the northern end of the island of Kerrera in Ardantive Bay west of Oban itself. Norman described RAF Oban as '...a desolate place with very little to do outside of the base, and atrocious weather most of the time'. After being surveyed by the RAF before the war it was deemed to be suitable for flying boat operations, and a fuel depot was established. At the start of the war in 1939, 209 Squadron arrived with their Supermarine Stranraer flying boats. An aircraft service area for the squadron had been built, along with a jetty, whilst headquarters facilities were at Dungallon House in Oban, and aircrew were billeted in the town. 209 Squadron re-equipped with Saunders-Roe Lerwick flying boats, a type which was not successful, and which suffered a high loss rate; eleven of the 21 built were lost, mostly in accidents. In 1940, 209 Squadron was replaced at RAF Oban by 210 Squadron, which were equipped with the much more effective and famous Short Sunderland flying boat. Aircraft servicing on the Sunderland's was carried out alongside the jetty with cradles suspended from the wings and secured on mountings on each side of the engines.

210 Squadron's duties as part of 18 Group Coastal Command were anti-submarine patrols out into the Atlantic, along with convoy escorts, and ferry services. On 15th January 1941, after spending five months in Oban, 210 Squadron received orders to detach three Sunderland flying boats with pilots and crews, maintenance personnel and spares, to Freetown, Sierra Leone in West Africa for operations. The three aircraft, P9626E, L2163G, and T9041D, left for Pembroke Dock on 16th January at 1200 hours. During the next few days, Wing Commander (W/C) Fressanges, and Squadron Leader (S/L) Lombard, who were originally from 210 Squadron, joined the flight, which then became 95 Squadron. On 6th February 1941 at 0630 hours, the ground party with P/O Gibson in command, and consisting of twelve officers, seven Warrant Officers and senior NCOs embarked for Gourock along with 161 ORS, (Operational Research Station). They arrived at 1300 hours. Ten officers boarded the SS *Highland Brigade* at Glasgow the same night,

with three officers and the remainder of the party, including Norman, spending the night in the transit camp at Gourock. The following day at 1800 hours, all the officers and men who had spent the previous night in the transit camp boarded the ship. On the 8th the ship left in a convoy bound for Freetown, West Africa, sailing via through Gibraltar on its way to the new station in Sierra Leone. The journey was recorded as being '...without incident of note.'

Freetown could scarcely have been more different from Oban, with high temperatures and humidity. Norman said that after a few months they understood why it was historically known as 'the white man's graveyard'. Back in England Alma received a letter from Norman saying that he was now overseas, but he could not say where, or when he would return, but only that it may be some time. Alma knew that absence was to be expected if your partner was serving in the armed

95 Squadron Sunderlands patrolling the South Atlantic off West Africa, from their base at Freetown. Crown Copyright, by Royal Air Force official photographer, F/O Woodbine G.

services, and that this would probably continue for the duration of the war, if they lived that long.

The duties of 95 Squadron, which began on 24th March 1941, were to provide anti-submarine patrols over the South Atlantic, escort ships along the West African Coastline and attack any enemy shipping or U boats that they came across. At first, the biggest threat came from the Vichy French fighter units based in West Africa, and in July 1941 the squadron formed a Hawker Hurricane wing to deal with this threat. The wing remained part of 95 Squadron until October 1941, when it was formed into No. 128 Squadron.

Norman remembered the day that one of the Vichy French fighters, crashed into the ground near the airfield following an engagement with the Hurricanes. Along with a few others he was detailed to recover any parts of the aircraft that was left, which included the pilot who was still in the aircraft. Due to the aircraft crashing nose first into the ground, he had been thrown forward into the engine and the recovery was, as Norman said, '…most unpleasant.'

Engine failures on the Sunderland were commonplace, with aircraft having to force-land at sea, often with the loss of the entire crew. Although the squadron made few contacts with enemy submarines, and was involved in even fewer attacks, it was still considered effective; no ships were lost to U Boats within the area covered by the 95 Squadron Sunderland's for the entire time they were in West Africa. In March 1942, the squadron moved from Freetown to a new base at Jui, on the side of a crocodile-infested lake.

One day, Norman saw in the daily Routine Orders an appeal for Aircraft Fitters to volunteer for flying duty as Flight Engineers, these being needed to assist the pilots flying the new four-engine bombers that were rapidly coming into service, these being the Short Stirling, Handley Page Halifax and Avro Lancaster. He considered this and, considered it was his duty to offer up his skills, Norman was one of the first to volunteer.

Flight Engineer

Norman left West Africa for England on 12th September 1942 after a period of 18 months, arriving on 25th September. On arrival he journeyed to the Aircrew Selection Centre in Euston, London, for a medical exam to see if he was fit enough for aircrew duty. After checking his heart, eyes, ears, height, weight and virtually everything else Norman thought could be measured, the Doctor produced a chair. He told Norman to step up and down on the chair as many times as he could for 30 seconds, after which he would have his heart rate measured to ascertain his fitness. The clock started and Norman started to step up and down, managing well over 20 steps in the allotted time. The doctor thought that was excellent but said that the important thing now was Norman's heart rate. This had hardly climbed at all from his resting heart rate. The doctor was extremely impressed and stamped Norman's medical record as 'Fit for Aircrew.' He asked Norman how he managed to maintain this level of fitness; Norman told him that this exercise was taught to him by his adoptive father when he was a young lad and that from that day, he had been doing the exercise regularly throughout his life. Edwin Gunter's training had proved its worth.

Norman was then posted to RAF St Athan in South Wales for aircrew training as a flight engineer. The first part of the course covered the theory of aircraft engines, their construction, working, servicing requirement. Finally, they were taught how to operate the engines for maximum efficiency, particularly how to squeeze the maximum endurance out of them. After this part of the course finished, they moved onto studying the airframe of the Avro Lancaster bomber, covering the flying controls, fuel system, and hydraulics system which operated the undercarriage, the flaps, and various other controls. Then there was the vacuum pressure system, which drove the instruments, along with the automatic pilot, popularly known as 'George', the wheel brakes and other emergency apparatus. The aim of this course was to understand the whole aircraft. There was a visit to the Rolls Royce engine factory at Derby and a visit to the aircraft factory of A.V. Roe and Company, (Avro) at Chadderton, Lancashire.

Avro Lancaster cockpit showing the Pilot's seat, from the Flight Engineer's position.

Flight Engineer in the cockpit of a Lancaster (Crown Copyright).

Finally, there was a short Air Gunnery Course at RAF Penrhos, which involved classroom study on aircraft recognition, and the effective range of the Browning .303 machine guns. This was 300 to 400 yards, with a one second burst on a Browning .303 expending 10 rounds of ammunition. There was instruction on estimating the deflection when firing at an enemy aircraft. This was followed by training in an actual Frazer Nash gun turret. The whole idea of this course was for the Flight Engineer not just to understand the gun turrets as an integral part of the aircraft, but also to ensure that he could operate a gun turret during low-level mine laying when the bomb aimer was busy, or if a gunner became injured or killed during a bombing raid and the aircraft was under attack from enemy fighters.

With little time available for leave, my parents were married on Boxing Day, 26th December 1942 in Saint Mary's Church Twickenham, followed by a reception at the room above the Fox pub in Church Street Twickenham. The happy couple enjoyed a few days off and then Norman went back to training.

Following the completion of his Flight Engineer course, and the final exam which he passed, Norman received the coveted Flight Engineer's brevet and was posted to No. 27 Operational Training Unit at Lichfield in Staffordshire.

A photo of Norman and Alma's wedding photo including, in the background, Geoffrey Hartley and Nelly Hall.

At 27 OTU, Norman was given operational training in preparation for active service, flying in the Vickers Wellington bomber. Such training included occasional dropping of leaflets over occupied Europe. On 19th June 1943, Norman and his future crew were transferred from 27 OTU to 1654 Heavy Conversion Unit (HCU) at RAF Wigsley, 7½ miles from the centre of Lincoln. It was here that his crew came together for the first time. They trained on the Lancaster as the weather allowed, daily if possible, and covered not only various aspects of flying, bombing practice, fighter identification and evasion, but also practised parachute escape along with evacuation of the aircraft after ditching and climbing into the dinghy.

The crew, like most other crews, referred to each other by nicknames, usually a contraction of their surname. Hence Norman was always known as 'Jacko', Fred Mifflin as 'Miff,' Ernest Sandelands as 'Sandy', Maurice Toft as 'Tofty', and Frank Higgins as 'Pops', this because Frank Higgins was several years older than the rest of the crew, Walter Smith, the mid-upper gunner was inevitably known as 'Smudge', that being the generic nickname for anyone with his surname. The rear gunner, Norman Hugh Johnson, known to his family as Hugh, was known as 'Johnny'. Except for the more formal or solemn entries, the crew members are referred to by their nicknames, as that is how they knew each other.

Engine Theory to Under Training Air Engineers

Above: Flight Engineers attend a lecture on Engine Theory at RAF St. Athan.

Below: Groups of Flight Engineers study a Lancaster engine handling trainer, No. 4 School of Technical Training, RAF St. Athan (both photos courtesy of Flight Engineers Association)

'For Freedom'

The official 106 Squadron crest, with its motto, 'For Freedom'.

On 28th July 1943, the crew joined 106 Squadron, at that time based at Syerston in Nottinghamshire. 106 Squadron was a front-line heavy bomber squadron equipped with the Avro Lancaster. It routinely took part in the night-time bombing operations mounted by Bomber Command. 106 Squadron's motto was *'Pro Liberate'* (*'For Freedom'*). All 106 Squadron aircraft carried the code letters ZN, followed by an individual letter for that machine.

First formed on the 30th of September 1917, 106 Squadron fulfilled a corps reconnaissance role, moving to Ireland in May 1918, before becoming one of a vast number of squadrons to be disbanded in late 1919. It remained on the shelf until being resurrected at Abingdon on the 1st of June 1938. W/C Montgommerie had been appointed to command the squadron on the 8th of October, and during his periods of absence S/L Sheen stepped up. The squadron was initially equipped with Hawker Hinds, which were replaced by Fairey Battles, and a number of Ansons and Oxfords were also taken on charge. In May 1939, Hampdens arrived, and this type would remain with the squadron until well into 1942. The outbreak of war on the 3rd of September 1939 found 106 Squadron at Cottesmore in the county of Rutland, where it had resided for just two days. Each of Bomber Command's operational groups had been ordered to designate one squadron for group pool training duties, to feed new crews into the front line. This important role was handed to 106 Squadron, and it would be thus occupied for the entire first year of war.

In May 1939 the squadron Hampdens arrived, and this aircraft would remain with the Squadron until the later part of 1942 where it would be replaced by the Avro Manchester and subsequently the Avro Lancaster.

The Squadron had previously been commanded by W/C Guy Penrose Gibson, but he transferred earlier in the year to command the newly formed 617 'Dambuster' Squadron. Gibson, who was due some well-deserved leave following the completion of his latest tour of operations, was astonished when, on 14th March 1943, he was posted from his position as Officer Commanding, 106 Squadron to 5 Group HQ at St Vincents in Grantham. He believed at the time that he was being sent there to write a book, and with his customary stubbornness, felt that he should still be commanding 106 Squadron.

On 15th March Sir Arthur Harris met with the newly appointed A.O.C. 5 Group, Air Vice Marshall Sir Ralph Cochrane. Harris told Cochrane to form a new special squadron, to be commanded by Gibson, to train for an attack on the Ruhr Dams. When told that this was the real reason for his move, Gibson accepted the appointment willingly and did not give a second thought to the loss of his well-deserved leave. Gibson was allowed some degree of involvement in selecting the crews and quite naturally decided to select a number of those with whom he had spent time over the last twelve months while commanding 106 Squadron. Flight Lieutenant (F/L) John Hopgood was an automatic choice having completed his tour of operations back in October. F/L Dave Shannon, who was about to begin training with the Pathfinders at Wyton when he received a call from Gibson was also an obvious selection. Gibson's third choice was a Canadian Pilot Officer, Lewis John Burpee. Following the invitation from Gibson all travelled to Scampton along with their crews[7].

Very shortly after joining 106 Squadron, Norman's crew had their first personal experience of how dangerous flying as a member of Bomber Command could be. On 1st August 1943 they were detailed on a training flight on the veteran Lancaster R5614, squadron code ZN-Z. The flight was successful, and the crew were confident that they had all performed well. However, on approach to landing, and with the aircraft almost at the touchdown, the wind changed. Miff was struggling to keep the aircraft lined up on the centre of the runway and the Lancaster touched down heavily. Fred opened the throttles in order to go around but the crosswind was so strong that he struggled to keep the aircraft on the runway, resulting in a loss of control and the aircraft ended up in the overshoot area off the end of the runway. The undercarriage collapsed and the aircraft caught fire and was destroyed. The rear turret, containing 'Johnny' Johnson, broke away from the main fuselage and overtook the rest of the Lancaster, winding up some 50 yards ahead of the wreckage.

The crew managed to escape but all sustained injuries, the most serious being Norman breaking his lower left leg. Norman, with the rest of the crew, ended up in the medical centre where his left lower leg was put into plaster. However, not wishing the crew to continue without him, he refused medical advice to rest until the removal of the plaster in some six weeks' time. Therefore, his first few operations were flown with his leg in plaster, which he said did not hamper him in any way.

---

[7] Details from *RAF Bomber Command Profiles - 106 Squadron* by Chris Ward (Aviation Books Ltd., UK, 2022)

In a letter to his parents on 7th August 1944, sent from the RAF Hospital at Rauceby, near Sleaford, Lincolnshire, Johnny gave some details about the aftermath and mentioned having received a letter from Sandy:

'He told me in his letter that he hadn't told his wife about the crash, but that she had asked him in the morning, why he'd been saying in his sleep – "Where's Johhny, Frank, for Christ's sake where's Johnny."

This is because, presumably they went to the tail of the aircraft to look for me, but there wasn't any tail there.

Somehow it had, when it broke off, finished up about 50 yards in front of the nose.

This all sounds rather dramatic I know, but Miff who came to see me yesterday told me the same thing about the tail and said that being rather shaken they couldn't make out where I was for the moment. Anyway, it's nice to know that they all thought of me when they'd got out.

Miff couldn't say whether I'll be able to stick with the crew or not, but I know that he'll do his best to keep me with them. He doesn't know yet whether any blame will be attached to him but said that everyone seems to be regarding it as a very bad bit (of) luck, more than anything.

He told me however, that the Group Captain visited him in sick quarters on the station and was very nice, saying that he wasn't to blame.

I didn't know that Jack had been in a crash, and I think that it's rather hard luck if he has got a fractured spine[8].'

---

[8] The final sentence is somewhat enigmatic. It has been assumed by family members that Johnny is referring to Norman here, but the rear gunner would surely have known that the flight engineer had been with them. Norman had also suffered a broken leg, rather than a fractured spine. Finally, the crew apparently referred to Norman as 'Jacko' rather than 'Jack'. It is therefore possible that Johnny was referring not to

Johnny concluded his letter with some personal notes to his parents. This explains why his first op was delayed until November that year, rather than Johnny starting with the rest of his crew.

The Lancaster bomber, or 'Lanc' as the crews referred to it, was to become the most successful RAF bomber of the Second World War. It had a crew of seven, comprising the pilot, flight engineer, bomb aimer (the correct term being air bomber), who also operated the nose turret guns, navigator, wireless operator, mid upper gunner and tail gunner. The nose and mid upper turret had two Browning .303 machine guns with 1,000 rounds of ammunition for each gun. The rear turret had four Browning .303 machine guns with 1,000 rounds of ammunition for each gun. The rear turret was changed in many later Lancasters with the rear turret being fitted with two larger 50 calibre machine guns.

The aircraft had an overall length of 69 feet 4 inches, a wingspan of 102 feet, and height of 20 feet 6 inches. Its maximum speed was 282 miles per hour, with a cruise speed of 200 miles per hour. The Lanc was powered by four Rolls Royce Merlin engines, each generating 1,460 horsepower, these driving four 13-foot diameter de Havilland hydromatic three bladed propellers. The aircraft had six fuel tanks, three in each wing, which contained a total of 2,154 gallons of 100 octane petrol. This was coloured green, not only for identification purposes but to discourage theft, as it was also suitable for use in the few cars owned by RAF airmen at the time, and petrol for personal use was very strictly rationed. The normal bombload could be up to 14,000lb. The unobstructed bomb bay meant that the Lancaster could also carry the heaviest bombs used by the Royal Air Force during the war including the 4,000lb 'Cookie', 8,000lb 'Blockbuster' and 12,000lb. 'Tallboy' bombs. The Lanc was eventually adapted to carry the 22,000lb 'Grand Slam' earthquake bomb invented by Barnes Wallace, who also designed the famous 'Upkeep' bouncing bomb[9] used in the Dams Raid.

Norman, but to another airman he knew as 'Jack', this news perhaps having been given to him by his parents in a previous letter.

[9] Technically, the 'Upkeep' weapon was a mine, as it was detonated by hydrostatic pressure under water, rather than on impact.

The Lancaster had a maximum range of 2,530 miles, though with a full bombload of 14,000lb, this was reduced to 1,600 miles. As landing in Occupied Europe to refuel was clearly not an option, this meant that the furthest distance that a full bombload could be delivered was to a target some 800 miles away. Allowance had to be made for wind en route, time climbing to cruising height and forming up, and a usable reserve of fuel on return. All of these reduced the bombload in favour of fuel, meaning that at this stage in the war, a Lancaster could carry around 8,000 pounds of bombs to Berlin, whilst the Ruhr could receive significantly more explosive per aircraft. The fuel burn at full power was 460 gallons per hour, this being constantly controlled by the Flight Engineer to squeeze every last mile out of the Lancaster. The service ceiling was 24,500 feet with a climb rate of 720 feet per minute at a weight of 63,000lb.

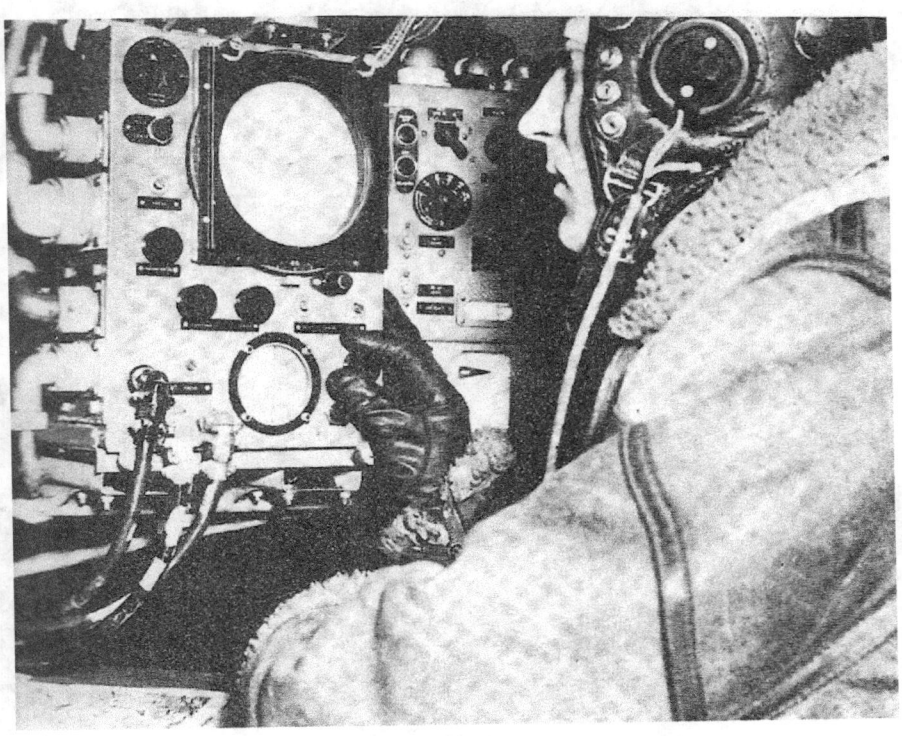

A navigator tuning his H2S set (Crown Copyright)

Gee receiver fitted to the Navigator's station in a Lancaster.

There was also a downward-looking radar system, H2S, used by either navigator or the wireless operator, depending on circumstances. This provided a rudimentary electronic image of the ground and was usually of adequate resolution to identify major features on the ground, such as rivers and lakes. H2S also incorporated an enhancement, *Fishpond*, used by the wireless operator, which worked on a frequency of 3 Gigahertz, and alerted the wireless operator to the presence of an enemy fighter. Unfortunately, H2S used a transmitter fitted to the aircraft which could be detected by German nightfighters fitted with a FuG 350 Naxos receiver, so this system initially had to be used with discretion. However, when a Luftwaffe Ju88 nightfighter was captured, examination of the Naxos set showed that, whilst it might be able to detect a bomber stream, it was ineffective at guiding the fighter to an individual bomber. A more effective German system, *Flensburg*, was guiding the fighters to the bomber's other fighter detection system, *Monica*. As a result, *Monica* was removed and use of H2S was unhindered.

The navigator was assisted in his task by the installation in the Lancaster of Gee, a receiver for a navigation system of synchronised pulses transmitted from the UK. The device calculated the aircraft's position from the time delay between pulses. The range of the Gee receiver was limited as it relied on line-of-site from the transmitter. At around 22,000 feet the effective range was 300 to 400 miles, though this could vary with atmospheric conditions, and the system was later vulnerable to enemy jamming. The system had a whip type aerial mounted just ahead of the mid upper turret on top of the fuselage.

The flight engineer was expected to know his aircraft inside and out and be able to cope with any emergency whether arising from mechanical faults or enemy action. He was practically minded and able to make split second decisions, as a delay in reacting to the emergency could result in the crash of the aircraft and injury or death for the crew.

Photo overleaf: The Wireless Operator's station in a Lancaster. On the left is the H2S screen; upper right is the wireless transmitter and lower right is the wireless receiver.

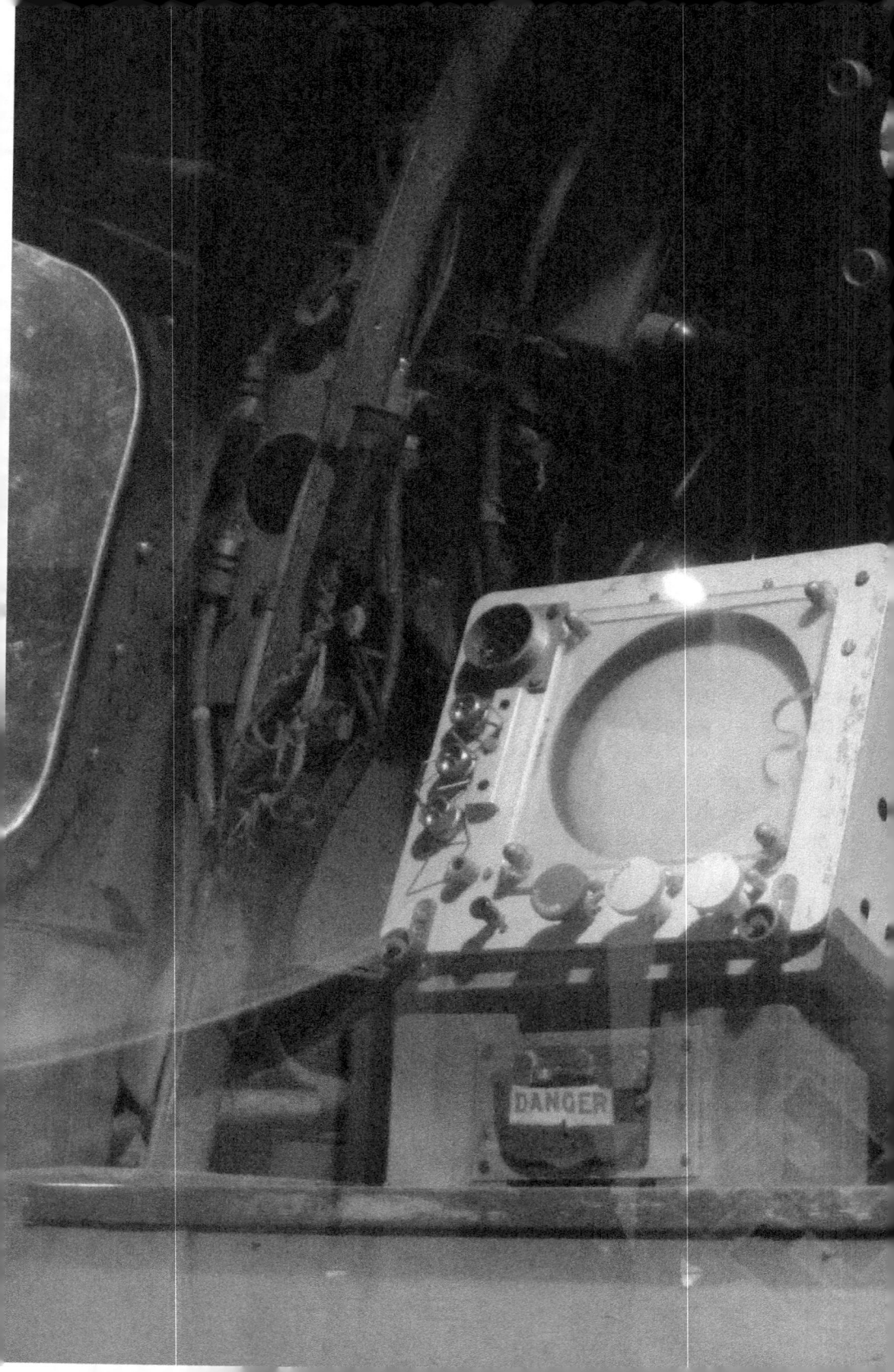

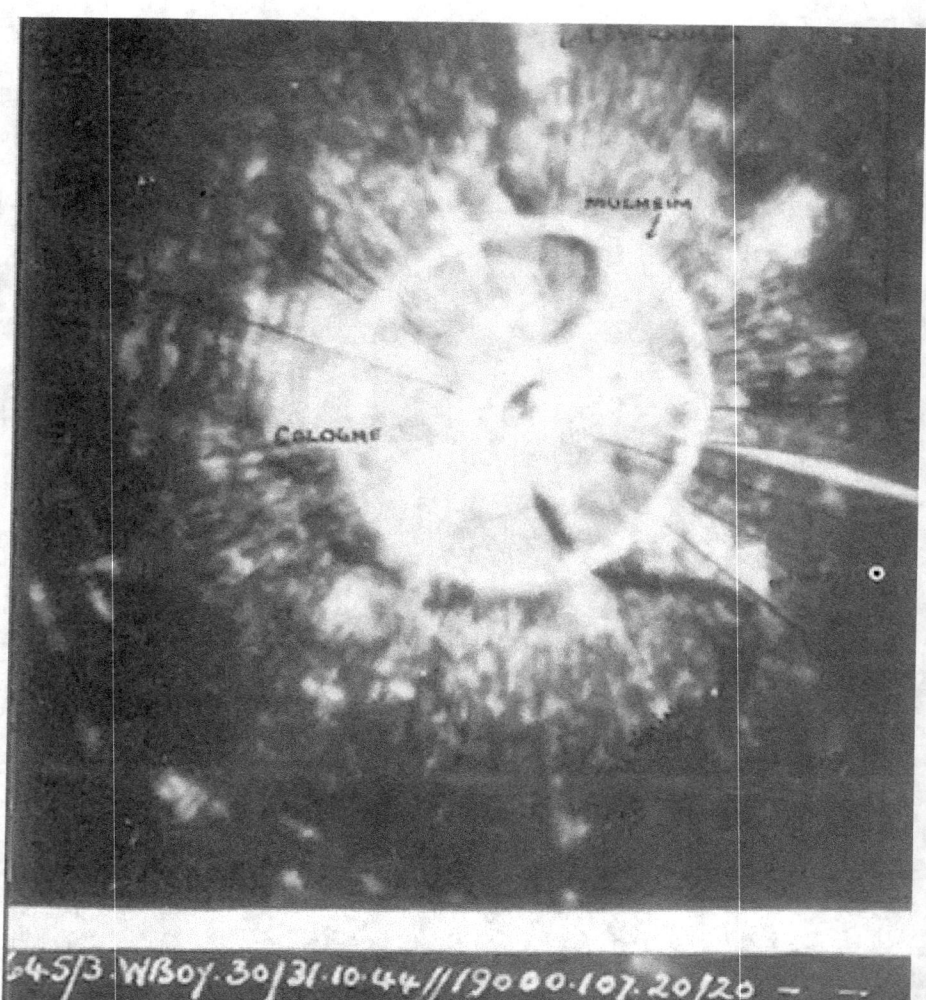

The image on an H2S screen, taken just after bombing Cologne on 30/31st October 1944. The caption relates that the aircraft, 'C' of 156 Squadron from RAF Warboys, was flown by P/O Bartleman. They bombed from 19,000 feet on a heading of 107 degrees, having been guided to the aiming point by using 'Gee' (Crown Copyright).

He had to monitor full time the four engines via some 20 gauges, making constant adjustments to the engine settings to allow the maximum fuel efficiency and greatest range, and control the electrical systems, along with the propeller and throttle controls. The flight engineer also assisted the pilot, which, when necessary, could include flying the aircraft if the pilot was killed or wounded or needed to use the Elsan lavatory in the rear of the aircraft. Whilst few, if any, flight engineers flew a pilot-less bomber back to a safe landing in England, they could at least hold the aircraft straight and level while the rest of the crew bailed out. Towards the end of the war, Bomber Command losses reduced to the extent that supply of new pilots exceeded the demand from casualties, and many pilots were reassigned to fly as flight engineers.

Norman always carried a tool bag into the aircraft with what he deemed to be useful bits and pieces along with some tools that could all be useful in an emergency, he stowed the bag out of the way in the casualty area of the Lancaster.

The crew were now fully-fledged and ready for operations. They were expected to complete 30 before being reassigned for a 'rest'[10], if of course they survived that long. Bomber crew survival rate was little more than one in every two from operational flying, but there were also considerable losses during training as well. Taking an example 100 airmen, 55 were killed on operations or training including those that died because of wounds, four were injured, in varying levels of severity on operations or active service, twelve were taken prisoner of war, some wounded, two having been shot down would manage to evade capture, and 27 would survive a tour of 30 operations.

Despite these abysmal odds, they accepted the risks and still climbed into their bomber's night after night. These men were prepared to serve their country and give whatever it took to do their duty, and yet, after the war, RAF Bomber Command aircrew were treated extremely poorly

---

[10] The 'rest' usually entailed being posted to a training unit, to pass on their experience and expertise to new crews. As the accident rate amongst trainee aircrew was very high, this was definitely not a safe posting. After six months they would expect to return for a second tour, usually of 20 ops.

KEY TO *Fig. 3*

FLIGHT ENGINEER'S
PANEL
LANCASTERS I & III

68. Ammeter.
69. Oil pressure gauges.
70. Pressure-head heater switch.
71. Oil temperature gauges.
72. Coolant temperature gauges.
74. Fuel contents gauges.
75. Inspection lamp socket.
76. Fuel contents gauge switch.
77. Fuel tanks selector cocks.
78. Electric fuel booster pump switches.
79. Fuel pressure warning lights.
80. Emergency air control.
81. Oil dilution buttons.

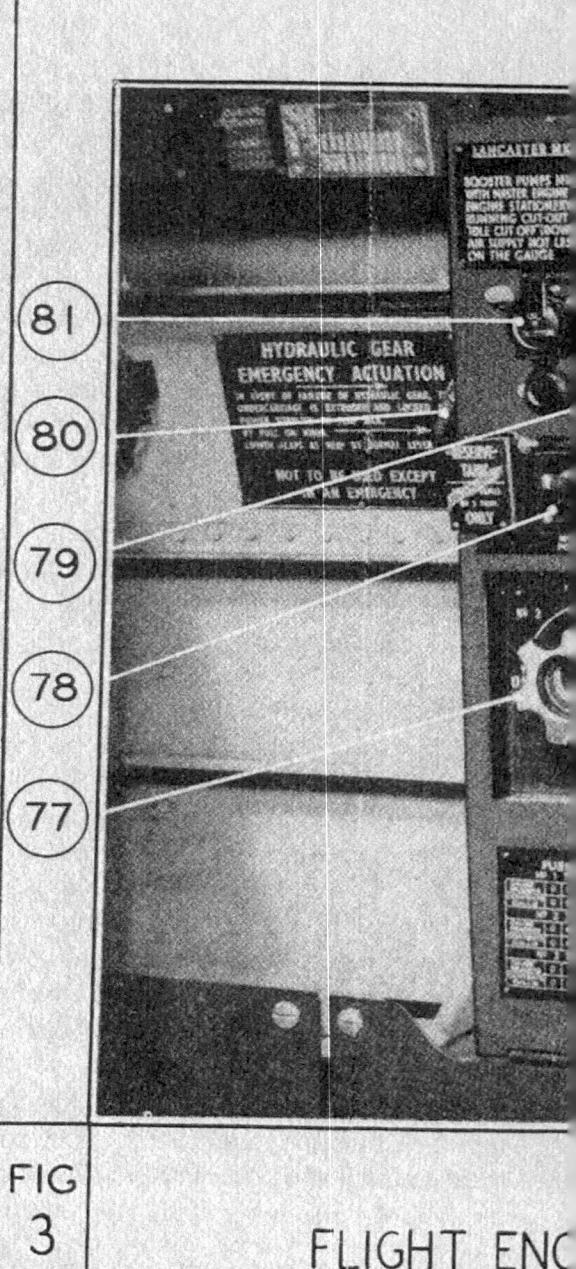

The Flight Engineer's panel in a Merlin-powered Lancaster

(from The Lancaster Manual, Air Ministry 1942-45, Crown Copyright)

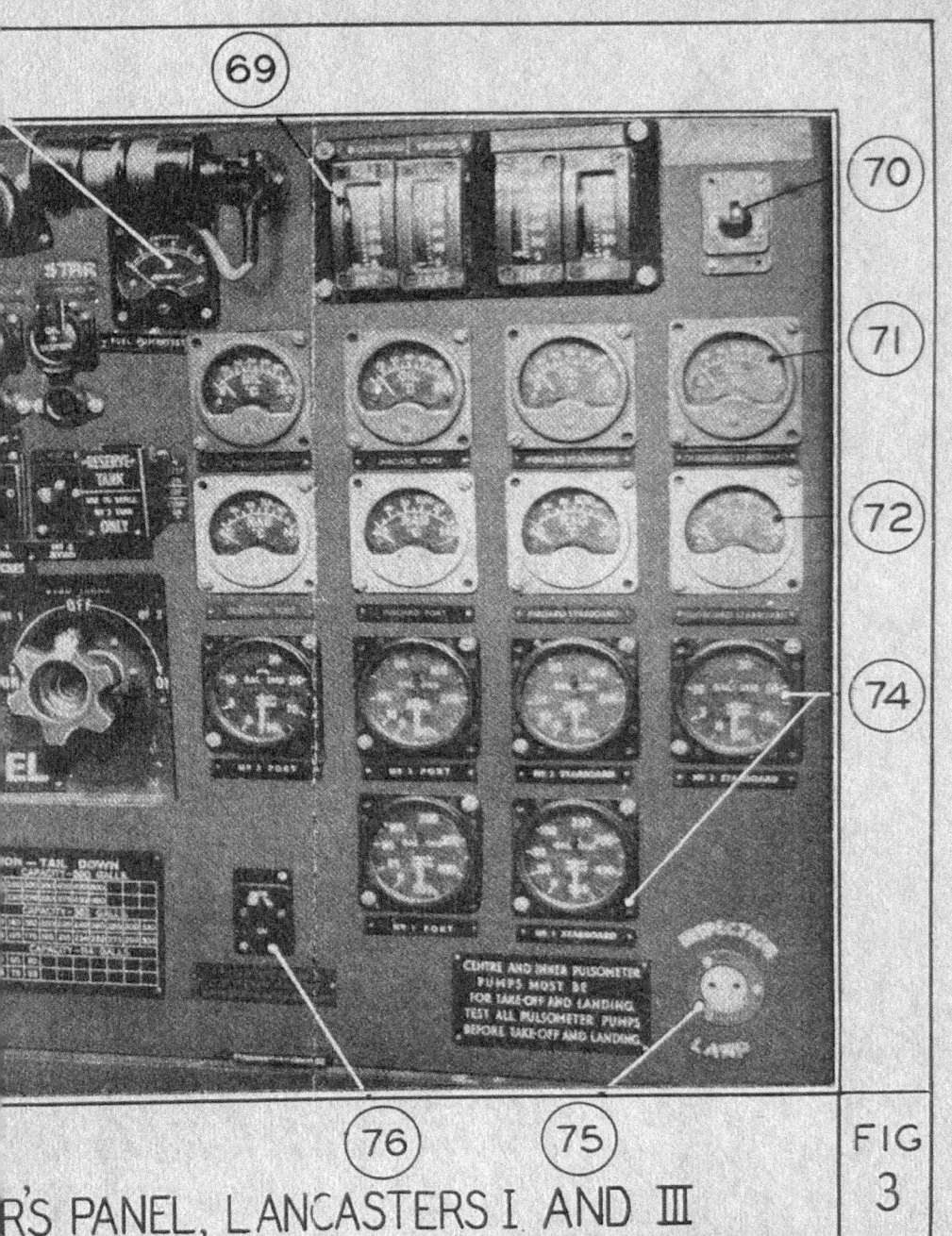

FIG 3 — R'S PANEL, LANCASTERS I AND III

WAAFs waving off a Lancaster crew at Syerston.

Some of the crew. From left: Frank Higgins, Maurice Toft, Hugh Johnson, Ernest Sandelands and, on the right, Fred Mifflin.

because of an emerging perception that operations like Dresden resulted in unnecessarily high numbers of civilian casualties. Indeed, the belief that Bomber Command only bombed German cities in order kill as many German citizens as possible, and actually had done little that was of any use in bringing the war to an end still prevails to this day. That was clear following the much-delayed Bomber Command Memorial in Green Park London, which has suffered attacks by people who quite happily refer to the members of Bomber Command, and their leader, Air Chief Marshal Sir Arthur Harris, as 'murderers'.

It should be noted that, with the exception of a few pacifists, who in any event would not have been tolerated by victorious Nazis, this view of the efficacy of the bombing campaign only really emerged once an allied victory appeared certain.

F/O Fred Mifflin was Norman's pilot.

A thumbs up from Fred Mifflin.

Part Two: Operations

The following part of the book gives the full details of Norman's operations including reasons for the target selection. It is hoped that these assist the reader to understand the justification for the attack on them. If people understood why these operations were carried out in the way that they were, perhaps the paradigm around Bomber Command could be changed.

Bomber Command aircrews operated as a team; each member was mutually dependent on the others, and every man had a vital part to play in ensuring that the aircraft reached its target, dropped its bombs, and returned safely to base. The crew all shared the same experiences and dangers.

Norman described being in a squadron as like being part of a large family. Everyone tended to know what is going on and felt involved in everything, especially operations. Even though they might not have been personally involved in whatever was going on, they still felt included as it was their squadron.

The first of 106 Squadron's operations that Norman remembered after his arrival was on 17th and 18th August 1943. This was the attack on the V2 rocket experimental site at Peenemunde in the Baltic. 106 Squadron supplied nine Lancasters to a force of 597 aircraft for this attack in which there were three aiming points: the housing estate, which were the living quarters for the scientists and workers, the V2 assembly sheds, and thirdly the experimental site.

The bomb load for the 106 Lancasters was one 4,000lb 'Cookie', six 1,000lb and two 250lb bombs. The weather en route to the target was excellent and as the Lancasters of 106 Squadron arrived over the Baltic coast they found the operation well under way. Group Captain Searby from 83 Squadron was overhead the target and directing the target marking as well as the bombing. He experienced some problems early on when he noticed that some of the Pathfinder markers had fallen onto the Trassenheide camp for the forced workers, which was a mile or so to the south of the housing estate target. Many of these workers, who had been taken there by Nazis as slaves, were trapped in their wooden barracks and were killed or wounded in the bombing. However, this error was rectified, and the operation then proceeded much as originally planned. As a result of this, ultimately effective, operation the development programme for the V2 rockets was delayed, and the Germans had to relocate the testing programme eastwards into Poland beyond the range of Bomber Command.

On operations, the festivities started with an operational briefing, which was attended by all members of the crew. The crews assembled, and the senior officers took their seats at the front of the room. A curtain covering the front wall was drawn back, revealing a large map of Europe along with ribbons showing the track from base to the target and back. Several subsidiary boards contained relevant information relating to the operation, such as cloud layers, flare colours, times on target, and so on. The crewmen paid careful attention, as their lives depended on understanding and remembering the information on the boards, along with that given in briefings by the various subject matter experts. These covered meteorology, signals, enemy defences, and the sequence of attack. The winds and weather en route to, over, and returning from the target were of the utmost importance.

Throughout the day, the ground crews, comprising fitters, armourers, and other technicians, had been preparing the Lancasters for the operation. Each aircraft was checked and, if necessary, test flown earlier in the day by the crew. Each Lancaster had its own assigned ground crew who took pride in, and considered that they owned, that aircraft. The ground crew faced an agonising wait as the crew 'borrowed' their Lanc for each op, until crew and machine returned several hours later. All too often, though, their dispersal remained empty and that was emotionally hard on the ground crew.

These ground crews were the unsung heroes of Bomber Command, a fact that all flight crews knew and appreciated. As each squadron might have up to 30 large aeroplanes on its strength, the luxury of hangar space for more than a few was simply not available. Therefore, routine maintenance and minor repairs were carried out by the technicians in the open air, on the dispersal pan. By their very nature, airfields are open expanses of ground with no shelter from adverse weather, so the ground crews were exposed to the elements all hours of the day, literally come rain, sleet, snow, or blazing sunshine.

There was pressure on each squadron to maintain as high a level of serviceability as possible, especially if Group HQ was calling for a 'Maximum Effort'. In preparation for the next operation, the aircraft needed to be refuelled, the navigational and electronic equipment, which was secret, would be brought to the individual aircraft and installed prior to each operation, and the designated bomb load would be delivered on a series of trolleys.

To targets in the western part of Germany, including the ever-popular Ruhr, each Lancaster often carried a bomb load totalling 11,000 to 12,000 pounds. These were usually a mixture of General Purpose, High Explosive and incendiary bombs. The largest size routinely carried was the 4,000-pound 'Cookie'. Some Lancasters were able to accommodate the 8,000-pound 'Blockbuster', which was in effect two 'Cookies' welded together. The purpose of these particular bombs which were basically metal dustbins full of high explosive, was to blast open buildings, especially to remove their roofing, which would allow the smaller incendiary bombs to set fire to the interiors. Even when the bombs were yet to be fused, they had to be handled with care, especially the 'Cookies' which had a thin case.

The bomb trailer once loaded would be towed by a tractor to the fusing hut, where the bomb would have its transit plugs removed, and the detonators and firing pistol installed. The firing pistol had a small windmill which turned as the bomb dropped through the airflow and thereby armed the bomb. This had to be wired in place to stop it being turned by the wind or by the slipstream from the propeller of an aircraft while on its journey from the bomb dump to the aircraft, the bomb doors of the Lancaster were closed by the aircraft's hydraulic system, which required the engines to be running. When the bomb trailer arrived, the 'Cookie' was installed first, hoisted into position by hydraulic winches. Once in position the rest of the bomb load would follow and, when the full bomb load had been installed, the safety wires would be removed. With the Lancaster now fuelled, bombed up and tested it was ready for the crew.

Once the briefing was finished the crew headed for the dining hall. The Women's Auxiliary Air Force (WAAF) ran a round-the-clock kitchen for the aircrew conducting operations over Europe. and their evening pre-flight meal was usually eggs and bacon with beans or sausages. Sometimes chips and a pint of milk were added, and occasionally steak. Despite the severe rationing in place throughout the war, it was thought that downed aircrew would stand a much better chance of survival if after bailing out they landed with a full stomach rather than hungry. Therefore, they received special treatment, but only when they were 'on ops.'. The food was forced down knowing that this may be their last meal. There was no discussion about the target as they all knew the importance of security.

Following the meal, they went to the huts where the flying kit was maintained and stored. They would sign for their parachutes and harnesses; the crew being supplied with chest-mounted parachutes. Only the pilot had a parachute fitted to the rear of his harness and this doubled up as his cushion on the metal pilots' seat in the cockpit of the Lancaster. The pilots generally thought that the parachute was as hard as concrete. There was inevitably some comedian who, when signing for his parachute, that would remark, "If it fails to work, can I bring it back?"

The airmen then drew the keys to their personal lockers which were in the flying kit hut and don their own personal flying clothing. Norman, like many other airmen, always flew in his sheepskin-lined Irvin flying jacket over the top of his battle dress, with his parachute harness over the top. They already had on their thermal underwear over which they wore their RAF uniform. They pulled on their silk socks, outer thermal socks, and then their fur-lined flying boots, all of these being necessary for the extreme cold at high altitudes. 40 degrees below zero was commonplace.

They then left the hut and climbed into the back of the trucks that conveyed them out to their allotted and waiting aircraft. The crews were required to be in the aircraft one hour before their designated take off time. Once at the aircraft each pilot signed the Form 700 to say that he found everything satisfactory, and he accepted receipt of one airworthy aircraft. For some crew members, 'Wakey-Wakey' tablets were issued by the Medical Officer on request. These were Benzedrine Sulphate which would maintain alertness, especially on the return journey.

Once at the aircraft the Flight Engineers' duties involved checking that all the external covers had been removed, the flying controls and undercarriage safety strut covers on the aircraft taken off, and that the aeroplane was ready for flight. The filler caps on the petrol tanks had to be checked for security before priming the engines with petrol ready for start-up. With pre-flight checks done by the Flight Engineer, both outside and inside the aircraft, the crew boarded, each took up their station and carried out their own respective checks. The Flight Engineer then secured the entrance door, stowed the crew ladder and went to his position beside the pilot.

The starter trolley arrived and was connected to the aircraft. When the order came, he then started the engines and assisted the pilot with the preparations for take-off. the starboard inner engine would be started first as this engine drives an onboard electrical generator. Next came the starboard outer engine, the port inner engine and finally the port outer engine.

As the engines started, the pilot and Flight Engineer began the litany of pre-take-off checks: engines set to 1200 rpm, engine pressures and temperatures in the green or rising, ground/flight switch to 'Flight', altimeter set, instrument vacuum check, radiator shutters open, brake pressure 300 pounds per square inch. Then, if he was satisfied that all was well, the Flight Engineer signalled 'Chocks Away!' to the ground crew by crossing then uncrossing his hands.

The pilot released the brakes and increased power sufficiently to start the aeroplane rolling slowly forward. Leaving the dispersal, it joined the others along the perimeter track. The checks continued: autopilot control out, dead reckoning compass set, aircraft trim set for take-off, propellers fully up, fuel selection 1 and 2 tanks selected, booster pumps on, flaps set for take-off. The pilot called to each crew member individually to make sure all was well. Eventually the line of snaking bombers reached the end of the active runway, where the controller's caravan was parked, and from where each aeroplane would receive a morse signal with its code letter, and a green light. The pilot was expected to be ready for an immediate take off.

As each aircraft began its take off run another one took its place at the runway's end. The engines were run up to full power and the pilot released the brakes. The aircraft started to accelerate down the runway, each engine set to 3,000 rpm with +14 inches of boost[11]. The Flight Engineer used his left hand to work the throttles, watching the temperatures and pressures of the four engines, while the pilot kept the aircraft heading straight down the runway. This was to guard against the throttles moving backwards and reducing the fuel flow at this critical time.

The take-off speed of a Lancaster, depending on its weight and the wind, was between 95 and 105 miles per hour. The pilot held the Lancaster onto the runway to get close to 105 miles per hour, the extra speed helping the heavily laden Lancaster start its climb. The Lancaster, laden with 2154 gallons of fuel burning at 460 gallons per hour at full throttle, 12,000 pounds or more of explosive, seven crew members and an overall weight of up to 65,000 pounds, slowly became airborne. As it slowly climbed, and on the command of the pilot, the Flight Engineer retracted the undercarriage to reduce drag. This was the most critical stage of flight, and an engine failure now would spell disaster. At around 800 feet the pilot called for the flaps to be retracted; at 1,000 feet and safely airborne, the Flight Engineer throttled back the engines to the setting for continuous climb, and the Lancaster headed to the rendezvous point which the bomber had to pass at its allotted time.

---

[11] Boost is the term used for the pressure in the inlet manifold in pounds per square inch above the normal atmospheric pressure.

At 10,000 feet the crew would put on their oxygen masks, and at 13,000 feet the Flight Engineer would change the supercharger to a higher ratio known as S gear, in order to maintain the power in the thinning atmosphere. By this time the Lancaster was usually crossing the English coast and the navigator set a course for joining the main bomber stream, after which the crew anticipated the call of 'Enemy Coast Ahead". This procedure was followed by every Lancaster bomber.

Operation 1: Leverkusen, 22nd / 23rd August 1943

Aircraft assigned: Lancaster DV182.

Crew:
Pilot: Sgt. F.M. Mifflin
Flight engineer: Sgt. N.C. Jackson
Navigator Sgt. F.L. Higgins
Bomb aimer: Sgt. N.H. Toft
Wireless operator Sgt. E. Sandelands
Mid upper gunner Sgt. W, Smith
Rear gunner Sgt. W.N. Wait

Bomb load: 1 x 4,000lb. 1410 x 4lb. 80 x 30lb.
Take off: 21.05 hours.
Time of landing: 02.10 hours.
Duration of operation: 5 hours and 5 minutes.

Bomber Command detailed a total of 462 aircraft: 257 Lancasters, 192 Halifaxes, and thirteen Mosquitos. 106 Squadron's contribution numbered eleven Lancasters. The IG Farben chemical plant was chosen as the aiming point for this raid. This was an important German chemicals company that manufactured various substances including synthetic oil. It also manufactured the Zyklon B gas used to exterminate millions of European Jews in the Holocaust.

The crew knew the importance of the target and wanted to do a good job and destroy the factory. They were also anxious to complete their first sortie and get at least one under their belt. They were understandably nervous; each man trying to do his absolute best and remember everything learnt in training. The gunners were scrutinising the skies from the moment the aircraft crossed the coast of England, scanning left, right, up and down, searching the skies for fighters, ready to call it out to the pilot if any were seen.

With the course set for the bomber stream and then the enemy coast, the Lancaster began its long climb to its designated altitude of 20,000 feet, at a climb rate of 750 feet per minute. This would take the best part of half an hour.

On this operation 106 Squadron was led for the first time by S/L Howroyd. The weather that night was clear all the way up to the target, but when the target area was reached, they found 10/10ths cloud which rose to a height of 20,000 feet. The target and surrounding area were completely obscured by dense clouds, and the conditions left no alternative but to bomb with the use of sky markers, which was the least accurate method of target marking. Sky markers are TIs (TIs) which could be fused for both ground and air burst. The air burst markers resembled upturned fir trees when ignited in the air and hung under their parachutes. The Germans referred to these markers as 'Christmas trees' because of their shape.

S/L Howroyd aimed for the sky markers from his bombing height of 19,000 feet at 00.20 hours. He reported seeing fires below the clouds and like most of the other crews present witnessed large explosions. The Pathfinder flares which had been dropped to mark the target from a much lower altitude were not seen at all. Norman's aircraft arrived directly over the target at the crew's allotted time, which was six minutes before the flight commander. With no sky markers in sight the only alternative for them, as it was for other crews, was to bomb the target on the estimated time of arrival over the target from the last Gee navigational fix. The bombs were dropped through the clouds at 00.14 hours from a height of 20,000 feet, and they could only hope that the bombs would hit the target. No results were observed but a few scattered fires were seen and one large explosion.

There were some isolated searchlights and moderate flak over the target area. Several fighters were seen, and even though some were so close that the gunners called out their presence to Miff, the two gunners did not engage them[12]. One of the squadron's Lancasters, JA876 piloted by P/O. J Forsyth, was attacked on four occasions by fighters during this operation but evaded them all and was not damaged. The return journey, which took more than two hours, was tense, waiting for an attack by fighters. Then, at last, they crossed the coast and began the descent over the English Channel. Sandy, the wireless operator, sent a message by morse code to base informing them that they were on their way home. In due course landing instructions were received and the flare path on the runway illuminated. Three Lancasters and two Halifaxes failed to return. One of the Lancs was from 106 Squadron. JA871 crashed close to Dusseldorf and Canadian F/O Kain, and all his crew were killed. They, like Norman and his crew, had only just started their first tour of operations.

There was no relaxation for the flight crews until their home base was in sight; only then could they come to believe that they had survived the operation. After landing, the aircraft was parked and shut down. The crew now had to meet with the intelligence officer for de-briefing, having first been served a cup of hot tea laced with rum. They were all extremely tired after the five-hour trip which involved intense concentration on their job under huge stress.

---

[12] It was common practice for gunners not to engage with enemy nightfighters unless these were attacking their own aircraft, or another alongside them. This was because the muzzle flashes and tracer would attract unwelcome attention.

The crew considered that they were extremely fortunate on their first operational sortie not to have been engaged by any of the fighters in the area, and only moderate flak. Like all the participating crews they were disappointed by the lack of visibility over the target area due to the cloud cover, but they knew that they had done the best that they could.

This was the only operation on which the crew flew DV182, squadron code ZN-S. This Lancaster was lost a fortnight later, shot down by a nightfighter during the attack on Mannheim, G/C Hodder, Station Commander at RAF Syerston, was flying as supernumerary crew in DV182 and was killed.

A post-raid analysis revealed details of the raid. It was suggested that the thick and heavy cloud cover, along with some of the bombers being affected by a partial failure of the 'Oboe' navigational signal from England, resulted in a scattered attack with bombs deposited onto a dozen other Ruhr towns. The IG Farben factory was untouched.

On the following night, 23rd/24th August, 106 Squadron was detailed for its first raid on Berlin since the previous March. However, Norman's crew, having completed their first operation earlier that morning, were not detailed for operational duties. The Squadron supplied thirteen Lancasters and in charge was the newly promoted B Flight Commander, S/L Crowe, this operation being his first of the month.

This raid on Berlin was to be the first for a new type of bombing method, deploying a Master Bomber who, while over the target, would control the raid giving instructions to the rest of the bomber stream on which Pathfinder markers to aim for. The Master Bomber on this occasion was a Canadian, W/C Johnny Fauquier, who in a previous life had been a bush pilot and was well known for his no-nonsense approach to life. Fauquier had previously commanded 405 (Vancouver) Squadron and would finish the war as a Group Captain, commanding 617 Squadron.

Despite the Master Bomber's best efforts, some of the bombs ended up falling into open country, and several outlying towns reported bombs exploding all around them. This was unavoidable with the equipment and techniques available at the time and became the norm during this campaign. However, despite the difficulties in finding the target from high altitude, over 2,600 buildings were destroyed, and this was the best result to date. The cost of Bomber Command aircraft and crews was enormous with the loss of 56 aircraft, the crew loss was 392 almost all killed, the largest loss yet suffered by Bomber Command, it was the Stirlings and Halifax's that suffered the highest percentage losses. All of 106 Squadron's aircraft returned unscathed.

For Norman's crew it would be four days until the next operation, but with little time to relax due to more daily training on target bombing and navigation. Norman sent letters home whenever he found the time, family of aircrew eagerly welcomed a letter or telegram, just so that they could know their loved ones were alive and well. Alma was at home in Twickenham expecting their first child, trying to keep busy, but like all partners and family of aircrew, not knowing if your loved ones were flying bombing operations that day or night, you would just wait for some sort of message or contact to let you know that for the moment, all was well.

Operation 2: Nuremberg, 27th / 28th August 1943

Aircraft assigned: Lancaster JA973

Crew:
Pilot: Sgt. F.M. Mifflin
Flight engineer: Sgt. N.C. Jackson
Navigator: Sgt. F.L. Higgins
Bomb aimer: Sgt. N.H. Toft
Wireless operator: Sgt. E. Sandelands
Mid upper gunner: Sgt. W. Smith
Rear gunner P/O. J.S. Toffin

Bomb load: 1 x 4,000lb. 1410 x 4lb. 80 x 30lb.
Take off: 21.05 hours.
Time of landing. 04.55 hours.
Duration of operation: 8 hours 33 minutes.

Bomber Command had had its sights on Nuremberg for some time. The city was an important industrial centre with companies such as engineering and manufacturing giants Siemens and MAN. Both firms contributed mightily to Germany's war effort. Siemens produced everything from communications equipment to electrical and mechanical components for U-boats, aircraft, and V1 and V2 rockets. Nuremberg's MAN company produced 40 percent of all Panther medium tanks built by Nazi Germany. MAN also built diesel engines for submarines, and manufactured artillery of every description. Altogether the city was home to over 120 armament companies.

Nuremberg was a long trip for any crew, especially one on only their second operation. The bomber stream's route through Germany was always planned, wherever possible, to avoid areas of flak. In the case of Nuremberg the most concentrated areas were around the Ruhr and Frankfurt, as well as the many nightfighter bases. The route was also designed to leave the enemy guessing for as long as possible the actual target. The Nuremberg route was quite direct with only two turning points on the long approach to the target.

The route on this occasion consisted of a straight run of around 265 miles across Germany before turning south for Nuremberg. This was an unusually long stretch for the bombers to fly and passed close to the Ruhr defences, the nightfighter beacons at Ida and Otto, and close to many of the Luftwaffe's airfields. During the planning for the raid, the met forecasts predicted a strong tailwind for this straight leg, which was expected to take just over an hour, and it was hoped that high clouds would give the bombers some protection. The straight route across Germany was designed to get the bombers to Nuremberg as quickly as possible and reduce the time that they were exposed to the enemy nightfighters.

The heading and length of the leg should still have avoided disclosing the identity of the target to the Germans. After completing the long leg, the bombers turned south for their run into Nuremberg. No route markers were dropped at the turning point as these invariably attracted the nightfighters. Once the turn south had been made, the final leg of 79 miles took around 20 minutes but passed extremely close to the Heinz fighter beacon.

The Pathfinders arrived before the main bomber force and found the city clear of clouds but difficult to locate on what was a very dark night. The H2S radar was not performing as well it might and even though the Pathfinders had marked the target accurately, some creep back developed. This was exacerbated by some communication problems which prevented the Master Bomber's instructions from getting through to some of the main bomber stream.

Bombing was carried out on instructions from the 'Master of Ceremonies', the Master Bomber and, on arrival over target area, Tofty located the aiming point, which was illuminated by the Pathfinder flares, with the centre of four green TIs in sight. He released their bombs from a height of 20,000 feet, at 00.47 hours. As the bombs were released, simultaneously a flare was dropped which lit up the ground sufficiently to show the target area aimed at.

A special camera within the Lancaster which took the photograph left the film exposed for several seconds as the flare was planned to burst when the bombs were halfway through their trajectory to the ground. The object of this exercise was to obtain a record of where the bombs were likely to impact, rather than the explosion itself. However, in order for this photograph to be obtained the pilot had to fly straight and level for a period of up to 30 seconds after the bomb release. This went against the crew's natural instinct to turn away as quickly as possible, rather than continue to fly straight and level over a well-defended target. This was a particularly stressful period of time.

Most aircrew feared anti-aircraft fire, known as flak, although statistically, they were more likely to be shot down by fighters. Shrapnel from exploding flak could cause extensive damage not only to the aircraft, but also injuries to the crew. It could result in serious injuries, especially if it struck the head or upper part of the body. The sight and sound of shells bursting nearby were unnerving to an aircrew and a near miss could cause the aircraft to jolt alarmingly.

On this occasion, however, the defences in the target area were poor, and no fighters were seen. The return journey was in darkness, as the moon had set and the route back was well clear of any major flak areas and nightfighter airfields. In avoiding these areas, it resulted in a long trip home lasting almost five hours.

Bomber Command lost 33 aircraft along with 231 crew, most of whom lost their lives but 106 Squadron came through unscathed. The crews were quietly confident that the raid had been successful, but the crews' photos showed that bombing positions were mostly between one and a half to five miles south-southeast of the aiming point and many of the bombs fell into open country.

For aircrew returning safely from an operation, relief at survival was the overriding emotion. Once home they could enjoy a hot meal and sleep in a warm bed. For the next day or two there might be no flying on operations and no training. RAF stations generally had good leisure facilities and there were frequent dances, mess parties and variety shows. Aircrew were given generous amounts of leave, with a seven day pass every six weeks and shorter periods granted during prolonged bad weather or after difficult operations. There was no leave yet due for Norman's crew so, after visiting Nuremberg, they were detailed to fly another operation, their third, just two days later, with Norman's leg still in plaster.

Operation 3: Mönchengladbach / Rheydt, 30th / 31st August 1943

Aircraft assigned: Lancaster ED358

Crew:
Pilot: Sgt. F.M. Mifflin
Flight engineer: Sgt. N.C. Jackson
Navigator: Sgt. F.L. Higgins
Bomb aimer: Sgt. N.H. Toft
Wireless operator: Sgt. E. Sandelands
Mid upper gunner: Sgt. W. Smith
Rear gunner: Sgt. H.J. Keenan

Bomb load: 1 x 4,000lb. 1320 x 4lb. 64 x 30lb.
Take off: 23.35 hours.

Time of landing. 04.50 hours.
Duration of operation: 5 hours 15 minutes.

Mönchengladbach and Rheydt are cities in Northwest Rhine-Westphalia, Germany, located west of the Rhine, halfway between Dusseldorf and the Dutch border. The Royal Air Force considered these cities important due to their armaments factories and railyards which were used by the Germans for all sorts of freight movements into Belgium and Holland. Railway yards and railway lines were the arteries of any country allowing the movement at speed of troops, armaments, produce and all things connected with that country's war effort.

When the briefing room curtain uncovered the target for that night, there were undoubtedly some sighs of relief at what appeared to be a short haul operation to the southwestern edges of the Ruhr valley. The bomber force was some 600 aircraft strong, of which fifteen were from 106 Squadron. The plan was an attack in two phases, with a separation time of two minutes as the Pathfinders relocated the aiming point from one town to the other. 106 Squadron had been enjoying a recent unbroken run of excellent serviceability, but this was to end this evening when F/O Roper lost his port inner engine while en route to the target and returned home.

As Norman's Lancaster, ED358, arrived over the target area the weather was 8/10ths cloud with tops of 10,000 feet, and good visibility. The aiming point was indicated by Pathfinder markers. Norman's bomb aimer, Tofty, aimed from 18,000 feet at the centre of a cluster of green TIs that were seen cascading at 02.30 hours. Their own results were not observed but fires in the target area appeared to be well concentrated. The later bombers, arriving at the target area after 02.30 hours, attacked Rheydt. The flak was very light, and no fighters were seen. As far as the operation was concerned, it all proceeded to plan and was deemed a success with both towns sustaining considerable damage, with a combined number of 2,300 buildings destroyed.

Despite the clear skies there was, as always, a risk of collision when flying at night, especially with the concentration of many aircraft over just one area. An RAF Halifax Mark 2 of 51 squadron, returning from the raid, collided with an Avro Lancaster, sustaining considerable damage to its port outer engine, fuselage and its port rudder being cut in two. The pilot of the Halifax found his aircraft uncontrollable below 180 knots of airspeed and consequently the landing back at his home airfield was extremely fast. The aircraft ran out of runway and came to rest on the grass beyond, fortunately with only light injuries to some members of the crew. In many such cases the crews of both aircraft were lost. 25 aircraft were lost during this raid, along with 175 crew, but for the third raid in succession all 106 Squadron participants arrived home safely. ED358 was another Lancaster living on borrowed time and would fail to return from Leipzig on the night of 20th / 21st October 1943, with the loss of P/O P. Hanavan and his crew of seven, which included a second bomb aimer, F/L G.C. Cooper.

With three days until the next operation Norman had time to write letters home to his parents and to his wife Alma. When crews were not on ops or training sorties, the evenings were spent either in the base bar or, if permitted, a trip to Grantham. On evenings of drinking or partying the excitement for the crew, like any other crew, was frenetic. It was of that peculiar quality that grips men who live their lives from day to day and night to night in mortal danger and well know that this brief moment of almost carefree existence, maybe only an hour or two, may be their last.

Operation 4: Berlin, 3rd / 4th September 1943

Aircraft assigned: Lancaster JA876

Crew:
Pilot: Sgt. F.M. Mifflin
Flight engineer: Sgt. N.C. Jackson
Navigator   Sgt. F.L. Higgins
Bomb aimer: Sgt. N.H. Toft
Wireless operator   Sgt. E. Sandelands
Mid upper gunner   Sgt. W. Smith
Rear gunner   Sgt. T. Astwick

Bomb load: 1 x4,000lb. 600 x 4lb. 48 x30lb.
Take off: 20.10 hours.
Time of landing.   04.10 hours.
Duration of operation: 8 hours.

When in 1939 the Second World War in Europe began, US President Franklin D Roosevelt issued a request to the major belligerents to confine their air raids to military targets. The British and French agreed to abide by the request upon the understanding that these same rules of warfare would be scrupulously observed by all their opponents. The British had a policy of using aerial bombing only against military targets and or infrastructure such as ports and railways of direct military importance. It was acknowledged that the aerial bombing of Germany would cause civilian casualties, but the British Government renounced the deliberate bombing of civilian property outside of the combat zone as a military tactic.

This policy was abandoned on 15th May 1940 following the German air attack on Rotterdam in which the Dutch city was subjected to heavy aerial bombardment by the Luftwaffe and almost destroyed. The objective was to support German troops fighting in the city, break Dutch resistance, and force the Dutch army to surrender. The bombing began at the outset of hostilities on 10th May 1940 and culminated with the destruction of the entire historic city centre on 14th May. The psychological and the physical success of the raid, from the German perspective, led the overall commander of the Luftwaffe, Reichsmarshall Herman Goering, to threaten to destroy the city of Utrecht in the same way if the Dutch Command did not surrender. The Dutch surrendered in the late afternoon of 14th May and signed the capitulation early the next morning.

Following this conduct by the Luftwaffe the Royal Air Force was given permission to attack targets in the Ruhr, including oil plants and other civilian industrial targets that aided the German war effort. These targets were of the utmost importance to the German war effort, however, with the technology available at that time it was almost impossible to hit a specific target from 20,000 feet, and so carpet bombing by large numbers of bombers concentrated over an area for as short a time as possible was tried and proved to be far more effective.

The battle for Berlin, which was launched by Sir Arthur Harris, Commander-in-Chief of Bomber Command, was to be a concentrated campaign against the German capital, although other cities continued to be attacked to prevent the Germans from concentrating their defences in Berlin. Harris believed this could be the blow that would break German resistance; it would cost between 400 to 500 aircraft, he said, but it would cost Germany the war.

Bomber Command detailed 316 Lancasters and 4 Mosquitos for this raid. 106 Squadron, commanded by S/L Holroyd, contributed eleven Lancasters to the bomber force. All were airborne either side of 20.00 hours and headed for the Dutch coast at Den Helder with the intention of a direct route to the target of Berlin. There was heavy cloud below them on the outward journey, but this had almost dissipated as the target was sighted. Due to the clear visibility the Pathfinders had laid ground markers, positioned over the aiming point but once again creeping back by five miles or so. However, on this occasion, it was not unfortunate, as the creep back was on the line of approach to the target and intersected the Siemens Stadt industrial district.

The bomber force started to arrive over the target just after 23.20 hours. As Norman's aircraft arrived over the target, Miff handed direction over to Tofty to line the aircraft up for the bomb run. After the nerve-racking procedure of "Left... left a bit more... steady... right... steady... steady... steady..." Maurice aimed and released the bombs at the centre of a cluster of three green TIs from 20,700 feet at 23.25 hours. Fires were seen burning in good concentration. The defences were very fierce, several fighters were seen, and once again came extremely close but their aircraft was not directly engaged. Then as they were leaving the target 'Smudge' Smith, the mid upper gunner called on the intercom and said that there was a Lancaster close on their port side and just forward of them, that was involved in a combat with a fighter. He asked permission from Miff to fire on the fighter to assist the other Lancaster, Fred gave his permission but said, "Be careful with the ammunition as we may need to defend ourselves." He then asked Sgt. Astwick, the rear gunner, if he could see the fighter, there was no reply, Fred called again and still heard no reply.

Norman disconnected his intercom and oxygen, clipped on one of the portable oxygen bottles and made his way back to the rear gunner's position. He slid open the doors to the rear turret to see Sgt. Astwick motionless in the seat, so shook him vigorously. This had no effect, so he dragged him backwards from the rear turret into the main section of the fuselage. Norman could hear 'Smudge' Smith firing at the fighter, which was clearly the major threat. Climbing into the rear turret, Norman aimed the four machine guns and fired short bursts at the fighter, which was still attacking the other Lancaster. He could see his and 'Smudge' Smith's tracer bullets flying straight into the fighter, as was the tracer from the guns of the other Lancaster, and the fighter broke off the attack.

Norman and Smudge thought that it may have been shot down but left it to the gunners of the other Lancaster to claim as they had been in actual combat with the fighter. Norman went back to Sgt. Astwick and dragged him to the casualty station where he laid him on the bunk. Norman could see no sign of injury and so made him comfortable and returned to the cockpit. During the trip back to base Sgt. Astwick regained consciousness, and said he was feeling well enough to return to his station. After arriving back at base Sgt. Astwick was sent to the medical officer for examination, but nothing was found that could have explained his losing consciousness. The aircraft oxygen supply to the rear turret was inspected and found to be fully operational, so with no obvious explanation for his incapacitation he was passed fit to return to operational flying. Norman joked later "...maybe he just fell asleep."

JA876 was one of only three Lancasters in which Norman flew operationally to survive the war, staying in service until November 1947.

S/L Holroyd, flying JA893, had just bombed from 20,000 feet at 23.37 hours when they were attacked by a nightfighter. A fierce combat ensued with the fighter, and the Lancaster received several hits, as did the fighter, which was shot down. The Lancaster was severely damaged, and some members of the crew were hit. P/O. Saxby, the bomb aimer, was killed, and the rear gunner, Sgt. McKenzie, sustained very serious wounds. The Lancaster ended up having to ditch 150 miles short of the English coast. One of the crew had operated the dinghy deployment lever inside the aircraft before escaping through the hatch. The survivors exited the sinking Lancaster and climbed into the dinghy though they to leave the body of P/O Saxby in the Lancaster. Before ditching the wireless operator had managed to send a message giving their position and requesting help, and within a few hours a Hudson of 279 Squadron located them and dropped a lifeboat. A naval launch was not far behind, and the rescue took place. Unfortunately, Sgt. Mckenzie, the rear gunner, died from his wounds shortly before the naval launch arrived. The launch took the surviving crew to Immingham on the north Lincolnshire coast arriving at 05.45 hours.

106 Squadron lost ED385 that night as well, with F/O Roper RAAF at the controls, probably due to damage sustained by fighter attacks. They crashed into the woods while east-northeast of Hanover on the way home, with the loss of F/O Roper and all his crew. The day following an operation, any losses were obvious from the empty tables and chairs in the dining hall but would seldom be mentioned. The crews all shared the same knowledge that the following night it may be them that did not return.

The operation was designated as partially successful due to the amount of destruction to the residential and industrial districts of Berlin. This came at some cost to Bomber Command of the loss of 22 Lancasters along with 154 aircrew. With the loss of a total of 125 aircraft and 875 crew on the Berlin operations that had taken place so far, it was decided by Bomber Command to put a hold on Berlin as a target until the long dark nights of winter would give better protection. This did not put the bombing campaign on hold as there were plenty of alternative targets which were important if the German war effort was to be stopped. After the next night off, Norman and his crew found themselves once again on the Battle Order.

Operation 5: Ludwigshafen-Mannheim, 5th / 6th September 1943

Aircraft assigned: Lancaster ED801

Crew:
Pilot: Sgt. F.M. Mifflin
Flight engineer: Sgt. N.C. Jackson
Navigator Sgt. F.L. Higgins
Bomb aimer: Sgt. N.H. Toft
Wireless operator Sgt. E. Sandelands
Mid upper gunner Sgt. W. Smith
Rear gunner Sgt. T. Astwick

Bomb load: 1 x 4,000lb. 900 x 4lb. 80 x 30lb.
Take off: 21.10 hours.
Time of landing 02.20 hours.
Duration of operation: 5 hours 10 minutes.

The target area was highly industrialised with major chemical production and oil infrastructure as the chief attractions. The combined target area of Ludwigshafen-Mannheim presented a formidable, heavily defended, challenge to the attacking bomber force.

Mannheim and Ludwigshafen are on opposite sides of the Rhine in Southern Germany. Bomber Command thought that the position of these targets lent itself to taking advantage of the creep back that had been occurring during the marking of aiming points by the Pathfinder force[13]. The plan was to mark an aiming point in the eastern half of Mannheim, with an approach from the west. The bombers would therefore fly directly over Ludwigshafen, with the creep back extending back across the western side of Mannheim, over the Rhine and onto Ludwigshafen on the west bank of the river. Bomber Command detailed 605 aircraft comprising 299 Lancasters, 195 Halifaxes, and 111 Stirlings, though 106 Squadron could contribute only eight Lancasters. The following explanation was entered in the Squadron's Operations Report Book:

> *No replacements being forthcoming to build up our depleted resources, the squadron could only offer eight aircraft for tonight's raid. The night proved disastrous.*

The weather that night forecast no clouds, and good visibility. This was to be the largest raid on Mannheim during the war.

106 Squadron had no senior pilots on duty that night, so the Station Commander, Group Captain Hodder, decided to take part and flew as eighth man aboard DV182, piloted by Pilot Officer (P/O) Robertson. After the Squadron had all departed either side of 20.00 hours, Flight Sergeant (F/Sgt) Hart had to abort and return to Syerston with an

---

[13] 'Creep back' resulted from the understandable tendency of some bomb aimers to release their ordnance no later than strictly necessary, so that a speedier exit from the target area might be possible. With several hundred bombers releasing their blast- and incendiary bombs as soon as they could be reasonably certain that they would at least hit the target fires, if not the actual TIs, the resultant fires tended to spread backwards along the line of attack. This was mitigated to a certain extent by 'backers-up' renewing the TIs, and exhortations of the Master Bomber to crews to bomb the TIs, not the flames.

unserviceable engine. Just five minutes later, F/Sgt. Turner touched down back at Syerston with an unserviceable rear turret. The other six Lancasters of 106 Squadron joined with the main bomber force and headed for the target.

The Pathfinder marking plan worked perfectly, ground markers were placed on the eastern side of Mannheim. The bombing was accurate, and severe destruction was caused to both Mannheim and Ludwigshafen. As Norman's Lancaster arrived over the target, Miff handed direction over to Tofty. At 23.12 hrs, Maurice released the bombs from 20,000 feet, aiming at the centre of a cluster of five green TIs which he saw cascading down. A photograph taken was plotted three miles from the aiming point. A large concentration of fires was seen. There was heavy and accurate flak over the target.

Photo Reconnaissance confirmed the raid had been a complete success and the creep back plan had worked perfectly. Both Mannheim and Ludwigshafen had suffered enormous amounts of damage to industrial buildings along with residential dwellings. The damage was exacerbated, as reported and recorded by the Ludwigshafen authorities, by almost 2,000 individual fires in their city alone.

There was a high cost to pay for the success. 34 aircraft along with 238 crew never made it back to base. As noted above, for 106 Squadron the night was indeed 'disastrous'. W4922, piloted by F/Sgt. Taylor. RAAF, crashed on the banks of the Rhine, killing all on board. P/O Robertson's Lancaster DV182, was attacked by a nightfighter and racked with heavy machine gun or cannon fire. P/O Robertson was killed outright and his flight engineer, Sgt. Cunliffe, was mortally wounded. As the Lancaster started to fall from the sky a fire broke out, but the bomb aimer, Flying Officer (F/O) Willatt, managed to bail out before the Lancaster crashed north-west of Karlsruhe. The loss of this aircraft claimed the lives of another six of 106 Squadron's airmen plus the equally unfortunate Station Commander, Group Captain Hodder.

ED801, Norman's aircraft on this raid, was later transferred to 1661 CU, then returned to operational service with 207 Squadron. After a further tour, the aircraft went to 1653 CU, where she survived a crash, and managed also to survive the war.

Following the raid on the 6th and 7th September there was a two week stand down for most of the Squadrons of 1 and 5 Groups including 106 Squadron. During this time there may have been an opportunity for some leave. If there was, it is likely that Norman travelled down to Twickenham to see his wife and family. Alma was expecting their first child and with the birth expected the following April there would no doubt have been a lot to organise[14].

Back at Syerston, when the crew was not on operations, there was almost daily training on navigation, bomb aiming, cross country and trial flights. In mid-1943 the Squadron's crews started training on a regular basis with a new piece of radar equipment codenamed *Monica*. This was mounted in the tail of the aircraft and was designed to warn bomber crews of an attack by a fighter from the rear. Unfortunately, *Monica* proved to be somewhat of a magnet to German nightfighters equipped with passive radar receivers that could be tuned to home in on the *Monica* transmissions. Bomber Command remained completely unaware of the German homing capability on *Monica* for some six months after its first use and many bomber crews paid for this oversight with their lives.

---

[14] The author recalls Alma telling him that she and Norman would talk a lot about the future, including how many children they would have. Norman, being adopted, wanted a large family. They discussed where they would live and the type and size of property they would like. All of this is quite normal for a young couple, but what was not normal was that both knew that at that moment such matters were just dreams. They knew that in reality, making any plans beyond Norman's next operation was futile, but they never spoke to each other in that negative way, preferring to maintain a positive mindset despite their own private apprehensions.

Operation 6: Hagen, 1st / 2nd October 1943

Aircraft assigned: Lancaster ED593

Crew:
Pilot:	Sgt. F.M. Mifflin
Flight engineer:	Sgt. N.C. Jackson
Navigator	Sgt. F.L. Higgins
Bomb aimer:	Sgt. A. Porritt
Wireless operator	Sgt. N. Woodward
Mid upper gunner	Sgt. W. Smith
Rear gunner	Sgt. J. Pears

Bomb load: 1 x 4,000lb. 1260 x4lb. 104 x30lb.
Take off: 18.00 hours.
Time of landing. 00.05 hours.
Duration of operation: 6 hours 5 minutes.

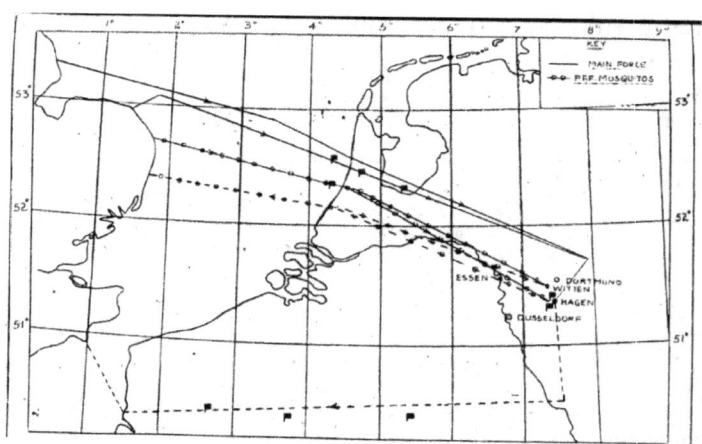

Routing of the various night raids of 1st / 2nd October 1943. These are from the records of Bomber Command and were hand-drawn as shown. The copies available are poor quality but worthy of inclusion. The black flags denote known losses of bombers (Steve Smith)

Hagen, which is situated at the eastern end of the Ruhr, just south of Dortmund. was well known at the time for its mining of coal and production of steel. The Ruhr, which had the largest coal deposits of anywhere in the world, contributed a huge amount to the ability of the German nation to wage war. The coal fuelled the power stations and every type of factory and business, so its importance was enormous. The steel produced at Hagen was shipped all over Germany for use in producing all forms of armaments and vehicles and was also used to reinforce the concrete that the Germans were using to construct more factories. On the night of 1st / 2nd October, Bomber Command sent an all-Lancaster bomber force of 243 aircraft. 8 Mosquitos were to provide the marking of the target using Oboe[15], 106 Squadron provided fifteen Lancasters with W/C Baxter as the officer commanding the force. The route, rather than crossing over the Lincolnshire coast was over Dungeness in Kent, this route was a means to avoid running straight through the Ruhr defences.

The weather that night was 10/10ths cloud, with the top of the cloud at 7,000 feet. The target was identified by Pathfinder markers, which had been laid directly over the aiming point; green TIs were seen cascading at 21.05 hours. After arriving directly over the target area, Norman's aircraft began its run into the target. Tofty released the bombs on the green TIs from 20,000 feet at 21.06 hours. The results were not seen but the bombing seemed to be well concentrated. The defences over the target were poor but there was considerable opposition on the journey in with both heavy and in some area's fierce flak despite the attempt to avoid the Ruhr defences.

According to the Bomber Command records, the raid was a complete success achieved on a completely covered target of relatively small size, with only a moderate bomber force and at a trifling cost. Analysis

---

[15] *Oboe* was a British bomb-aiming system developed to allow a target to be marked accurately in all weathers, day or night. The Mosquito aircraft being fast with the capability and manoeuvrability of a fighter was ideal for the role. The system's main limitations were (i) that it required line of sight to the beacon and so was effective only up to 250 miles and (ii) the marker aircraft had to fly a steady course in the run up to the release point for the TIs.

reported that apart from the residential damage, 46 factories and businesses had been destroyed, including a U-Boat accumulator battery factory, and the loss of production from this factory slowed down U-Boat output considerably.

Operation 7: Munich, 2nd / 3rd October 1943

Aircraft assigned: Lancaster JA876

Crew:
Pilot: P/O F.M. Mifflin
Flight engineer: Sgt. N.C. Jackson
Navigator   Sgt. F.L. Higgins
Bomb aimer: Sgt. A. Porritt
Wireless operator   Sgt. M. Woodward
Mid upper gunner   Sgt. W. Smith
Rear gunner   Sgt. J. Pears

Bomb load: 1 x 4,000lb. 600 x 4lb. 84 x 30lb.
Take off: 18.45 hours.
Time of landing: 02.55 hours
Duration of operation: 8 hours 10 minutes.

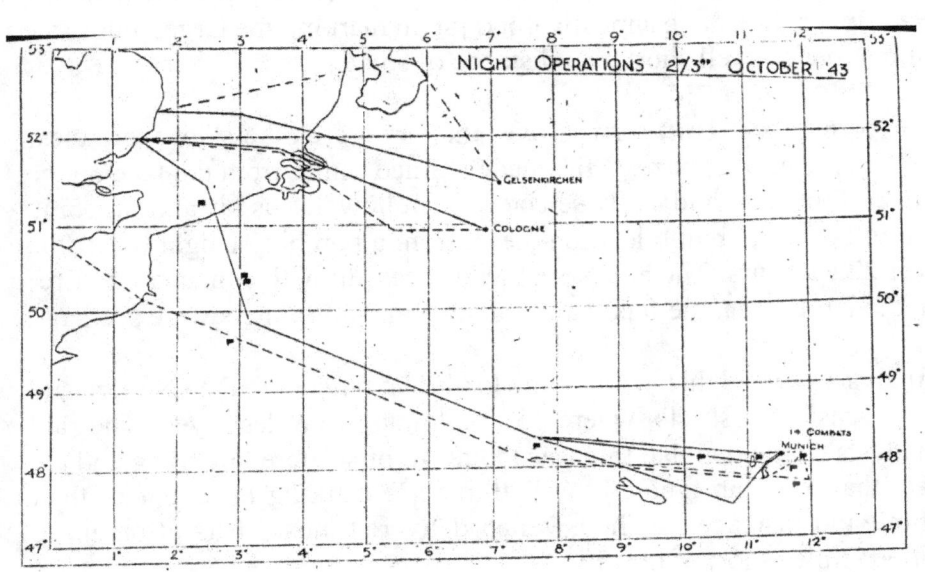

Norman and his crew were 'on ops' the same evening. Norman's pilot, Miff, had now received his commission and was a Pilot Officer.

Munich was always thought of as an especially valuable target by Bomber Command for two reasons. Firstly, it was a major industrial and transport centre, contributing mightily to the German war effort. Secondly, it was significant for propaganda reasons, because Munich was the birthplace of the Nazi movement in 1920, and the Nazi Party headquarters was located here. Munich was also where the Nazis constructed their first concentration camp, located ten miles to the west of the city.

Bomber Command detailed a force of almost 300 aircraft for the attack on Munich to which 106 Squadron contributed thirteen Lancasters. The squadron was led by S/L Howroyd who was the most senior pilot on duty that evening. All 106 Squadron pilots for this raid were officers. After taking to the air safely between 18.30 and 19.10 hours, one Lancaster, piloted by F/O Forsyth had a problem with his outer starboard engine and his flight engineer, Sgt. A. Woollag, after trying his utmost to rectify the issue, had to shut the engine down and they returned to base. All the remaining 106 Squadron aircraft made it safely to the target of Munich. It was a clear night over the target area and the Pathfinders had done a mostly good job in marking the target, but some of the markers fell short by a distance of some miles.

As Norman's aircraft arrived over the target area the skies were clear with some ground haze. Miff made a timed run in from the lake on the edge of the city, and Tofty selected the yellow TIs as his aiming point. He released the bomb load on these, from a bombing height of 21,000 feet 22.37 hours. The attack seemed successful with concentrated fires in the target area, the flak was moderate, and no fighters were seen.

Analysis showed that many bomb loads had fallen into the southern and south-eastern districts, where 339 buildings were destroyed. The raid analysts concluded that this was the result of scattered marking and the fact that 5 Group ignored the Pathfinder's marking in favour of their 'time and distance' method, which delivered most of its effort up to fifteen miles short of the city.

JA876 survived the war, being transferred to 1661 CU after her operational service. She was transferred to the Royal Aircraft Establishment after VE Day and took part in trials developing Decca navigation systems.

On 4th October 106 Squadron was detailed for the fourth consecutive night for an operation. The Squadron supplied eleven Lancasters for a raid on Frankfurt, the opposition was negligible, and all aircraft returned safely. Norman and his crew were not detailed for this operation.

There was now a period of day and night training along with operations detailed for the night of 5th / 6th October when 106 Squadron detailed fourteen Lancasters for each operation, but with the crews ready in their Lancasters the operations were cancelled.

Operation 8: Stuttgart, 7th / 8th October 1943

Aircraft assigned: Lancaster W4897

Crew:
Pilot: P/O F.M. Mifflin
Flight engineer: Sgt. N.C. Jackson
Navigator F/Sgt. F.L. Higgins
Bomb aimer: Sgt. M.H. Toft
Wireless operator Sgt. E. Sandelands
Mid upper gunner Sgt. W. Smith
Rear gunner Sgt. J. Pears

Bomb load: 1 x 4,000lb. 690 x 4lb. 72 x 30lb.
Take off: 20.45 hours.
Time down: 03.50 hours
Duration of operation: 7 hours 5 minutes

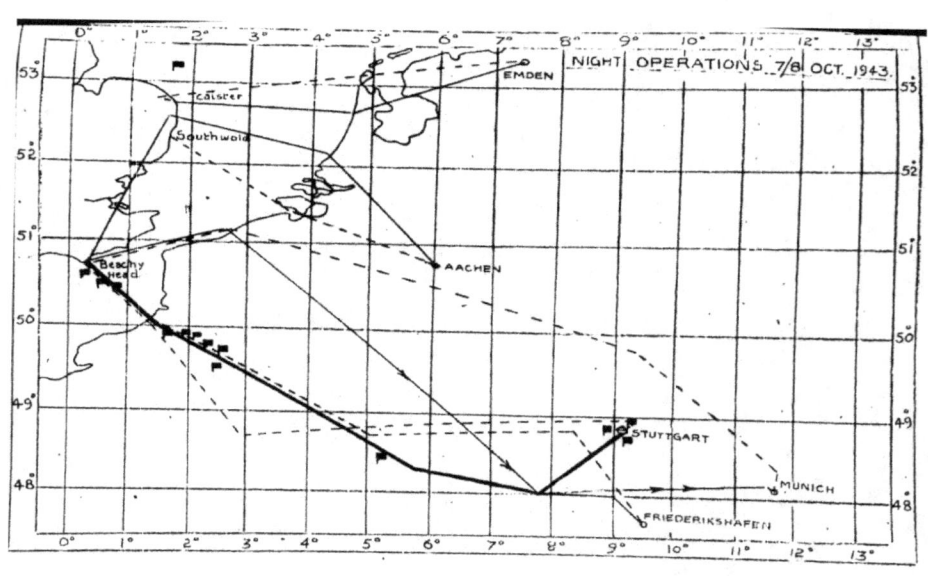

Stuttgart was a centre of industry with among others, the Bosch, Daimler-Benz plants, and the SKF factory which produced ball bearings. It was also an important rail hub for the rail traffic delivering armaments etc. all over Germany.

Bomber Command detailed 343 aircraft for the Stuttgart operation, fourteen of them from 106 Squadron. It was on this operation that Bomber Command included 101 Squadron's radio countermeasures (RCM) aircraft in significant numbers. 101 Squadron was part of 1 Group. The countermeasure equipment that these aircraft carried was called *Mandrel*, which was designed to jam the nightfighter's communication from ground to air. It was known to the crews as ABC, (*airborne cigar*). Each of the ABC Lancasters carried a crew of eight, the extra crew member operating the device. He would have a basic knowledge of German which would allow him to recognise the language and what was said when he heard it on the radio. It was his job, once having identified the German transmission to use the device to broadcast engine noise across all the radio channels in use, this would completely disrupt the communication between the ground stations and the nightfighters. The 101 Squadron Lancasters would also carry a normal bomb load which was reduced in weight by 1,000 pounds to compensate for the extra crew man and the equipment. After *Mandrel* proved to be effective in its operation, several of 101 Squadrons ABC Lancasters would join the main bomber force on all major operations, this was independent of whether other members of 1 Group were part of the operation.

F/Ls Claridge and Poore were the senior pilots on duty as the Lancasters of 106 Squadron started to become airborne from 20.45. After the aircraft formed up, they headed for Beachy Head. One aircraft piloted by P/O Richards had an unserviceable rear turret and had to return early.

The skies were clear for nearly all the outbound journey, but with around 50 miles or so to the target, clouds began to build, eventually reaching eight-tenths over the target, and the ground was no longer clearly visible. The Pathfinders had dropped route marking flares which identified the route to the target along with TIs on the target itself. The route to the target was reported as good and as Norman's Lancaster arrived over the target of Stuttgart, Tofty began his bomb run, dropping from 20,000 feet at 00.17 hours, but no results were observed owing to the cloud cover. Reflections of large fires were seen, there were very few searchlights but heavy flak, and no fighters were seen.

Post-raid analysis reported that the marking of the target had developed in two main areas, and the attack caused substantial damage to the city. 344 buildings were destroyed and more than 4,000 damaged. With the remarkably low number of just four aircraft and twenty-eight crew on board failing to return, it was believed that ABC had been a glowing success. However, there was a diversion operation flown by Mosquitos to Munich at the same time, and that may also have contributed to the low number of aircraft lost.

After serving with 106 Squadron, W4897 was transferred to 463 Squadron, RAAF. Operating with a crew consisting of Australian, British, and Canadian airmen, under F/Sgt. Stanley Lawson RAAF, she was lost without trace on the night of 1st / 2nd January 1944, attacking Berlin.

On 9th October nine Lancasters from 106 Squadron were detailed for an operation but this was cancelled due to fog. The fog was to remain for the rest of the month only lifting occasionally, allowing for more training day and night. The fog did lift on the night of the 18th which allowed for an operation to attack Hanover, 106 Squadron detailed thirteen aircraft, there was light flak over the target and many fighters. One of the 106 Squadron Lancasters received considerable damage from an attack by a fighter along with the rear gunner being injured but returned safely.

An operation was detailed for the 19th but cancelled due to fog. The following night the weather improved slightly to allow for an attack on Leipzig.

Operation 9: Leipzig, 20th / 21st October 1943

Aircraft assigned: Lancaster JA973

Crew:
Pilot: P/O F.M. Mifflin
Flight engineer: F/Sgt. N.C. Jackson
Navigator F/Sgt. F.L. Higgins
Bomb aimer: Sgt. M.H. Toft
Wireless operator Sgt. E. Sandelands
Mid upper gunner Sgt. W. Smith
Rear gunner Sgt. J. Pears

Bomb load: 1 x 4,000lb. 900 x 4lb. 96 x 30lb.
Take off: 17.30 hours.
Time down: 21.15 hours.
Duration of operation: 3 hours 45 minutes.

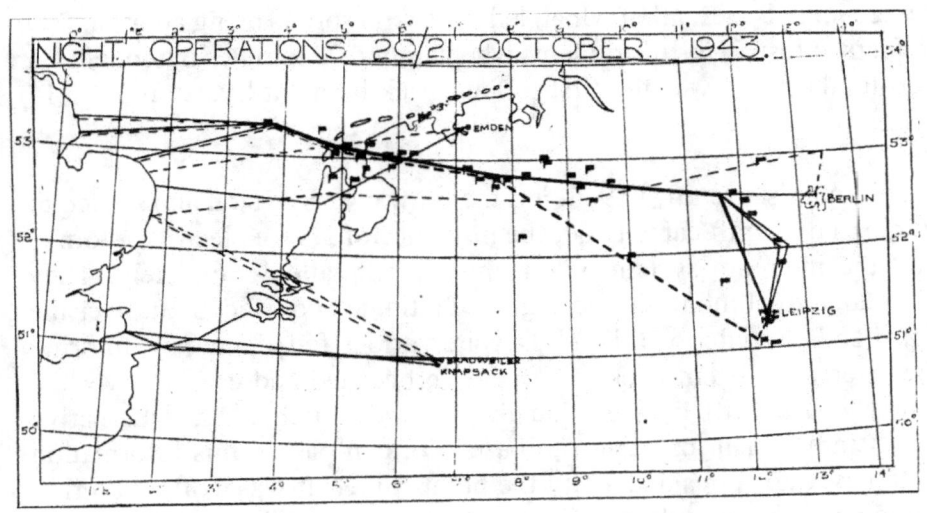

Leipzig is situated in Eastern Germany, midway between the city of Kassel in northern Hesse, and the Czechoslovakian frontier. It was a target of immense importance to Bomber Command for more reasons than the fact that it was the sixth largest city of the Greater German Reich. The city was home to no fewer than four factories which were producing the Messerschmitt Bf109 fighter. There was also a factory producing ball bearings, one of the most important components in the production of any type of armament or machinery with moving parts. Leipzig was also a very important railroad intersection in Germany at that time.

Bomber Command detailed 358 Lancasters for this raid, 1, 5, 6, and 8 Groups were all involved. 106 Squadron provided thirteen Lancasters which were led by the new A flight commander, S/L Dunn, on what was his first time in command of an operation. The previous commander, S/L Howroyd had taken part in an operation on 8th / 9th October to Hanover. His Lancaster DV272, after dropping its bombs, crashed seven miles to the south-west of Hanover. Only the bomb aimer, P/O Crumb, RCAF, survived the crash and was captured by the enemy.

S/L Dunn was airborne first at 17.00 hours. The weather on the outbound journey was nothing short of appalling with thick clouds that had their tops at 25,000 feet. There were violent electrical storms and severe icing issues, all of which led to several sorties being aborted. P/O Anderson lost all his instruments when around 90 minutes outbound. He had to abort and was the first to land back home at Syerston at 20.15 hours.

As Norman's aircraft, JA973, left the runway at Syerston and started to climb, the aircraft came under the influence of severe electrical storms, and the intercom system within the aircraft failed completely. They continued to climb to their designated altitude and headed out over the coast and en route to Holland. Despite various failed attempts to bring the intercom system back to life they proceeded and crossed over the Dutch coast. Miff decided that they would search for an alternative target rather than just return to base. Norman passed this information onto navigator Pops and Tofty the bomb aimer. It was Tofty who first came up with a possibility as he saw what looked like an airfield flare path off to one side of them, Pops consulted his maps and current position and identified the sighting as the aerodrome at Bergen Alkrinar. It was decided that this would be their secondary target, and they set course to fly directly overhead the aerodrome. The bomb load was dropped, and the bombs were seen to explode on or very close to Tofty's aiming point. Then they set a course for home.

For the rest of the squadron, continuing as planned, problems were still occurring. P/O Perry lost both his inner engines three hours after take-off, he was struggling to maintain altitude through the severe icing on his wings, he had to turn around and head back for home. The crew of this aircraft, as if not having enough pressure to deal with, were carrying a passenger, the new station commander Group Captain Pleasance.

The first member of the Squadron to arrive over the target was F/O Jardine, who bombed from 20,000 feet at 21.06 hours, aiming at the glow of fires that were reflected in the clouds as no route markers or TIs were seen at all. On his return he described the operation as '...a long and tedious trip which achieved doubtful results.' Just a minute behind was F/O Latham, who did see a yellow TI along with two sky marker flares. Hs bomb aimer used the yellow illumination and bombed from 14,500 feet. F/O Latham had been forced to shut down one engine on the outbound flight but continued with three engines, struggling to maintain altitude with the heavy bomb load.

On approach to the target S/L Dunn's bomb aimer spotted what he believed was a red TI and he bombed on that from 20,000 feet at 21.12 hours. This crew also returned with feelings of pessimism regarding hitting the target. F/L Boyle and his crew felt the same as they could find no route markers, TIs or sky marker flares, and so bombed on the estimated position from their last fix at 21.13 hours.

ED358 piloted by P/O Hanavan of 106 Squadron, failed to arrive back at Syerston. Information eventually came through that the aircraft had crashed in northern Germany with the loss of all eight crew on board; the aircraft had been carrying an additional bomb aimer, F/L Cooper, who was new to the squadron. All in all, the whole operation was seen as a failure.

JA973 was another 106 Squadron Lancaster that made her way to 463 Squadron RAAF. As was so often the case, she fell victim to the enemy defences on a visit to Berlin on 30th / 31st January 1944. Six of the crew of P/O Hanson RAAF, were killed, the sole survivor being the flight engineer, Sgt. Hughes.

There were only minor operations and training for the rest of the month, mainly due to more fog, which allowed the bomber crews nine nights to rest and pay visits to the local establishments for entertainment.

In November 106 Squadron were notified of a move of station from Syerston, to their new home base at Metheringham. This was an airfield that was still under construction, being built out of the farmland only a few miles to the west of Woodhall Spa. The airfield had few permanent buildings offering comfortable accommodation for those soon to arrive from Syerston, as most of the airfield was still under construction. 106 Squadron sent an advance party to start the process of transition; they found the conditions at Metheringham to be very basic and had to endure what could only have been described as a quite miserable existence due to the cold and damp. They had to sleep wherever they could find a comfortable place, which was usually either in the cookhouse or the messes.

On 5th November, five officers of 106 Squadron, along with 61 N.C.Os and airmen relocated to Metheringham in order to prepare for the arrival of the rest of the Squadron. It was on the 7th that 106 Squadron was notified that the aircraft, crews, and main party were to move to Metheringham the following day, with a farewell party at Syerston on the 9th and the final completion of the move on the 10th. these plans were changed when operations were scheduled for the nights of 8th / 9th November. However, ops were cancelled at the last minute. The Lancasters of 106 Squadron were now scheduled to be flown to Metheringham on the 10th, but this was to change yet again with another operation detailed, and 106 Squadron was ordered to prepare for that instead.

Operation 10: Modane, 10th / 11th November 1943

Aircraft assigned: Lancaster LM310

Crew:
Pilot: P/O F.M. Mifflin
Flight engineer: F/Sgt N.C. Jackson
Navigator   F/Sgt. F.L. Higgins
Bomb aimer: Sgt. M.H. Toft
Wireless operator   Sgt. E. Sandelands
Mid upper gunner   Sgt. W. Smith
Rear gunner   Sgt. R.S. Miller

Bomb load: 9 x 1,000lb.
Take off: 21.05 hours.
Time down: 04.35 hours.
Duration of operation: 7 hours 30 minutes.

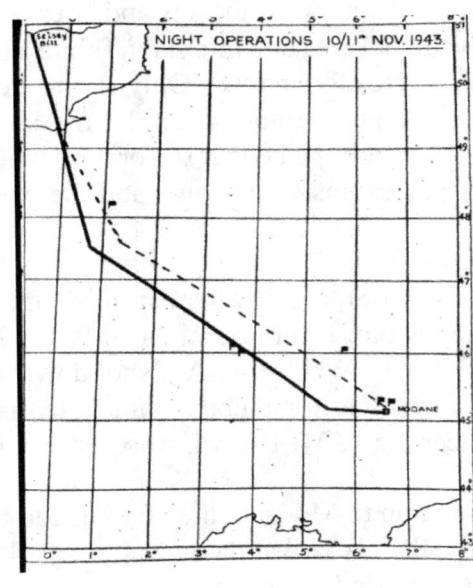

Bomber Command detailed 313 Lancasters for this operation from 1, 5, and 8 Groups. The operation was for these Lancasters to destroy the marshalling yards at Modane in Southern France. These were on the French side of a key Alpine tunnel on the main route to Italy. The intention was to disrupt this important rail hub used to supply materials between the Axis partners. 106 Squadron supplied fourteen Lancasters for this operation. This was a long round trip for the Lancasters, some of which were airborne for around nine hours, and the target would be very difficult to identify within the terrain that it was situated.

All 106 Squadron aircraft were airborne between 20.30 and 21.10 hours. Leading the Squadron on this operation was the senior pilot on duty, F/L Claridge. The Pathfinders slightly overshot the main aiming point on arrival over the target. The first 106 Squadron aircraft over the target was that of F/O Cooper; his bomb aimer lined up and dropped his bombs on the centre of six red TIs from 16,700 feet at 01.00 hours.

As Norman's aircraft arrived over the target the visibility was good with no cloud. Red spot fires were seen over the target along with Pathfinder TIs. Tofty delivered his bombs from 15,000 feet at 01.06 hours, aimed at the centre of some green TIs that he could clearly see cascading. The bombs were seen to explode amongst the TIs and fires. After bombing they continued over the tunnel area and into Italy, flying a long and large orbit before setting course for home. Only light defences were encountered. The bombing photographs taken by the Lancaster crews showed that all bombs were dropped either on, or within one mile of the target. The target suffered extensive damage, and the operation was a success.

LM310 was transferred to 61 Squadron after her time with 106 Sqn. She failed to return from Schweinfurt on the night of 24th / 25th February 1944 in the hands of F/L N.D. Webb RNZAF, shot down at 20,000 feet over the target area. All the crew members parachuted into captivity, except the flight engineer, Sgt. J.W. Brown, who lost his life.

On return from the operation to Modane, the 106 Squadron Lancasters landed back at Syerston, then later that day the aircrews flew their aircraft to their new base at Metheringham.

The following day saw training and familiarisation flights take place. There were a few issues reported by several crews with the airfield approach equipment and this needed to be rectified immediately if possible. The following day, 13th November, W/C Baxter with S/L Dunn's crew, flew a 50-minute inspection flight to test again the airfield approach equipment which he then deemed to be satisfactory.

The break in operations allowed a period of settling in for 106 Squadron at their new home. It was also a time that allowed for the replacement of their Lancasters with new ones which were equipped with H2S radar[16]. The new aircraft were made ready for the squadron's return to operations on 18th November. When the crews were settled in the briefing room, and the curtain was pulled back, they saw they would be going back to Berlin.

Lancaster maintenance at Metheringham

---

[16] This radar equipment would scan the terrain for up to six miles around the aircraft and give the navigator a virtual map of the ground, detailing towns, rivers, lakes and coastlines.

Operation 11: Berlin, 18th / 19th November 1943

Aircraft assigned: Lancaster DV229

Crew:
Pilot: P/O F.M. Mifflin
Flight engineer: F/Sgt. N.C. Jackson
Navigator F/Sgt. F.L. Higgins
Bomb aimer: Sgt. M.H. Toft
Wireless operator Sgt. E. Sandelands
Mid upper gunner Sgt. W. Smith
Rear gunner Sgt. N.H. Johnson

Bomb load: 1 x 4,000lb. 1,140 x 4lb. 60 x 30lb
Take off: 17.20 hours.
Time down: 00.50 hours.
Duration of operation: 7 hours 30 minutes.

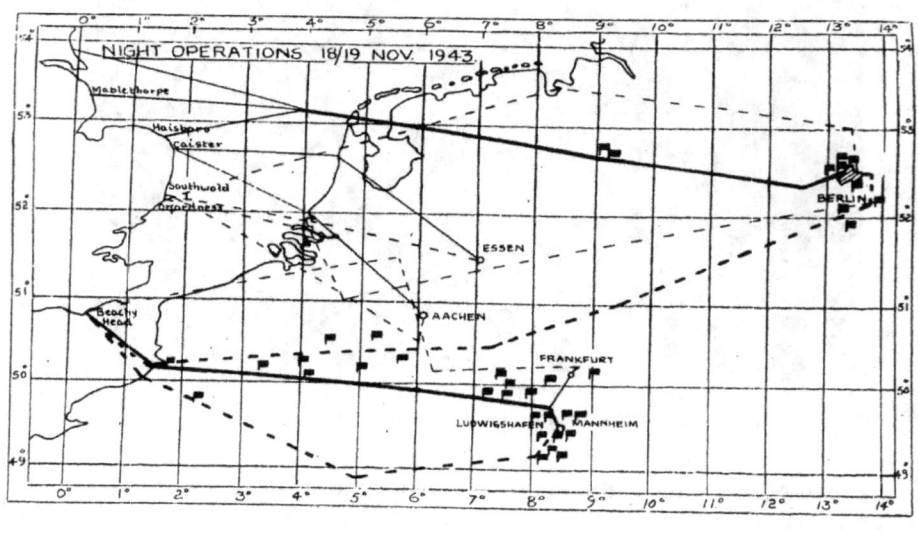

This was the first operation for 'Johnny' Johnson who had now returned from his spell in hospital, and recuperation, to rejoin Norman's crew as their rear gunner.

This was to be an all-Lancaster operation. Bomber Command detailed 440 of the type for the operation of which thirteen were from 106 Squadron. The 106 Squadron contingent was led by W/C Baxter, and he was one of the first to get airborne at 17.10 hours. All 106 Squadron aircraft were airborne by 17.35 hours. The route to the target took them over the Lincolnshire coast, out over the North Sea and then on a direct route just north of Hanover and onto Berlin. The attack plan was to approach from the west and fly over Berlin heading directly eastwards. As a means of confusing the German air defences, a second attack force made up of 400 aircraft, most of which were Halifaxes and Stirlings, headed to the south of Germany. Their targets were the cities of Mannheim and Ludwigshafen.

The weather that night was 10/10ths cloud over both targets which concealed the targets for many of the crews. On the journey to the target, Norman's crew experienced very heavy flak, with some exploding so close to the aircraft that the Lancaster was thrown around quite violently by the pressure waves of the explosions. They reached Berlin and with control of the aircraft handed over to Tofty they began their bomb run. Pathfinder markers were seen in the target area as well as one green TI seen cascading. The bombs were released from 21,000 feet at 21.10 hours, but results could not be observed owing to clouds though the TIs seemed scattered. They encountered no opposition over the target, and no fighters were seen. The return journey was once again one of what seemed like continuous attacks from the flak guns with accurate fire all around them.

The other 106 Squadron Lancasters all reached Berlin, and at altitudes of between 20,000 and 25,000 feet aimed their bombs at either TIs, or sky markers that were seen parachuting down. This was all done in a slot time of ten minutes from 21.00 hours. The results of their efforts were not observed due to the cloud cover, but most crews agreed that the attack was at best scattered.

Lancaster DV229 with the 463 Sqn RAAF crew of Joe Foster (rank unknown) (IBCC Archive).

For most of the crews the flak that night was light to moderate, however, F/O Forsyth ran into a heavy and accurate flak on the return journey and lost one engine. P/O Gibbs, flying Lancaster JB642 had finished his bomb run and had turned for home, when his mid-upper gunner, Sgt. Smith, had a problem with his oxygen supply due to his oxygen supply tube breaking, he lost consciousness and sustained severe frostbite, Sgt. Birch, the rear gunner, was having trouble manoeuvring his rear turret and declared it unserviceable. This aircraft flew the return journey at the extremely unusual altitude of 29,000 feet, with little means of defence the higher altitude may well have been the safest place. The aircraft landed safely on the south coast of England at Tangmere.

Analysis showed that the bombing had been scattered with no point of concentration; it was a very similar result in Mannheim and Ludwigshafen, but it was reported that the diversion tactic seemed successful with only nine Lancasters lost in the Berlin raid. The Mannheim and Ludwigshafen force suffered greater losses after nightfighters were vectored into the area and 23 aircraft failed to return with the loss of 161 crew. DV229 joined numerous other Lancasters in transferring to 463 Sqn RAAF, eventually failing to return from an attack on Orleans on 10th / 11th June 1944. Apparently fired upon by Royal Navy guns, DV229 lost two engines after leaving the target area. The pilot, P/O Joseph John Fletcher RAAF remained at the controls whilst his crew bailed out. He was killed in the ensuing crash, but his crew survived, four as POWs but the other two managed to evade the enemy.

In a letter to his parents on 19th November 1944, Johnny wrote:

> *'Incidentally, I was initiated last night, by going on my first raid, which was on Berlin. Wasn't too bad at all, apart from the intense cold.'*

106 Squadron armourers bomb up a Lancaster.

Operation 12: Berlin, 22nd / 23rd November 1943

Aircraft assigned: Lancaster JB612

Crew:
Pilot: P/O F.M. Mifflin
Flight engineer: F/Sgt. N.C. Jackson
Navigator F/Sgt. F.L. Higgins
Bomb aimer: Sgt. M.H. Toft
Wireless operator Sgt. E. Sandelands
Mid upper gunner Sgt. W. Smith
Rear gunner Sgt. N.H. Johnson

Bomb load: 1 x 4,000lb. 1260 x 4lb. 72 x 30lb.
Take off: 16.40 hours.
Time down: 00.20 hours.
Duration of operation: 7 hours 40 minutes.

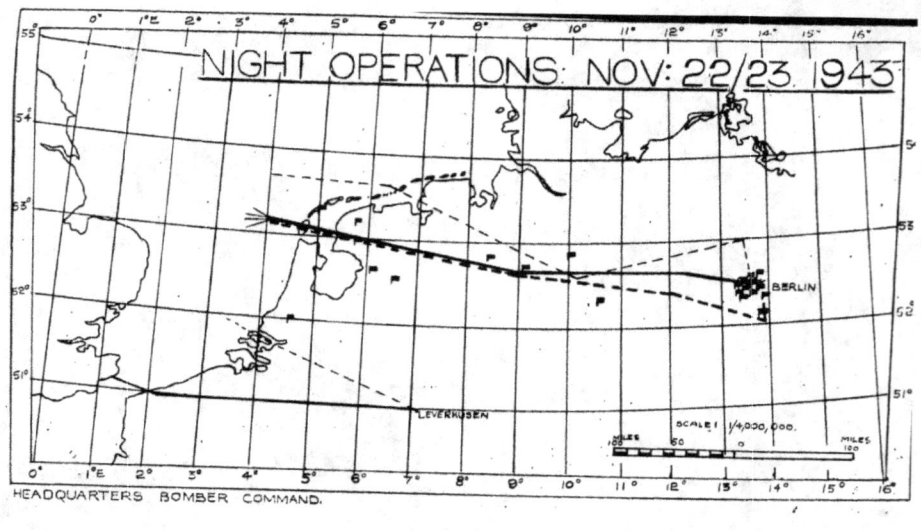

As the crews waited in the operations room for the night's target to be revealed there was, as always, a level of hope that it would be a target close to home. The crews knew that the chances were that it would not be, and then as the target was revealed, there were a few gasps and sighs of resignation as they all saw that the target for that evening was once again Berlin. Bomber Command called for a maximum effort and 764 aircraft were made ready throughout all the squadrons, the largest bomber force yet sent to Berlin. 106 Squadron put forward sixteen Lancasters with S/L Crowe leading, on his first op since September.

After taking off, Miff, at the controls of Lancaster JB612, headed for the Lincolnshire coast and to the forming up point over the North Sea. The route was almost the same as the previous operation and with the same return journey which was reciprocal. This was a very dark night with 10/10ths cloud cover, as Norman's Lancaster arrived over Berlin, a very good concentration of Pathfinder flares and markers were seen and used as the target. The bomb run was made at 21,000 feet and at 20.14 hours the bombs were released. The results could not be seen due to cloud cover, but good fires were observed and one enormous explosion at 20.22 hours.

Some of the other members of the squadron were having problems, P/O F.E. Garnett's Lancaster JB566 was hit by flak around 35 minutes short of the target, resulting in a fire in the starboard inner engine. They jettisoned their bomb load at 19.25 hours and turned for home. P/O Gibbs' aircraft was suffering from problems that resulted in the crew having to abort the operation and turn for home. F/O Harvey was the third member of 106 Squadron to turn back, due in his case to a complete failure of their navigation equipment.

The rest of the squadron reached the target but found poor weather conditions with complete cloud cover. S/L Crowe managed to locate the target by means of Pathfinder red flares with green stars, and he bombed on these from 19,000 feet at 20.05 hours, but again it was not possible to see below the cloud cover. It appeared to him that a concentrated attack was what was happening. A few members of the squadron still over the target area at 20.22 hours reported seeing a massive explosion.

This was in fact a very successful raid which left massive destruction from the west to the centre of Berlin. The destruction included 3,000 houses along with 23 industrial premises and factories. The raging firestorms also burnt out many more houses and 175,000 people were made homeless.

The weather on that night was so bad that it grounded the nightfighters. Bomber Command lost 26 aircraft and 182 crew, though only a few of these were lost in the target area itself. This was judged as being modest considering the number of aircraft involved in the operation and the target being Berlin. It was the Stirling bombers that were suffering disproportionally compared with the other aircraft, and Harris decided that this could no longer be tolerated. Once the surviving Stirlings had arrived back at home the type was withdrawn from active service over Germany.

Many of the 106 Squadron aircraft on returning to England from Berlin were diverted because of the extremely bad weather at home. They eventually returned to Metheringham during the day, arriving to find that orders had been issued for a return operation to Berlin that night. This placed enormous pressure on the ground crews and armourers to supply a full complement of Lancasters ready for the night's operation. The crews worked with enormous effort but only six Lancasters could be ready to add to the all-Lancaster force of 365 aircraft.

Norman's crew were not detailed for this operation, in common with many of the crews that had participated in the previous two raids on Berlin. 106 Squadron departed Metheringham shortly after 17.00 hours with F/L Grinder as the senior pilot on duty. The same route as before was used and the German nightfighter controller on picking up the main force correctly guessed the target. The Germans were now using a running commentary system to direct their fighters, known as *Sahme Sau*, (tame boar). However, the system was now being tapped into by RAF radio operators, and misleading instructions were being given from England. In total 46 of the bombers returned to base early. It was thought that the stress and strain on the aircrews from back-to-back operations to Berlin may have had a part to play in this, although F/O Harvey, part of the 106 contingent of six Lancasters, was forced to returned early as severe icing was preventing him from climbing above 12,000 feet. This was the second operation that F/O Harvey had to abort due to severe icing.

As the Pathfinders approached Berlin the glow of the fires which were still burning from the previous raids were clearly visible through the clouds. With the Pathfinder TIs clearly identified by the main force as they arrived over the target, there were many aiming points. The five remaining Lancasters from 106 Squadron arrived over the target and bombed from between 19,000 and 21,000 feet between the times of 20.01 and 20.14 hours. These aircraft all returned safely home. This was another successful raid to which 106 Squadron had contributed, 2,000 more homes destroyed as well as many industrial buildings. Bomber Command lost 20 Lancasters and 140 crew. These last two operations on Berlin were seen as the most successful of the entire Berlin campaign.

Operation 13: Berlin, 26th / 27th November 1943

Aircraft assigned: Lancaster JB612

Crew:
Pilot: P/O F.M. Mifflin
Flight engineer: F/Sgt. N.C. Jackson
Navigator: F/Sgt. F.L. Higgins
Bomb aimer: Sgt. M.H. Toft
Wireless operator: Sgt. E. Sandelands
Mid upper gunner Sgt. W. Smith
Rear gunner Sgt. A.E. Johnson[17]

Bomb load: 1 x 4,000lb. 1050 x 4lb. 40 x 30lb.
Take off: 17.30 hours.
Time down: 01.00 hours.
Duration of operation: 7 hours.30 minutes.

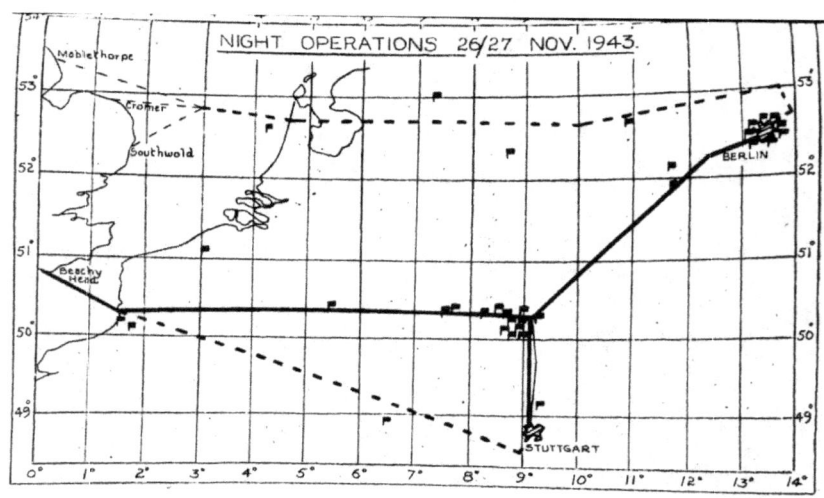

---

[17] Although the 106 Squadron Ops Record Book shows the rear gunner as Sgt. A.E. Johnson for this op, no such air gunner appears to have been in the squadron at the time. It is reasonable to assume that Sgt. N.H. 'Johnny' Johnson flew with the crew as usual, and the initials were simply erroneous.

This was the fourth operation to Berlin for 106 Squadron in nine nights. Good fortune had blessed the squadron with no aircrew lost for five weeks, though the whole squadron knew that this run of luck would eventually run out.

This was again to be an all-Lancaster force comprising 443 aircraft, eighteen of which were provided by 106 Squadron. Those responsible for the routes had decided that they needed to make the identity of the target less predictable. On this occasion a diversionary operation by a main force of Halifaxes would target Stuttgart, and a more complex route to the targets was planned. Both the Lancaster and Halifax forces departed England over Beachy Head and then made their way to the French coast. From there they were to turn east, fly across Belgium to a position just north-east of Frankfurt where the two forces would part company, the Halifaxes flying on a southerly course to Stuttgart and the Lancasters on a north-easterly course to Berlin.

The new route was flown in fairly good weather en route to the target and over enemy territory. Miff and Norman recorded that some of the aircraft below their altitude of 23,000 feet appeared to be in difficulty as a large number of jettisons were seen. As Norman's crew on board JB612 arrived over Berlin the weather remained clear. The bomb run was to be from west to east across the city. The Pathfinder Lancasters approaching from the south had overrun the aiming point to the north-west by some distance but with the clear skies and the markers being plentiful, finding the target for the main bomber stream proved to be without difficulty. The target area was covered in a smoke haze which hung over the city, and green TIs were seen to be cascading at 21.23 hours. Tofty aimed straight at the green TIs and the bombs were released from 23,000 feet at 21.24 hours. They observed their bombs heading straight for the TIs and the bombing was seen to be concentrated. There were heavy fires observed. The crew reported the defences over the target were found to be very heavy with flak explosions seemingly all around them on the way into the target and on the way out, some fighters were seen but they were not directly engaged. After bombing the stream made a turn of 180 degrees for a direct flight back, routing between

Hanover and Bremen. They then crossed the Dutch coast near Egmond and crossed the North Sea back to England.

For 106 Squadron the senior pilots on duty were F/Ls Boyle and Ginder. ED873, with P/O Neal at the controls, started to develop a problem with their starboard-outer engine, which was surging. Neal shut down the engine, jettisoned the bomb load, and returned to Metheringham on three engines. While attempting to land he overshot the landing and the Lancaster crashed close to the airfield with only one crew member, the rear gunner, sustaining a slight injury. JB592 was piloted by F/O van Hoboken DFC, at 32 years of age the oldest pilot in 106 Squadron. His aircraft crashed north-east of Frankfurt en route to Berlin. Brussels-born Jaques van Hoboken was killed along with all his crew. P/O Hinckley's JB593 had to choose a secondary target, Koblenz, due to his navigator, P/O R.A. Roberts, suffering from sickness. That target was bombed from 20,000 feet at 19.56 hours, and they arrived safely back home at 23.55 hours.

F/O Cole of 106 Squadron also reported seeing large numbers of bombs being jettisoned outside of the searchlight belt. The reason for these jettisons was explained in a book written by Martin Middlebrook, who explained that the A.O.C of 1 Group, Air Vice Marshall Rice, had conducted some tests to ascertain the maximum tonnage that a Lancaster could carry without the undercarriage starting to sustain overload. Therefore 1 Group Lancasters on this raid were carrying a larger bomb load than 5 Group Lancasters, which reduced the ceiling at which they could operate. As additional altitude brought greater safety, some of the crews jettisoned part of their surplus bombs when over enemy territory.

All returning crews reported the huge number of fires and dense smoke along with some sightings of large explosions sometime after they had left the target area.

Analysis indicated that this was a successful operation. Despite the Pathfinders overshooting the target area aiming point, most of the bombing managed to land within the city of Berlin. Some of those that did not fall within the target area fell in the industrial areas and suburbs of Siemens Stadt and Tegel, and 38 war industry factories were destroyed.

28 Lancasters failed to return, with the loss of 196 aircrew, which for Bomber Command was a depressing 6.2 percent loss rate. In addition, 14 Lancasters crashed on return to England. 106 Squadron had operated 83 sorties during the month of November, and it was only this raid that saw the failure to return, of one Lancaster, and the loss of one at home.

Operation 14: Berlin, 2nd / 3rd December 1943

Aircraft assigned: Lancaster JB612

Crew:
Pilot: P/O F.M. Mifflin
Flight engineer: F/Sgt. N.C. Jackson
Navigator: F/Sgt. F.L. Higgins
Bomb aimer: Sgt. M.H. Toft
Wireless operator: Sgt. E. Sandelands
Mid upper gunner: Sgt. W. Smith
Rear gunner: Sgt. N.H. Johnson

Bomb load: 1 x 4,000lb. 117 x 4lb. 68 x 30lb.
Take off: 17.00 hours.
Time of landing: 00.05 hours.
Duration of operation: 7 hours 05 minutes.

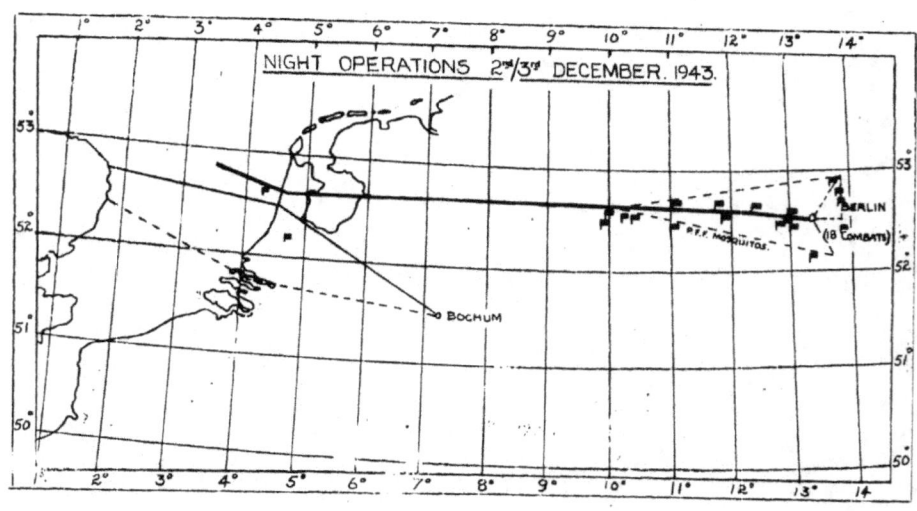

The Battle of Berlin continued with an all-Lancaster operation comprising 378 aircraft, sixteen of which were from 106 Squadron. F/Ls Claridge and Ginder were the senior pilots on duty. The route to the target was a reversion to the direct route across Holland and then straight on to Berlin, returning the same way. There were no diversionary tactics employed to confuse the nightfighter controllers, and they quickly realised that the target was to be the capital Berlin, therefore nightfighters were over the target and waiting for the bombers to arrive. The winds over Berlin were reported inaccurately and the bomber stream became spread out over a large area.

The outbound journey proved to be straight forward and with good visibility, but as Norman's crew in JB612 approached Berlin, they found 10/10ths low cloud over the target area and very heavy flak. Red sky markers with green stars were seen, along with red and green TIs, and four green TIs seen to be cascading. Tofty used these markers for his aiming point, bombing from 20,500 feet and timed at 20.20 hours. It was observed as a concentrated attack with many explosions and fires seen. After the required photograph had been taken, and as they started to leave the target area and make their turn to set course for home, Sandy called out that they were being tracked by a fighter. The two gunners, Johnny and 'Smudge' Smith, waited, scanning the sky for the fighter to appear, their tension if not already at its highest level went even higher. Norman Johnson in the rear turret was the first to see the fighter and called out on the intercom to Miff, 'FIGHTER! 1,000 yards...coming in from above and directly behind...900...800...NOW!!!'

Smudge in the mid-upper turret could see the fighter and zeroed in his guns. '700!' called the rear gunner, '600...500...400 yards...WEAVE!!!' Miff immediately turned the Lancaster to the right, and both gunners started to fire directly at the fighter. Simultaneously the fighter fired on the Lancaster, which was extensively damaged. The fire from the two gunners was accurate and flew straight into the fighter, which turned away, possibly having been damaged or even shot down.

Norman checked the aircraft instruments and saw that the temperature and pressures on the starboard outer engine were now at maximum. The engine had been damaged in the attack but the fuel tanks in the wing had not been ruptured, Fred Mifflin put the aircraft into a steep dive, an accepted practice to try to put an engine fire out, this was successful, and the aircraft returned to level flight. Norman shut down the engine, closed its fuel line and fired the engine fire extinguisher inside the engine as a precaution. The priority was to extinguish any threat of an engine fire return, so having done so he now altered the RPMs on the remaining engines as necessary to compensate for the loss of the starboard outer engine. Another critical task for Norman was to reduce the drag of the stationary propeller on the aircraft. When rotating as normal, the propeller blades are angled to provide thrust by driving the airflow backwards. With the engine stopped, the surface of the stationary blades caused an enormous amount of drag so, to prevent this, the propeller was 'feathered' by turning the blades edge-on to the airflow. To accomplish this, the Lancaster was equipped with four engine propeller feather switches, situated on the panel to the right of the throttles. When the switch for the stationary propeller was pressed, the blades automatically rotated to reduce the drag.

With the aircraft now on three engines, but without the weight of the bomb load, they started the long journey home, the gunners straining their eyes into the night sky for the arrival of another fighter. They were then surrounded by a heavy and accurate flak barrage and the Lancaster was hit again. The flak explosion was so close that the pressure from the blast threw the Lancaster violently upwards. It was obvious that the aircraft had suffered more damage and Norman needed to how much, what, and where it was. The remaining three engines all looked good on the instruments, so Norman asked Miff to check his flying controls. Fred reported that he had no elevator control at all, though the elevator trim was OK, as were his aileron and rudder controls. Pulling back the control column, Fred felt there was no resistance at all.

Norman immediately disconnected his intercom and then his mask from the main oxygen supply and connected it to a portable oxygen cylinder. There were portable oxygen cylinders, each providing around ten minutes of oxygen, placed in various positions around the aircraft, enabling the crew to leave their position if necessary. Norman left his position in the cockpit and climbed back through the aircraft to inspect the damage. With a torch in one hand, he started to work his way back through the aircraft.

A succinct entry in the 106 Squadron Ops Record Book describes the bare bones of a difficult trip to Berlin.

Once past the wireless operator, Sandy, he turned on the torch, being careful not to interfere with the crew's night vision. He inspected the fuselage of the Lancaster as he went. Working towards the rear of the fuselage, just past the mid upper gunner position he saw large holes in the port side of the fuselage, so he took a closer look. He found that the elevator push-pull tube that ran from the pilots' control column, along the inside of the left-hand side of the fuselage to the elevators, had been severed. He went to his tool bag which was stored in the casualty station and pulled out a short piece of steel wire about half an inch thick, two U-bolt clamps, and a spanner. Norman returned to the rear of the aircraft, disconnected the portable oxygen cylinder in order to save its air supply, and connected himself to the main oxygen supply outlet. This oxygen connection point was just below the mid upper gunner's position and was one of several such points located throughout the aircraft. Norman stood directly under 'Smudge' and shouted to him to call Miff on the intercom and tell him to hold the control column in the neutral or middle position. He knew that the elevators on the tail of the aircraft would be in the neutral position as the aircraft was flying straight and level. When he had confirmation from Smudge that that this had been done, Norman returned to the damaged control rod and spliced the severed control rod together using the steel cable and the U bolt clamps. With the spanner he bolted the clamps down as tightly as possible, then shouted up to Smudge to ask Fred to try the control column for elevator control. Norman watched the control rod and saw it worked perfectly. Smudge relayed a message from Miff that all was OK now and that Norman was a miracle worker. Norman shouted back that he was just doing his job and his duty. He disconnected his mask from the main oxygen supply outlet, reconnected the temporary oxygen cylinder, and returned to the cockpit. Patting Miff on the shoulder, Norman reconnected his intercom, then plugged his oxygen mask into the main oxygen supply, and they made for home. The whole of the return journey was made on three engines with Norman constantly balancing them for maximum performance.

It was this attack on the aircraft that made Norman consider how to deal with the aftermath of an attack that punctured the fuel tanks in the wings of the aircraft and started a fire. That type of damage could not be dealt with from the cockpit, and would therefore lead to the aircraft being lost, with the crew bailing out over enemy territory. All aircrew knew the possible consequences of descending into enemy territory, as they were now looked upon by the German population as *Terrorfliegers*, terror flyers, who brought only death and destruction. and if they were captured by the local population they could expect to be attacked, or even shot or lynched. Thus, it was that Norman came up with a contingency plan, which in his mind, was quite practical.

The other members of 106 Squadron also made their way towards Berlin. However, P/O Richards had to return to Metheringham due to severe icing, and F/O Jardine found himself over the western side of Berlin with an intercom that had become unserviceable en route, and now a windscreen that was so severely iced up that he could not see through it. Having been informed by the navigator they were over Brandenburg, which lies on the southern outskirts of Berlin, he decided that that would suffice as a secondary target, so the bombs were released, and they turned for home.

All other members of 106 Squadron reached the target area of Berlin and released their bombs on the markers which were visible through the cloud. The bombing was between 20.19 and 20.32 hours. There was too much cloud cover to make a judgement on the results of the bombing, but it was widely thought that the attack was scattered at first, becoming more concentrated as the attack went on.

The winds were still causing problems and stretching the bomber stream wider and wider, this allowed for the nightfighters to pick off stragglers. ED874 with P/O Neal in command, who a week before had returned on three engines and landed at Tangmere on the south coast of England, was attacked, brought down and crashed around ten miles to the north-east of the centre of Berlin. He was killed along with all his crew.

Analysis confirmed that the attack was scattered, and bombs had dropped mostly in southern districts and open country but also stated that some useful industrial damage was caused both to the east and the west of the centre of Berlin. 40 aircraft failed to return with the loss of 280 aircrew.

On the following night Bomber Command detailed 527 Lancasters and Halifaxes for an operation against the city of Leipzig. The previous operation to Leipzig, in October 1943, had been cancelled due to dreadful weather conditions. 106 Squadron briefed thirteen crews for this op with a late departure time just after midnight. Once all airborne and formed up, they crossed the Lincolnshire coast and then joined up with the main bomber stream. The bomber stream then set a direct course for Berlin as a feint to place confusion and doubt into the mind of the German nightfighter controller. The controller presumed that Berlin was to be the target once again and vectored his fighters to intercept the bomber stream on their direct course, but he lost them as they turned south for Leipzig. The weather over the target was ten-tenths cloud cover but Pathfinder release point flares were seen, and the bombs were aimed at these. All 106 Squadron aircraft bombed between 03.58 and 04.11 hours from 20,000 to 23,000 feet. Analysis confirmed that the attack had been successful with much damage caused to industrial and residential buildings. 24 aircraft failed to return with the further loss of another 168 aircrew, it was suggested that they were slightly of course on their return journey, encountered the Frankfurt defence zone, and were shot down. All 106 Squadron Lancasters returned safely.

There was no operational flying for almost the next two weeks due to the weather moon period, this allowed for intense daily training especially on the use of H2S radar.

On 16th December 483 Lancasters were detailed once again for an attack on Berlin. They were to be accompanied by ten Mosquitos with a planned direct route to the target. 106 Squadron detailed fifteen Lancasters. On this raid there was to be a diversionary element, but this was on the return journey. The idea was for the returning bomber stream to route on a north-westerly heading towards the Baltic and then over the North Sea by way of southern Denmark. The German nightfighter controller once again correctly identified Berlin as the target and nightfighters were amongst the bomber stream early and multiple combats were taking place all the way to Berlin and over the city itself. 106 Squadron Lancaster JB638, with P/O Storer in command, was attacked on its way to the target, and shot down north of Osnabruck in the region of the Mittelland Canal, crashing at Achmer. P/O Storer and all his crew were killed.

The operation was deemed to be moderately effective with no real concentration of the bombing, the bombs falling mainly in the residential area. 25 aircraft were lost on this operation along with 175 aircrew, but that would not be the end of the losses that night. As the exhausted crews arrived back over England after eight hours aloft, a blanket of thick fog descended over the stations mainly of 1, 6, and 8 Groups in Northern England. With little or no fuel reserves to fly to alternative airfields further south, the fatigued crews flew around blindly in the murk desperately trying to find somewhere to land. Between 11.00pm and 1.00am, 29 returning Lancasters crashed or were abandoned by their crews, tragically 150 airmen lost their lives. Having survived the operation to Berlin, and back, only to lose their lives to the weather back home clearly shows how dangerous being a member of Bomber Command aircrew really was, and the outstanding courage of those that served.

4 copies sent 5 Group 7/12/43

P/o. Mifflin

(1A)

118

SECRET

From :- No. 106 Squadron, R.A.F.
To   :- The Station Commander, R.A.F., Metheringham, Lincs.
        (For onward transmission to H.Q. No. 5 Grp. RAF.)
Date :- 3rd.Dcr.1943.
Ref :- 106s/S.109/Air.

COMBAT REPORT

1.	On the night of 2/3rd. December 1943, Lancaster 'U'., detailed to attack BERLIN, was attacked by a JU88 at 20.25 hours, shortly after leaving the target area.

2.	Prior to the attack, the Lancaster starboard outer engine had been hit by flak, and set on fire. The captain (P/O Mifflin) had just succeeded in extinguishing it by diving steeply, when the e/a was sighted dead astern at 400 yards. The Lancaster pilot was immediately instructed to corkscrew port and almost simultaneously, the e/a opened fire with machine gun and cannon tracer. The rear gunner replied with a short burst, but all four guns eventually jammed, the stoppage being caused by hits registered from the e/a on the gun feed ducts. The Mid Turret was out of action owing to the starboard outer engine being feathered.

3.	The JU88 was seen to break away on the starboard beam up after having caused extensive damage to the Lancaster, mainly on the starboard side of the fuselage.

4.	No searchlights or other phenomena was seen either before or during the combat, and no lights were carried by the e/a.

5.	At the time of the combat the Lancaster was at 16,000 feet flying on a course of 100°M at an I.A.S. of 190 m.p.h.

Page 1 of the Combat Report submitted by Fred Mifflin after the close encounter with a Ju88 nightfighter.

6. Vis. was very good, with 5/10ths. cloud at 8000 ft., and it is assumed that the fire in the starboard outer engine first attracted the e/a.

7. Although 'Monica' had been serviceable prior to the encounter, no aid was received from this device.

R/Gnr. 1516279 Sgt. Smith W.
(No. 7 AFU. and No. 14 OTU)

M/U Gnr. 1396602 Sgt. Johnson N.H.
(No. 4 AGS. and No. 14 O.T.U.)

Pilot Lieutenant,
For Wing Commander Commanding
No. 106 Squadron, R.A.F.

Squadron Commander's Remarks:

No remarks. Aircraft cat AC. R.E.Baxter
W/Cdr. Commanding No. 106 Squadron, R.A.F.

Station Commander's Remarks:

No claim
W.W.McKechnie G/Cpt.
G/Cptn. Commanding No. 106 Squadron, R.A.F.

Combat Report page 2. No claim for a victory was submitted.

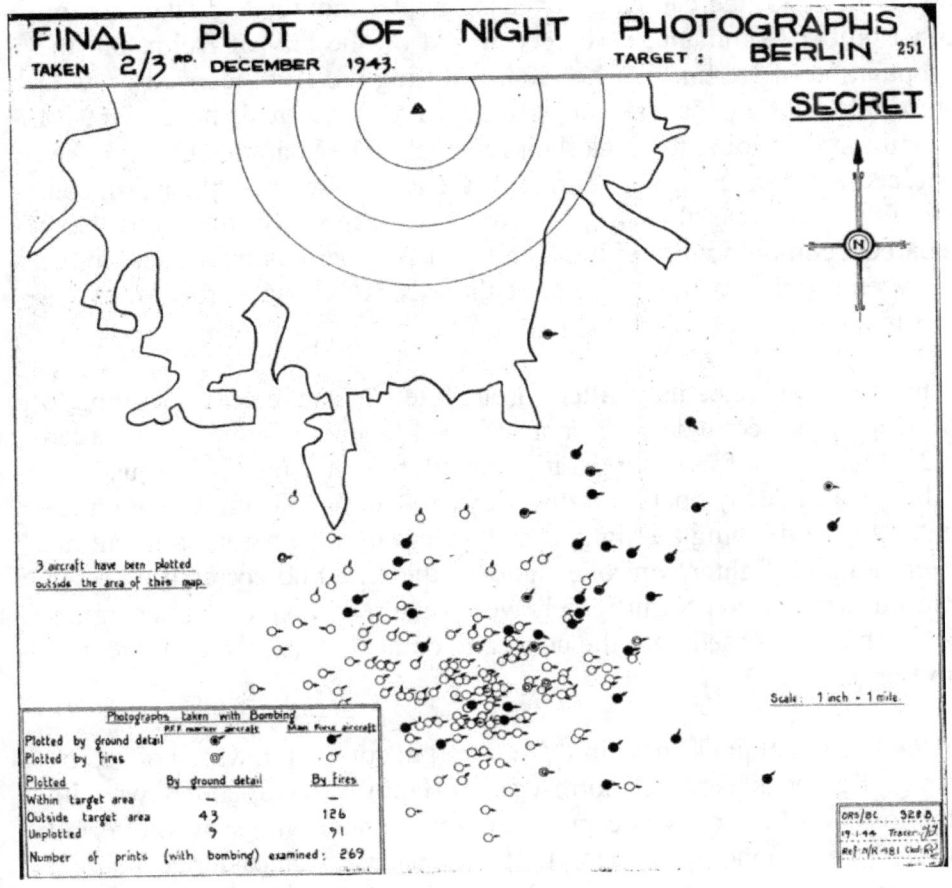

There were to be three more raids in December: Frankfurt on the 17th, Berlin on the 23rd, and again on the 29th. On these three operations alone, 77 aircraft failed to return with the loss of all crews, some 539 men. Without doubt the campaign over the winter months had taken its toll on Bomber Command, as indeed it had on the city of Belin, but the population of Berlin, like Londoners during the Blitz, carried on with fortitude, stating that, as far as they were concerned, no amount of bombing was going to break their resolve[18]. They paraded through the streets with banners proclaiming that the RAF may break their walls but would never break their hearts. However, deep down, they must have shared a common wish with the crews of Bomber Command that in the new year, Berlin would cease to be the focus of attention for Harris and his planners.

This wish was to be unfulfilled for a while yet, as the next operation to Berlin was scheduled on 2nd January 1944. Bomber Command detailed 421 Lancasters for this operation, with fifteen from 106 Squadron. There was a decoy operation flown by Mosquitos to Hamburg, with the intention of drawing the fighters away from the bomber stream, but the German nightfighter controller ignored the feint and correctly guessed Berlin as the target. Nightfighters were vectored into the bomber stream as soon as it crossed over the coast and combats took place all the way to Berlin.

JB643 of 106 Squadron, with P/O Garrett in command, was attacked by a nightfighter as it crossed north-west of Hanover. It was shot down with the loss of all the crew except for the rear gunner who survived to fall into enemy hands. A second 106 Squadron Lancaster with P/O Holbourn in command came under attack from a nightfighter close to Berlin and was shot down. P/O Holbourn along with all his crew lost their lives. There were 28 aircraft lost that night which meant the loss of another 196 aircrew. Sixteen of the Lancasters were believed to have been shot down on the way to the target.

---

[18] Under the Nazi regime, to do otherwise, of course, was tantamount to defeatism, so a brave face was definitely advisable.

On the following night, 3rd January, 383 aircraft were detailed for yet another attack on Berlin. 106 Squadron briefed twelve crews for this operation and eight Lancasters were airborne before one Lancaster came off the taxiway[19], and put a wheel into the mud. It became bogged down and unable to move, blocking the path to the runway for the remaining four Lancasters who had to abort their operations.

Perhaps unsurprisingly, the German nightfighter controller guessed the target would be Berlin and set a trap with his fighters waiting between Bremen and Hanover for the bomber stream. However, the fighters did not encounter the bomber stream until it was over Berlin and then the combats started. 27 Lancasters were lost that night including ten from the Pathfinders; another 189 aircrew were lost.

After a break in operational duties due to the weather, leave, and some cancelled operations, Norman's crew were detailed for their next operation on 20th January.

---

[19] This was also known as the peri-track.

Operation 15: Berlin, 20th January 1944

Aircraft assigned: Lancaster JB612

Crew:
Pilot: P/O F.M. Mifflin
Flight engineer: F/Sgt. N.C. Jackson
Navigator: F/Sgt F.L. Higgins
Bomb aimer: Sgt. M.H. Toft
Wireless operator Sgt. E. Sandelands
Mid upper gunner Sgt. W. Smith
Rear gunner Sgt. N.H. Johnson

Bomb load: 1 x 4,000lb. 1050 x 4lb. 60 x 30lb.
Take off: 16.25 hours.
Time down: 23.35 hours.
Duration of operation: 7 hours, 10 minutes.

In the briefing room, as the curtain drew back, the crews were probably not surprised that the target was, yet again, Berlin. This was to be a large raid consisting of 759 Lancasters and Halifaxes, including sixteen Lancasters from 106 Squadron. The departure times at Metheringham were earlier than normal and began at 16.30 hours. This meant that once airborne the crews could see the other aircraft all heading for the rendezvous point which was over the North Sea. The crews knew that the aircraft in the stream flew close together, but in the half-light of that late January afternoon it was quite alarming to see how close they actually were.

The heavy losses recently on the Berlin raids had made the planners realise that diversionary tactics were needed, rather than a direct route. The plan for this operation was to form up over the North Sea, cross into Germany near Bremen, and then to approach Berlin from the north-west. To cause confusion in the minds of the German nightfighter controllers, a small contingent of Mosquitos flew over Kiel and Hanover and then headed off in different directions from the main bomber stream.

Unfortunately, the German controllers remained unconfused; the nightfighters were ready and infiltrated the bomber stream to the south of Kiel. The nightfighter controllers were once again engaging in the use of the *Sahme Sau* control technique, the fighters forming up around radio beacons and given a course to fly straight into the bomber stream by a running commentary. For Norman's crew, the route to the target was unnerving with many fighters and combats seen. The two gunners were at their highest level of concentration, scanning the darkness whilst waiting for a warning from Sandy that they were being tracked by a fighter. However, on this trip they were not directly engaged.

As they approached the target area, the flak was only moderate, which was welcome, and they found ten-tenths-cloud with tops varying from 10,000 feet and up to 18,000 feet. The target was identified by Pathfinder sky markers and red TIs. Direction of the aircraft was handed over to Tofty and the nerve-racking bomb run began with the red TIs as his aiming point. He then spotted a wide circle of release point flares and decided that these would be his aiming point, which made the bomb run a little bit longer and put everyone's nerves even more on edge. The bombs were released at 19.39 hours from a height of 22,000 feet.

According to the squadron Operations Record Book, no specific results were observed but fires were seen through the clouds along with large explosions. Norman's crew saw much fighter activity on the return journey, and they expected to be attacked themselves at any time. On this night, however, they made it back unscathed. All the remaining 106 Squadron Lancasters reached the target and again found it covered with a ten-tenths cloud. The sky markers and TIs were clearly visible to the crews, however most of the crews, like Norman's, aimed their bombs at clusters of release point flares, these being sky markers. They bombed in a ten-minute time frame from 19.35 to 19.45 hours.

After the Lancasters completed their bomb runs they turned for home, flying south-west and heading for a point just north of Leipzig. From this point the route went due west; on this part of the route home fighter activity was clearly evident and there were many engagements. The fighter presence reduced as the bomber stream neared Brunswick and the fighters started to turn away, as their fuel and ammunition ran low. With the bombers now north-east of the Ruhr, the route was to the north-west and into northern Holland, crossing over Terschelling Bay and leaving enemy territory behind them.

22 Halifaxes and thirteen Lancasters had been lost on this operation, and two Halifaxes crashed on return to England. 245 aircrew would be missing from the dining rooms of their stations next morning, though mercifully 106 Squadron came through unscathed. At debrief the crews could only guess at the results of their efforts due to complete cloud cover and many speculated that the bombing was concentrated mainly in the eastern districts of Berlin. It was not until another four operations on Berlin had taken place that reconnaissance aircraft, due to the cloud cover improving, could finally get photographic records of the damage. This meant that no specific damage could be attributed to the earlier raids.

Norman and his crew had to wait less than 24 hours for their next operation.

Operation 16: Magdeburg, 21st / 22nd January 1944

Aircraft assigned: Lancaster JB612

Crew:
Pilot: P/O F.M. Mifflin
Flight engineer: F/Sgt. N.C. Jackson
Navigator F/Sgt. F.L. Higgins
Bomb aimer: Sgt. M.H. Toft
Wireless operator Sgt. E. Sandelands
Mid upper gunner Sgt. W. Smith
Rear gunner Sgt. N.H. Johnson

Bomb load: 1 x 4,000lb. 1350 x 4lb. 56 x 30lb.
Take off: 19.55 hours.
Time down: 03.25 hours.
Duration of operation: 7 hours 30 minutes.

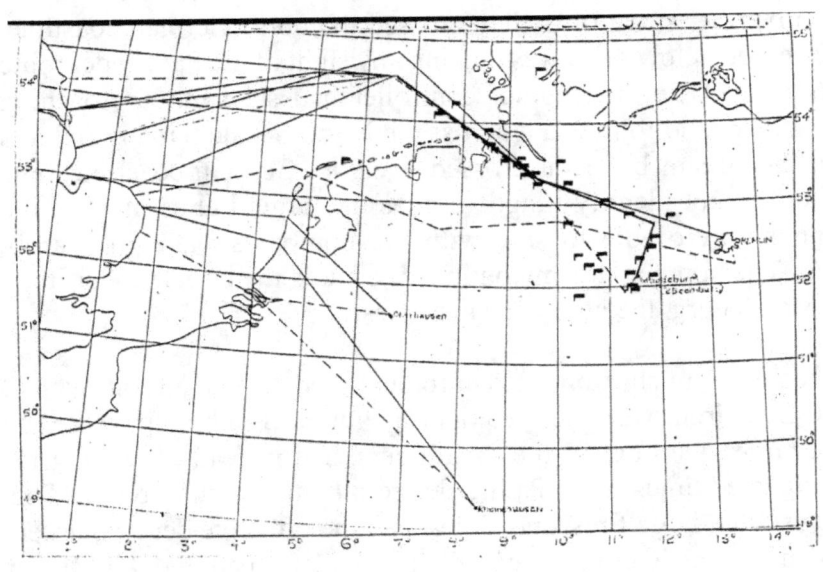

106 Squadron was to supply fourteen Lancasters for an attack on a new target, Magdeburg, along with two others to participate in a diversionary raid on Berlin. Magdeburg was a major industrial centre deep in the German Reich. The Polte Armaturen- und Maschinenfabrik factory in the city was one of the largest ammunition producers in the world. There were also plants producing synthetic oil from lignite coal. The raid was a heavy attack with 648 aircraft taking part, comprising 421 Lancasters, 224 Halifaxes and three Mosquitos. There was also a diversionary attack on Berlin consisting of 22 Lancasters and twelve Mosquitos, which was intended to confuse the fighter controller.

At Metheringham, the earliest away of 106 Squadron's contingent was JB534 with F/O J.B. Lathan at the controls at 19.40 hours. Seven Lancasters bound for Magdeburg, and one Lancaster bound for Berlin, had managed to get airborne before the second Berlin-bound Lancaster became bogged down while taxiing in the darkness. This aircraft blocked the way for all the remaining seven Lancasters bound for Magdeburg.

Norman's Lancaster JB612, along with the six other Lancasters for Magdeburg that had got airborne before the taxiway incident, continued over the Lincolnshire coast and out over the North Sea to form up with the main bomber stream. As they crossed the north German coastline, the thick cloud below them was making any sight of the Pathfinder route markers futile. The nightfighter controller had seen the approaching bomber stream and followed it across the North Sea, and many fighters were in the stream before it crossed over the German coastline. The controller did not identify Magdeburg as the target but as most of the nightfighters were able to stay with the bomber stream this hardly mattered. The bomber stream continued towards the target, and as they neared Magdeburg, the cloud began to clear.

The winds were much stronger than forecast and several aircraft which, like 106 Squadron, were now equipped with H2S radar, arrived early over the target, well before the Pathfinders, and instead of waiting for their designated time, or the Pathfinder zero hour, began to bomb. This bombing started large fires, and along with the effective decoy markers laid down by the Germans, completely undermined the Pathfinder attempts for a concentrated attack on their red TIs which were dropped at 22.50 hours. The 106 Squadron Lancasters all dropped on clusters of green TIs between 22.59 and 23.13 hours.

Tofty bombed from 21,000 feet at 23.13 hours, on five green TIs he could see cascading earthwards. Large fires were seen and a particularly spectacular purplish-red explosion at 23.18 hours. They reported that the flak opposition was spasmodic, some light and some very heavy, and no fighters were seen. All 106 Squadron aircraft returned safely but that was the not the same for all squadrons.

57 aircraft were lost, nearly nine percent of the force, along with 399 aircrew. 35 of the bombers lost were Halifaxes, representing a type loss rate of more than fifteen percent. It was thought quite probable that three quarters of the losses were due to German nightfighters. This was a huge loss for a new target, and it was believed that a large amount of the bombing was ineffective and indeed a wasted effort. In the aftermath of this raid there was serious disagreement between Air Ministry and Bomber Command over the conduct of the RAF Bomber Command offensive, this was seen by the Air Ministry as non-cooperation with their bombing policy. This led to a new directive on 28th January 1944 forcing Arthur Harris and Bomber Command to cooperate in a combined Anglo-American assault against the German aircraft industry.

There were a few days with no operations for 106 Squadron and so flying training was carried out day and night. The next scheduled operation was on the evening of 25th January. 106 Squadron crewed up seventeen Lancasters, which duly paraded on the taxiway ready to go to rearrange Frankfurt. With 25 minutes to go a signal was sent to all the waiting Lancasters to scrub the operation, and they returned to their parking positions and shut down. It would be two days before the next operation.

Operation 17: Berlin, 27th / 28th January 1944

Aircraft assigned: Lancaster JB612

Crew:
Pilot: P/O F.M. Mifflin
Flight engineer: F/Sgt. N.C. Jackson
Navigator F/Sgt. F.L. Higgins
Bomb aimer: Sgt. M.H. Toft
Wireless operator Sgt. E. Sandelands
Mid upper gunner Sgt. W. Smith
Rear gunner Sgt. N.H. Johnson

Bomb load: 1 x 4,000lb. 900 x 4lb. 48 x 30lb.
Take off: 17.40 hours.
Time down: 01.50 hours.
Duration of operation: 8 hours 10 minutes.

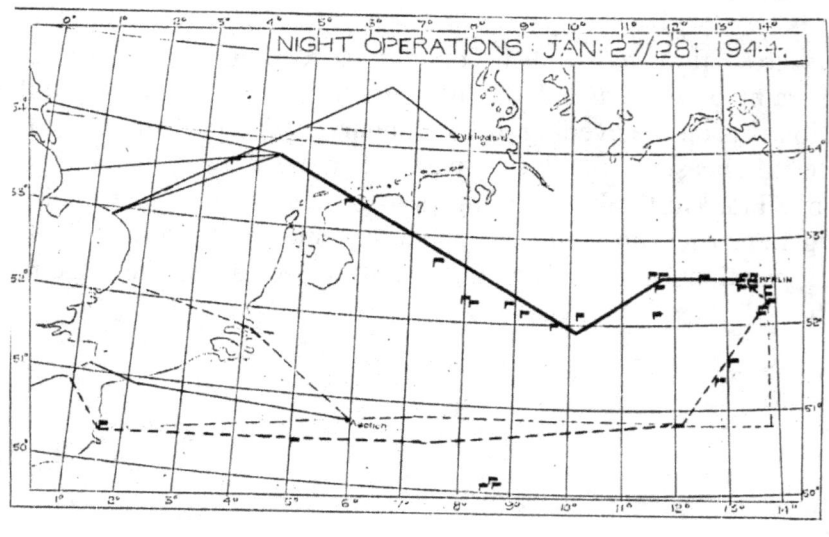

This was to be a 515-Lancaster operation to Berlin, with seventeen from 106 Squadron, led by F/L Ginder. All aircraft were airborne between 17.40 and 17.55 hours. Once formed up, the plan for the raid was for the main force to head for the German Bight as if on a mine laying operation, then turn south-east towards central Germany. It was hoped this would suggest to the nightfighter controller that the bomber stream was heading for an attack on Hanover, Brunswick, Magdeburg or Leipzig. Then, at an arranged point, the main force would turn to the north-west and onto Berlin, while some Mosquitos continued along the route suggesting a force of heavies was continuing towards one of the other cities. The Mosquitos dropped dummy route markers to add to the impression that this was a sizeable force. There must have been an element of success in the plan as lower numbers of nightfighters were reported in the main bomber stream than on recent raids.

JB612 followed the planned route towards Berlin and arrived over the target to find ten-tenths cloud cover with tops at around 12,000 feet. The Pathfinders had laid *Wanganui*[20] sky marker flares and release point flares, and these were clearly seen at the target. When control of the aircraft was handed over to Tofty, he saw a concentration of release point flares and aimed with the centre of these in his sights. They bombed from 21,000 feet at 20.40 hours and 30 seconds. No results were seen, but they saw large explosions and the glow of many fires. There was only light flak, and no fighters were seen.

Many of the squadron, including the leader F/L Ginder, reported large explosions at the target and F/O Perry reported clearly seeing the glow of fires on his return journey from a distance of 150 miles. Other issues for the squadron were that P/O Anderson returned to Metheringham

---

[20] Bomber Command had developed three main methods of target marking. *Newhaven* used H2S to identify the target, which was then marked trusting that equipment to be right. Backers-up reinforced the TIs with further flares. *Parramatta* involved dropping TIs blind, or with the aircraft's position over the target indicated by *Gee* or *Oboe*. *Wanganui* marking involved the use of parachute flares when the ground was concealed. If *Oboe* marking was relied on, the codename was prefixed with *Musical*. The unusual and seemingly random codenames were generated by three of the personnel in the Bomber Command operations room being asked where they hailed from.

early due to both mid upper and rear gun turrets being inoperable. Sgt. Moxey, along with his crew, were new to the squadron. They became unsure of their position on the way back home and requested and received four fixes from the radar station at Southampton which enabled them to find the south coast of England, they then made a safe landing at Middle Wallop. They were joined there by P/O Rosser and crew, whose navigator became very unwell not long after leaving the target and was placed in the casualty station of the aircraft. This led to the bomb aimer having to move up to the navigator's seat, he then managed to plot their positions and give headings for P/O Rosser to get them safely down at Middle Wallop.

Analysis reported that the bombing had been scattered over a wide area and once again many of the bombs fell onto outlying areas, but there was fresh damage within the city itself. This was achieved with the loss of 33 Lancasters along with 231 aircrew.

Norman's next operation followed in less than 24 hours.

Operation 18: Berlin, 29th January 1944

Aircraft assigned: Lancaster JB612

Crew:
Pilot: P/O F.M. Mifflin
Flight engineer: F/Sgt. N.C. Jackson
Navigator F/Sgt. F.L. Higgins
Bomb aimer: Sgt. M.H. Toft
Wireless operator Sgt. E. Sandelands
Mid upper gunner Sgt. W. Smith
Rear gunner Sgt. N.H. Johnson

Bomb load: 1 x 4,000lb. 900 x 4lb. 48 x 30lb.
Take off: 00.15 hours.
Time down: 08.20 hours.
Duration of operation: 8 Hours 05 minutes.

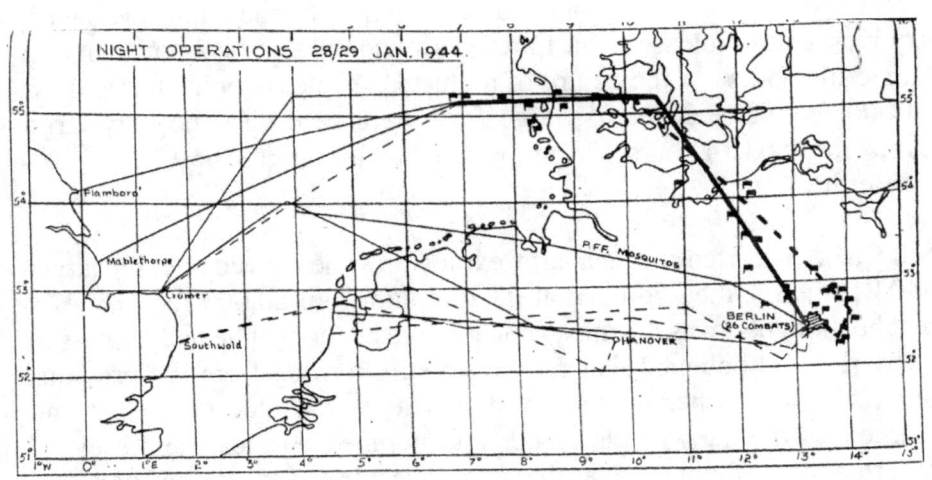

The planners for this operation decided that the main operation would get airborne just after midnight on the 29th. Diversionary operations were to take place earlier in the evening which included a Mosquito raid on Berlin itself, a mine laying operation to Kiel Bay, and a spoof attack on Hanover, but this did not stop the fighter controller concentrating most of his fighters over Berlin. Bomber Command detailed Halifaxes to join in the operation with the Lancasters to total 677 aircraft. 106 Squadron made ready seventeen Lancasters led by S/L Crowe.

After forming up, the route to the target that night for the bomber stream was out over Denmark and then straight onto Berlin. The return trip was to be the reverse. As the bomber stream headed towards Denmark there was an unusually large number of early returns, numbering 66 aircraft, which was almost ten percent of the bomber force. 106 Squadron had two early returns. P/O Pezzaro received a message from his rear gunner that his turret was completely inoperable. Meanwhile F/Sgt. Milne, flying JB663, developed engine problems, and despite the best efforts of his flight engineer Sgt. F.J. Butcher to correct the rough running engines, they could not continue.

When Norman's aircraft arrived over the target shortly after 03.00 hours, the target was once again covered in ten-tenths cloud with tops around 10,000 feet. The target had been marked by the Pathfinders with sky marker and release point flares. Tofty completed his bomb run and aimed his bombs at the centre of a cluster of release point flares from 21,000 feet at 03.27 hours, large fires were seen and one very large explosion at 03.14 hours. They reported that this was the best attack seen on Berlin.

S/L Crowe reported seeing a large explosion as he arrived over the target at 03.15 hours, then bombed at 03.25 hours from 20,000 feet. He said that he thought it was the most concentrated attack that he had witnessed on Berlin and believed that fires were still burning from the previous night's attack. Other crews reported that they could see the ground markers in the gaps of the clouds and bombed on these, and they all reported that to them this was the most concentrated attack they had seen on this target.

Analysis revealed that many bombs did indeed fall into the western and southern districts of the city, where around 180,000 people were bombed out of their homes, and scores of administrative and public buildings were severely damaged. They also said that much of the attack was again wasted on outlying areas. For their efforts Bomber Command lost 46 aircraft along with 322 aircrew that night.

Operation 19: Berlin, 30th January 1944

Aircraft assigned: Lancaster JB612

Crew:
Pilot: P/O F.M. Mifflin
Flight engineer: F/Sgt. N.C. Jackson
Navigator: F/Sgt. F.L. Higgins
Bomb aimer: Sgt. M.H. Toft
Wireless operator: Sgt. E. Sandelands
Mid upper gunner: Sgt. W. Smith
Rear gunner Sgt. N.H. Johnson

Bomb load: 1 x 4,000lb. 1050 x 4lb. 64 x 30lb.
Take off: 17.15 hours.
Time down: 23.45 hours.
Duration of operation: 6 hours 30 minutes.

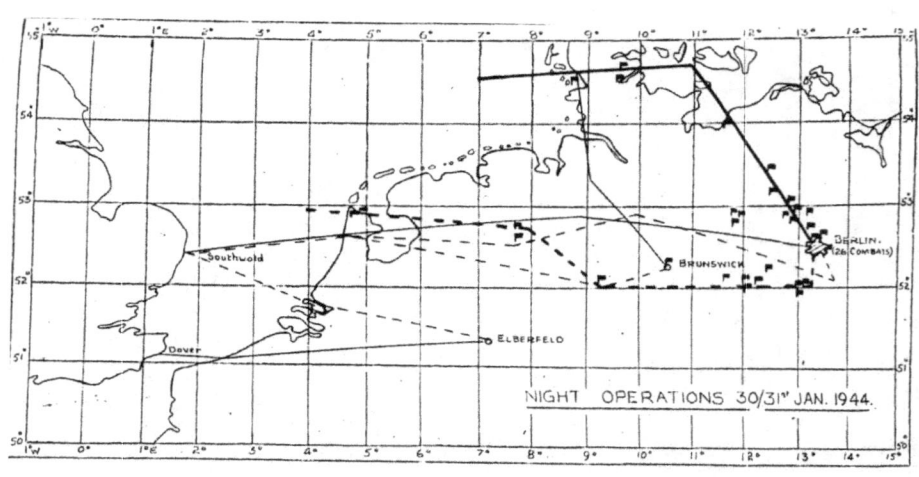

534 aircraft were readied for yet another operation on Berlin, many with the same crews who must have been feeling the strain. For Norman's crew, amongst others, it was the third consecutive night on which they would be braving the defences of what the crews referred to as the 'Big City'. Whilst all operations demanded constant focus for every member of the crew for the duration of the flight, Berlin was especially arduous, running the gauntlet of the ferocious defences for eight hours or more. Minimal rest before getting back into the aircraft and airborne again took a massive physical and mental toll on these young men.

106 Squadron detailed seventeen Lancasters for this operation. JB612 flew over the Lincolnshire coast and out over the North Sea to rendezvous with the bomber stream. The plan was to route to Berlin from the northwest after crossing the Schleswig-Holstein Peninsular, whilst the exit route after bombing was to head for the south of Brunswick, and then to the top of northern Ijsselmeer, and onto the Dutch coast. As JB612 approached Berlin, the cloud cover was once again almost complete, nine-tenths, with tops at about 8,000 feet. The target was indicated by sky markers and green TIs. With the aircraft under the direction of Tofty, JB612 started the bomb run and Tofty aimed at the centre of the concentration of green TIs, dropping the bombs from 21,000 feet at 20.25 hours. They reported that the concentration of fires was very good. The route was reported as good, and, unbelievably, despite their fatigue, the Operations Record Book states that '...on the whole, it was quite a pleasant trip.'

The Lancasters from Metheringham started to get airborne for this operation at 17.10 hours, with P/O R. Hinkley, flying Lancaster JB593 first off, five minutes before Norman. P/O Pezzaro had to abort his flight, for the second operation in a row, this time due to a defective engine. All the other crews arrived safely over the target to find up to ten-tenths cloud cover. Sky markers and green TIs indicated the target, and all 106 Squadron aircraft bombed on these in an eight-minute slot from 20.25 hours. The crews, on returning, reported seeing many fires in what appeared to be a concentrated and successful attack.

There was only one reported incident, and one aircraft lost for 106 Squadron. F/O Forsyth's Lancaster was attacked by a nightfighter, and hit in the bomb bay, directly below the pilot's seat. The fighter was driven off by the gunners and, luckily, it did not return. F/O Forsyth and his crew landed safely back at Metheringham, on what was their 29th trip. This was not the case for ND336 flown by P/O Kirkland, RAAF and his crew, who were shot down, and they crashed into the North Sea. P/O Kirkland's body was washed ashore on the Frisian Island of Vlieland, five weeks after the crash, but the other members of the crew were never found.

Analysis reported that severe damage had been caused to the city and outlying areas during this operation. It had been a successful operation, but for the loss of 33 aircraft and a further 231 aircrew.

There now followed a fortnight without operations for 106 Squadron, which gave them a respite to rebuild their energy after the gruelling and hazardous operations that they had flown since November. This was also a time for more training, including the new *Fishpond*[21] fighter warning radar which had just arrived. There was the usual training of high-level bombing and cross-country navigation at night, known to the crews as 'Bullseyes'. These were training exercises which involved mock raids, with the bombers having to navigate cross country to locate their target, and RAF nightfighters carrying out mock interceptions.

---

[21] *Fishpond* was an enhancement of the H2S scanner which could give early warning of approaching night fighters at a distance of up to 30 miles.

Operation 20: Berlin, 15th /16th February 1944

Aircraft assigned: Lancaster JB612

Crew:
Pilot: F/O F.M. Mifflin
Flight engineer: F/Sgt. N.C. Jackson
Navigator: F/Sgt. F.L. Higgins
Bomb aimer: Sgt. M.H. Toft
Wireless operator: F/Sgt. E. Sandelands
Mid upper gunner: Sgt. W. Smith
Rear gunner: Sgt. N.H. Johnson

Bomb load: 1 x 4,000lb. 900 x 4lb. 64 x 30lb.
Take off: 17.35 hours.
Time down: 00.05 hours.
Duration of operation: 6 hours 30 minutes.

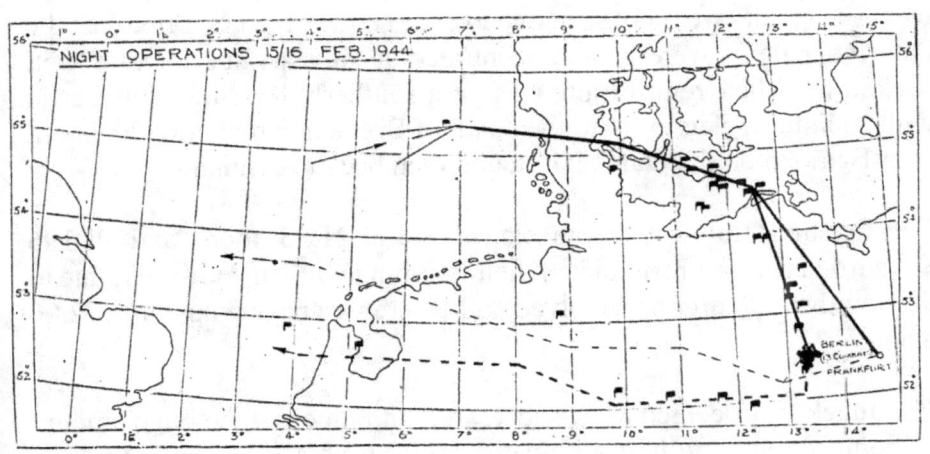

This downtime came to an end on 15th February, when 106 Squadron was required to supply nineteen Lancasters for the largest bomber force to date to attack once again Berlin. A total of 891 aircraft, including more than 500 Lancasters and 300 Halifaxes, were to deliver a record 2,642 tons of bombs on the city.

The operation planners had once again laid on diversionary operations in an effort to cause confusion in the mind of the fighter controller. A mine-laying operation was undertaken in Kiel Bay prior to the large bomber formation crossing this area. There was also an attack by Mosquito aircraft on Berlin and further east, an attack on Frankfurt-an-Oder.

After JB612 was airborne, Norman's crew began forming up with the rest of 106 Squadron, then the formation cleared the Lincolnshire coast and joined with the main bomber force over the North Sea. The outward route was to take them on a north-easterly heading towards the coast of southern Denmark, then turn onto a new heading of south-east which would take them directly to the target. Norman's aircraft arrived over the target area just after 21.00 hours, where they found ten-tenths cloud cover with tops at 10,000 feet. Pathfinder markers were seen at the target and Tofty aimed at one green target indicator which was seen cascading at 21.14 hours. His bombs were released at 21.25 hours from 22,000 feet. The results were not seen due to cloud cover; they reported that the Pathfinder flares were well concentrated at the start but not very well backed up. Their return route was on a southerly heading from Berlin with a slight dogleg to fly to the south of Bremen, which took them out over Egmond on the Dutch coast, and then back to England.

The finishing time for the attack was set at 21.35 hours, and all 106 Squadron crews had completed their bombing by then. However, due to the number of aircraft involved, other crews arrived up until 22.00 hours.

The attack was deemed to be successful with much of the huge amount of bomb tonnage falling within the built-up area of Berlin. Analysis reported that 1,000 homes had been destroyed as well as 500 wooden barracks which were being used as temporary housing. Many industrial buildings, such as factories, warehouses, storehouses and administration buildings were also hit. There were over 1,100 individual fires that the emergency services reported they had to deal with. This all came at the cost to Bomber Command of 43 aircraft and 301 aircrew.

106 Squadron did not lose any of their Lancasters during the operation, but F/O Forsyth, for the second operation in a row, was to experience issues that must have seemed to him, designed to stop him and his crew finishing their tour of 30 operations. Flying JB641, he was carrying an additional crew member, P/O. E.W. Carey[22], who may have come to think that he should have flown with another crew. After successfully bombing the target at 21.10 hours, from 20,000 feet, the aircraft was hit by incendiaries from another aircraft above, and considerably damaged. F/O Forsyth, along with his crew, managed to get the Lancaster back to Metheringham, landing at 00.01 hours. The aircraft was extensively damaged and according to the Squadrons operation book it was categorised AC, meaning that it was far beyond repair for the ground crews, and required outside contractors, or a specialist unit to repair the aircraft at Metheringham.

Lincolnshire had many bomber airfields, and on a night like this there were many aircraft arriving back over the Lincolnshire countryside at similar times. Some of the airfields had circuit patterns which overlapped, and vigilance was paramount, even though all the crews would have been fatigued by the constant focus and concentration demanded by flying operations, especially the Berlin raids. It was after midnight when JB534 of 106 Squadron, with P/O Dickerson in command had joined the circuit pattern for Metheringham. He was flying the downwind leg of the circuit when the aircraft crashed into the ground killing five members of the crew, P/O Dickerson, Sgt. Baffay, F/O Lewis, Sgt. Pauley and Sgt. Hills. The two gunners were taken to hospital with severe injuries but survived. An investigation was held into the crash which concluded that, whilst the aircraft was on the downwind leg of the circuit, the bomb aimer spotted another aircraft

---

[22] In all probability P/O Carey was a new pilot flying as 'second dickey' on an operational flight to gain experience. All too often, they were lost before carrying out ops with their own crew.

directly in front of them. The mid upper gunner said that he heard a shout of alarm on the intercom from the bomb aimer to P/O Dickerson alerting him to the other aircraft and telling him to dive immediately. P/O Dickerson immediately pushed the control column forward to put the aircraft into a descent under the other aircraft to avoid a collision, but in the darkness, and bad weather, JB534 descended too low, the aircraft hit the ground and broke up.

That was the final operation to Berlin for Norman's crew. They had flown ten operations to the Reich capital in total. Norman thought that this was not far off a record for a Bomber Command crew. The city was far from destroyed as Harris had hoped; it was a very large city and had most definitely suffered greatly from the attacks that took place from November to mid-February but had not been brought to its knees. The distance for the crews to fly to attack Berlin and the level of defence made this a very difficult target, and the Luftwaffe proved that it was now at its most lethal. Bomber Command had suffered mounting losses of aircraft, during this campaign 274 heavy bombers were lost on the Berlin operations alone, with the loss of 1,918 aircrew. The value of these raids must surely have been questionable in the minds of Bomber Command.

Harris now decided to leave Berlin alone for the time being. This was to enable his forces to be directed wholeheartedly towards *Operation Argument*, part of the effort in line with the *Pointblank Directive* of June 1943. The intention was to eliminate the *Luftwaffe* in Western Europe as an effective fighting force by the time of the planned *Operation Overlord*, the invasion of Europe that summer. The day bombers of the USAAF would attack aircraft production on the ground, enticing into the air enemy fighters, so that they could be shot down by the American Mustangs and Thunderbolts. Meanwhile by night, the RAF was to obliterate aircraft and aero-engine plants on the ground. This would start immediately, in what became known as 'Big Week.

There was an air of 'hurry up and wait' over the next few days as operations were arranged for each of the following three nights for 106 Squadron, only to be cancelled, but this was soon remedied.

Operation 21: Leipzig, 19th / 20th February 1944

Aircraft assigned: Lancaster JB612

Crew:
Pilot:	F/O F.M. Mifflin
2nd Pilot	F/O F.C.W. Clement
Flight engineer:	F/Sgt. N.C. Jackson
Navigator	F/Sgt. F.L. Higgins
Bomb aimer:	Sgt. M.H. Toft
Wireless operator	F/Sgt. E. Sandelands
Mid upper gunner	Sgt. M. Singh
Rear gunner	Sgt. N.H. Johnson

Bomb load: 1 x 4,000lb. 990 x 4lb. 40 x 30lb.
Take off: 23.45 hours.
Time down: 06.30 hours.
Duration of operation: 6 hours 45 minutes.

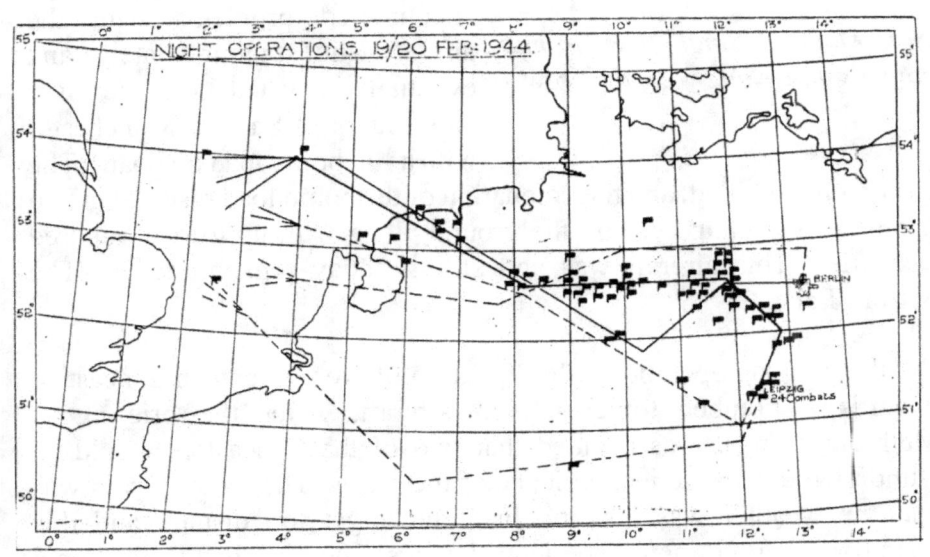

Norman's second attempt to visit Leipzig was to involve him in one of the worst nights of the war for Bomber Command. As noted previously, Leipzig's aircraft and aero-engine plants meant it was an obvious choice to herald the start of 'Big Week'.

Sgt. Mohand Singh flew as mid upper gunner on two of the crew's ops.

There was a rotation of crew members, usually for training purposes, and Sgt Walter Smith, Smudge, the mid upper gunner, was replaced by Sgt Mohand Singh. Sgt Mohand Singh was to fly the following two operations with Normans crew before the return of Smudge, he then transferred to another crew within 106 Squadron. Sadly, Sgt Mohand Singh was killed in the July of 1944 while acting as rear gunner on Lancaster ZN-S. This aircraft took off from Metheringham as one of 106 Squadrons contingent to a large bomber force, they encountered problems with the aircraft almost immediately and eventually crashed near the river and houses in Salford Manchester with a full bomb load on board. The crew were all killed, and the detonation of the bomb load resulted in two people losing their lives on the ground along with up to one hundred casualties. This aircraft was and still is today remembered as The Salford Lanc.

For this Leipzig operation, 106 Squadron offered seventeen Lancasters towards a bomber force of 823 aircraft. After the briefing at Metheringham, it was decided that two of the Lancasters would be withdrawn due to the inexperience of the crews. The reason given was that the weather was just too bad, the target too distant, and this operation required more experienced crews. The planners decided on a diversionary tactic, a mining operation taking place in Kiel Bay, which it was hoped would attract the nightfighters to that position. It was also planned that the aircraft would join well-defined waves, the Lancasters of 106 Squadron being positioned in the first, second, third and sixth waves.

P/O Clement, who was along for the experience, joined Fred and Norman in the already-cramped cockpit, and it appears that Fred entrusted the newcomer with taking the controls. The Lancaster started its take-off down the runway, and as the aircraft reached 95 miles an hour, rather than the usual 105 miles an hour, the aircraft started to become airborne. This was too slow a speed to keep a fully laden Lancaster in the air, so Fred shouted to Clement to keep the machine on the runway and build up speed to avoid the stall. As well as the fuel load required to reach Leipzig and return, they also carried close to 10,000lbs of bombs, along with the additional crewman. Norman, not waiting for P/O Clement to react, reached over with his left foot and placed it onto the control column and pushed it forward and held it place to hold the Lancaster onto the runway until the desired speed was reached before lifting off. P/O Clement apologised and said that he would have to watch that one in the future.

After taking off, and joining the other fourteen 106 Squadron Lancasters, Norman's aircraft crossed the coast and flew out over the North Sea to form up with the main bomber stream. The outward leg was to cross the Dutch coast and then fly directly to Leipzig. The plan was to have the 106 Squadron Lancasters over the target between 04.00 and 04.19 hours. The nightfighter controller tracked the incoming bomber stream and directed the nightfighters to meet the bombers as they crossed the Dutch coast. The attacks started as they did so, and degenerated into a slaughter of the bombers, which continued all the way to Leipzig. There was also a stronger than forecast tail wind and many of the main force aircraft arrived over the target ahead of their scheduled time. Discipline prevailed and, rather than simply dropping their bombs and turning immediately for home, they started to orbit around the target waiting for their allotted time. While orbiting 20 aircraft were shot down by flak, and there were two collisions between bombers resulting in the loss of a further four aircraft.

As Norman's Lancaster arrived over the target, and with Miff back at the controls, they found ten-tenths cloud with tops up to 12,000 feet. Tofty saw aiming point flares, and red and green TIs to which he guided the aircraft. He aimed at one release point flare and bombed from 23,000 feet at 04.00 hours exactly. No results were observed due to the cloud cover, and it was too early in the attack to expect fires.

The complete cloud cover made photo reconnaissance a worthless exercise. The returning crews were very much in agreement that this was a concentrated attack describing large explosions along with many fires. The validity of confirming these reports was not possible, but what was in no doubt was the price that Bomber Command had to pay for this operation. Sadly for 106 Squadron ME630, a Lancaster with F/O Leggett and his crew on board was shot down by a nightfighter as they were approaching Leipzig. The crew all managed to bail out, but tragically F/O Leggett fell into a lake and drowned; the rest of the crew were taken prisoner.

It was clearly evident that of the aircraft taking part in the raid, it was the Halifaxes that were most vulnerable, losing over thirteen percent of their number. Bomber Command decided that enough was enough and withdrew the Halifax aircraft from any further operations over Germany. This followed the earlier withdrawal of the Stirlings in the previous November. A staggering total of 78 aircraft were shot down resulting in the loss of 546 airmen. This has been Bomber Command's worst operation of the war in terms of total losses; sadly, this record toll did not remain the worst for long.

The crews would have been fatigued, especially after their last two long range operations, but they were almost always on duty and ready to be called for the next operation. The rest time after the Leipzig operation was just seventeen hours and 35 minutes before, they were taking off for their next operation.

Operation 22: Stuttgart, 20th / 21st February 1944

Aircraft assigned: Lancaster JB612

Crew:
Pilot: F/O F.M. Mifflin
Flight engineer: F/Sgt. N.C. Jackson
Navigator F/Sgt. F.L. Higgins
Navigator P/O W.B. Wilkinson (under training)
Bomb aimer: Sgt. M.H. Toft
Wireless operator F/Sgt. E. Sandelands
Mid upper gunner Sgt. M. Singh
Rear gunner Sgt. N.H. Johnson

Bomb load: 1 x 4,000lb. 1050 x 4lb. 40 x 30lb.
Take off: 00.45 hours.
Time down: 06.45 hours.
Duration of operation: 6 hours 40 minutes.

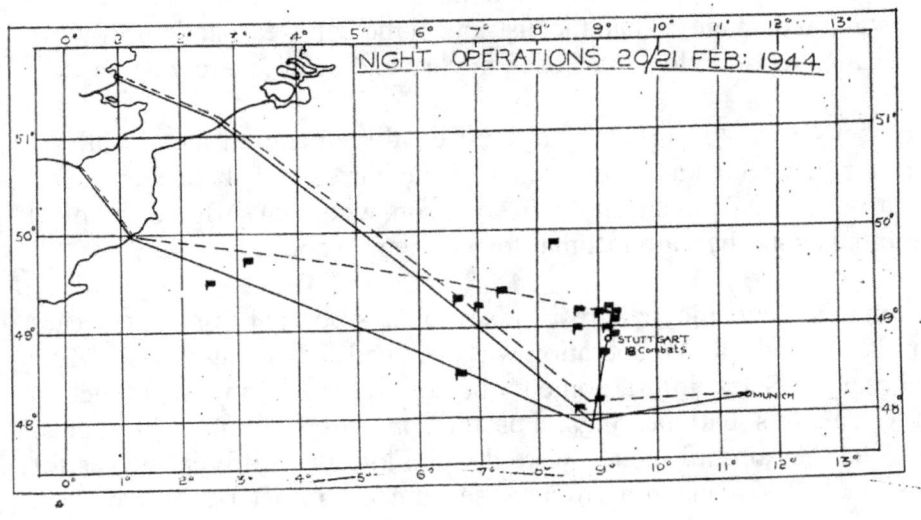

Bomber Command detailed close to 600 aircraft for this operation, which was a second visit to the city for Norman. Thirteen Lancasters were supplied by 106 Squadron. The targets for this visit were again the aircraft industry factories in and around the city.

Two hours before taking off, Bomber Command had detailed a diversionary exercise by way of a Mosquito attack on Munich, a secondary diversionary exercise was by way of using many aircraft from the training units who flew out over the North Sea and flew a heading towards the Dutch coast but orbited well before reaching the coast as if forming up for an operation. Both spoof operations had the effect of attracting the nightfighters which meant that as Norman's Lancaster, along with the main bomber force, crossed over the French coast heading for Stuttgart there was no fighter opposition to deal with.

As JB612 approached the target area they encountered only three-tenths cloud with tops at around 6,000 feet. The Pathfinders had delivered their red and green TIs and release point flares over the target, and it was all clearly visible, as indeed was the target. Tofty lined up the Lancaster for the bomb run, aimed at some green TIs and released the bombs at 04.01 hours from 23,000 feet. They reported seeing a very large explosion at 04.05 hours and concentrated fires in the target area.

Analysis reported that the central districts of Stuttgart had suffered substantial damage, as had the districts in the north-east and north-west. They also reported that the Bosch factory had been severely damaged.

Bomber Command lost nine aircraft on this operation along with 63 aircrew, 106 Squadron survived with no losses but there were early returns for F/O Penman, and P/O Anderson, who both suffered technical problems with their aircraft that forced them to abort.

Norman's crew enjoyed a rest for seven days but that was not the case for 106 Squadron. An operation was arranged for the night of 24th/25th February to Schweinfurt, home to the major factories in the production of Germany's ball bearings. For this operation Bomber Command detailed 734 aircraft, which were divided into two different waves for the attack. 106 Squadron provided seventeen Lancasters, three in each of the first and second waves of the first attack which consisted in total of 392 aircraft.

The squadron put its main effort, eleven Lancasters, in the second attack, which totalled 342 bombers. Three 106 Squadron crews acted as Pathfinder back-ups, four were in the third wave and four in the fourth. The waves were to be separated by two hours with the intent of catching the nightfighters on the ground refuelling and rearming as the second wave arrived over the target. The target was clear of clouds and with good visibility, the Pathfinder markers were clearly evident. The crews believed that the attack was successful. In the first attack, five of 106 Squadron's Lancasters completed the operation but one returned early. All eleven in the second attack were successful, four photos were taken and plotted; three were within two miles and one within one mile of the aiming points. All 106 aircraft returned safely to Metheringham.

Following the raid, photo reconnaissance could not report the damage done as the interpreters could not distinguish between the night's effort and the destruction from the raid of the American Eighth Air Force the day before. 33 aircraft failed to return with the further loss of 231 aircrew. With the second wave suffering losses by a margin of 50 percent less than the first wave, this showed that there was an advantage to be gained by dividing the main bomber force.

The following night an operation was detailed for an attack on the City of Augsburg deep in Southern Germany. This was another divided force operation with two waves and 106 Squadron provided thirteen Lancasters for the first wave.
During this operation 21 aircraft were lost along with 147 aircrew. These were less than previous raids where the bomber stream had not been divided into waves, and so Bomber Command decided that splitting the bomber stream into waves was the way ahead for future large raids into Germany.

With the last few days of February, heavy snowfalls arrived over the country and Lincolnshire was not spared. Everybody at Metheringham was kept busy clearing the snow to keep the airfield operational.

Operation 23: Stuttgart, 1st / 2nd March 1944

Aircraft assigned: Lancaster JB612

Crew:
Pilot: F/O F.M. Mifflin
Flight engineer: F/Sgt. N.C. Jackson
Navigator: F/Sgt. F.L. Higgins
Bomb aimer: Sgt. M.H. Toft
Wireless operator: F/Sgt. E. Sandelands
Mid upper gunner Sgt. W Smith
Rear gunner Sgt. N.H. Johnson

Bomb load: 1 x 4,000lb. 750 x 4 1lb. 68 x 30lb.
Take off: 23.10 hours.
Time down: 07.00 hours.
Duration of operation: 7 hours 50 minutes.

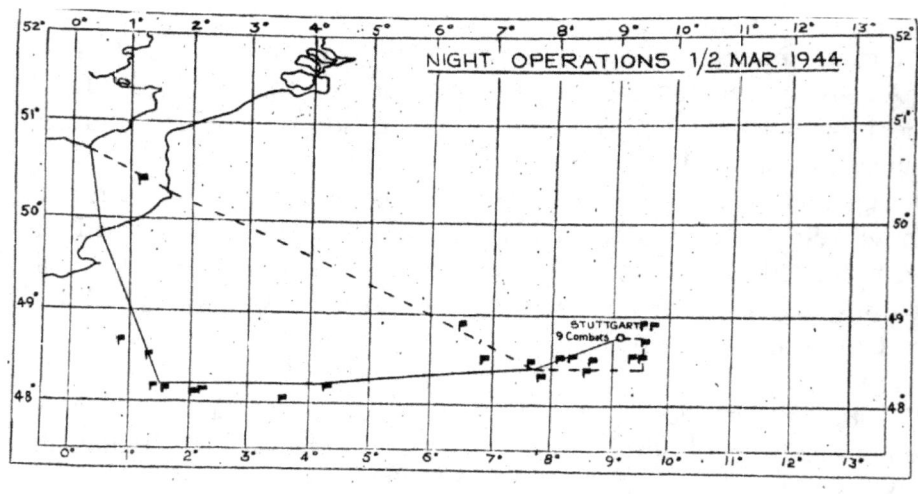

Operations resumed on the first day of March with notification of another raid on Stuttgart. Bomber Command detailed a force of over 550 aircraft with the inclusion of sixteen Lancasters from 106 Squadron.

As JB612 cleared the south coast of England they formed up with the main bomber stream. The weather over the English Channel was very heavy cloud with good visibility above. As they approached the target there was no fighter opposition, possibly due to the heavy cloud cover on the whole outward route, which rose to around 15,000 feet. On the run up to the target, the Pathfinder *Wanganui* flares were seen along with red and green TIs, but these had all disappeared at the time of the bombing. Tofty dropped the bombs on the glow of fires seen through the clouds from 22,000 feet at 03.10 hours. One large explosion was seen but otherwise no results were observed. The return journey was aided by the complete cloud cover, and they arrived safely back at Metheringham without incident.

All crews were debriefed on returning. They thought that the attack was ineffective and scattered due to the heavy cloud cover even though many big explosions had been observed. Without doubt, there was an air of disappointment regarding this attack. However post-raid analysis suggested the attack had been effective, with most of the bombing concentrated into the central, northern and western districts. This caused extensive damage to Stuttgart. 106 Squadron had delivered 66 tons of bombs on this operation, and this was the highest in 5 Group.

The Bomber Command losses for this operation were quite low in consideration to other raids; four aircraft failed to return but even so that meant another 28 aircrew were lost.

The day-to-day life on a bomber station is one of constant activity if the weather allows, and on the run up to Norman's last operation, this activity is listed as taken directly from the Squadrons Operation Book.

3rd March. Local flying plus extension of flying training. Cross Country exercises and high-level practice bombing.

4th March. Eleven aircraft were detailed for an operation but due to a snowstorm the operation was cancelled.

5th March. Eleven aircraft detailed for an operation but due to fog the operation was cancelled.

6th March. Eight aircraft detailed for an operation but once again the operation was cancelled. During the day high level bombing exercises were carried out.

7th March. Cross Country and bombing exercises carried out during the day and practice bombing at night.

8th March. No Flying. W/C E.K. Piercy, who is shortly to take over command of the Squadron, arrived from Syerston.

9th March. Fog at night. Training in the afternoon, formation and R/T practice.

10th March. 30 aircraft attacked an aircraft factory at Chateauroux.

11th March. No flying, one new crew successfully completed a night bullseye exercise.

12th March. Extensive training, high level bombing, formation bombing, air-to-sea firing.

13th and 14th March. Local flying training.

On 15th March Bomber Command detailed 818 aircraft to bomb Stuttgart, in another attempt to wipe out this important target. The 106 Squadron contingent was led for the first time by its new Commanding Officer, W/C Piercy.

In addition to the main force, six Lancasters from 106 Squadron co-operated with 617 Squadron, the *'Dam Busters'*, in an attack upon Woippy, near Metz. Acting upon instructions from the Master Bomber from 617 Squadron, the six Lancasters from 106 Squadron were to drop flares to illuminate the target. Unfortunately, however, the factories were obscured by ten-tenths cloud and, acting on instructions received over the target, the operation was abandoned, and the bombs brought back to base.

Norman's crew were one of twelve detailed for an attack on Munich, but the operation was cancelled three quarters of an hour before take-off, with the crews already in their Lancasters preparing to go.

After shutting down, Norman's crew climbed out of their Lancaster and made their way back to the flying kit hut to deposit their parachutes. As he did so, Norman was given a message to report to the Commanding Officer. The CO informed him of another operation that night which was getting ready for the off, but the flight engineer in the crew of P/O J.C. O'Leary, Sgt. E.L. Mortimer, had reported sick and they needed a replacement. Norman was told by the CO that he would like him to volunteer for the operation.

Norman said, "You would like me to volunteer? That sounded like an order, sir."

"Well, I suppose that's correct," the CO replied.

"Well in that case sir, I volunteer," was Norman's only reasonable option!" This was to be the operation in which Norman got one ahead of the rest of his crew.

Operation 24: Clermont-Ferrand, 16th/17th March 1944

Aircraft assigned: Lancaster JB292

Crew:
Pilot: P/O J.C. O'Leary
Flight engineer: F/Sgt. N.C. Jackson
Navigator   Sgt. J.E. Williams
Bomb aimer: Sgt. R.A. Snowden
Wireless operator   Sgt. G. Mellor
Mid upper gunner   Sgt. A.E. Johnson
Rear gunner   Sgt. R.S. Killer

Bomb load: 8 x 1,000lb. 1,000 x 4lb.
Take off: 19.15 hours.
Time down: 03.15 hours.
Duration of operation: 8 hours.

Another very important target for Bomber Command, Clermont-Ferrand, in the Auvergne region of central France, was home to the Michelin rubber tyre factory, which supplied enormous amounts of rubber tyres to the German war machine.

Bad weather did not prevent the six Lancasters from 106 Squadron taking off to assist 617 Squadron once more. The weather over the target area was ten-tenths cloud but with good visibility, and the 106 Squadron aircraft located the target itself on H2S radar and visually. The Pathfinders dropped their flares accurately and the target was brilliantly illuminated. The 617 Squadron aircraft leading the attack dropped red spot fires and the subsequent bombing on these markers was both accurate and concentrated. The aircraft from 106 Squadron then went into the attack.

Norman's Lancaster made two bombing runs, the first from 12,000 feet at 23.03 hours dropping high explosives, and the second from 10,000 feet at 23.10 hours dropping incendiaries. Two very large explosions were seen along with large fires and thick black smoke rising to 11,000 feet. There were no fighters seen, just a few searchlights and light flak. Several photographs were taken by the squadron which showed a good concentration of bombing on the target. The operation was deemed successful.

JB292 was lost on 7th / 8th May 1944, under the command of P/O Cyril Bartlett. Tasked with bombing an ammunition depot at Salbris, the Lancaster was probably shot down by a nightfighter with the loss of all on board.

It was around this time that Norman had noticed Miff starting to show signs of depression and stress, so he and a few of the crew persuaded Fred to see the Medical Officer, or Quack, as they all referred to him. The Medical Officer diagnosed extreme fatigue, along with stress. This was probably due to the long-range bomber operations the crew had been flying, around the eight-hour mark on average, especially Berlin, against which Norman and his crew had chalked up ten operations. Norman always thought that may have been a record number of operations to Berlin for 106 Squadron. Maybe, he considered, that was too many, and that most crews probably visited Berlin on between two and six operations[23]. The outcome was that Fred was stood down from flying operations for a few weeks to allow him some rest time to recover. In most cases this rest period was all that was needed by those who suffered extreme stress and fatigue from the almost constant operations. The rest of Fred's crew were still available for operational duty if required, and Norman and Tofty were selected for the next operation on Frankfurt.

There was a stand down from operations for 106 Squadron on the 17th and no flying training.

---

[23] By this time Fred and Norman had completed 23 ops including several of the worst nights for Bomber Command. An analysis of the specific loss rates for the ops they had undertaken (see Appendix 1) shows that their chances of having survived so far was 34%.

Operation 25: Frankfurt, 18th /19th March 1944

Aircraft assigned: Lancaster ED593

Crew:
Pilot: S/Ldr. A.O. Murdoch
Flight engineer: F/Sgt. N.C. Jackson
Navigator   Sgt. D. Clark
Bomb aimer: F/Sgt. M.H. Toft
Wireless operator   P/O. W.F. Collins
Mid upper gunner   Sgt. E.A. Hatch
Rear gunner   Sgt. J.E. Rees

Bomb load: 1 x 4,000lb. 1200 x 4lb. 96 x 30lb.
Take off: 19.15 hours.
Time down: 01.15 hours.
Duration of operation: 6 hours.

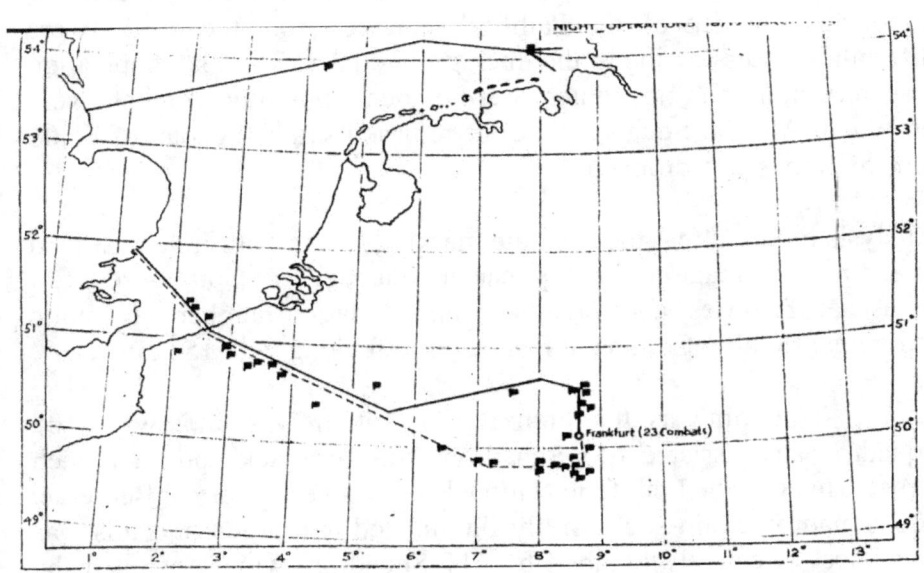

The city of Frankfurt was a major industrial city with a great variety of factories producing all manner of materials for the German war machine including the V.K.F. ball bearing plant. Bomber Command detailed 846 aircraft for the attack, which was to be split into five waves, with a total of 3,000 tons of bombs. 106 Squadron detailed thirteen Lancasters for this raid and they were divided amongst the waves with two each on the first and second, and three each on the third, fourth and fifth waves.

106 Squadron was led by W/C E.K. Piercy, the squadron's new CO, whilst Norman and Tofty flew with 'B' Flight commander S/L Murdoch. There was one early return for 106 Squadron; soon after F/L Sprawson took off at 19.10 hours, he experienced both his starboard engines overheating and had to return to base.

There was no cloud over the target area, but there was, however, a thick ground haze. The Pathfinders had laid their markers, and they were clear to see. Tofty aimed at the centre of a concentration of red and green TIs and released his bombs from 23,000 feet at 22.02 hours. There were no fires seen but one very large explosion was seen at 22.03 hours. P/O Bartlett mistook the release point flares at the target for route markers and overshot Frankfurt; he decided to turn south and bomb an alternative target, Mannheim. The other 106 Squadron Lancasters all located the target and bombed on the Pathfinder markers, but the results were difficult to assess owing to the thick ground haze. The Flak opposition was very light, and no fighters were evident and so no combats were observed. All 106 Squadron aircraft returned safely. A total of 6,506 tons of bombs was dropped.

Analysis reported that the accurate marking by the Pathfinders had led to extensive damage to the city, causing damage to 5,500 houses, 100 industrial factories and premises, and a large number of public buildings. Bomber Command lost 22 aircraft along with 154 aircrew.

At the same time as the Frankfurt operation was underway, 106 Squadron also assisted 617 Squadron with an attack upon a French target. This was the Poudferie Nationale explosives factory at Bergerac. 106 Squadron again successfully illuminated the target, and this was then most effectively bombed by 617 Squadron, which included the

ED593 was christened 'Admiral Prune II' whilst with 106 Squadron

(Aviation Books Ltd.)

dropping of six 12,000lb *'Tallboy'* bombs. 106 Squadron then assisted in fanning the general conflagration by dropping fourteen and a half tons of incendiaries. All the participating aircraft managed to take photographs of the target, and subsequent photographs by the Photographic Reconnaissance Unit revealed very extensive damage. All aircraft returned home safely.

ED593 survived the war, being transferred from 106 Squadron to No. 5 Lancaster Flying School in May 1944, having survived at least 71 ops. She was christened *Admiral Prune II* whilst with 106 Squadron. Her predecessor, W4118 *Admiral Prune* was something of a pin up for the squadron and was often flown by W/C Guy Gibson during his time with the unit. W4118 was lost on 4th / 5th February 1943 on a raid against Turin.

It would be four weeks until Norman's next operation, time for him to enjoy seven days' leave before returning to Metheringham. Generally, if the crews were not flying on operations, then they would be involved in training operations which took place on most days and nights weather permitting. This was not the case for 106 Squadron as a whole, the squadron kept on operating, flying operations as required. The squadron Ops Record Book records the following over the following weeks:

106 Squadron Lancasters prepare to leave for Frankfurt on the night of 22nd / 23rd March 1944

19th March. 106 Squadron detailed thirteen Lancasters for an operation on Munich, however, due to the appalling weather the operation was cancelled.

20th March. 106 Squadron detailed thirteen aircraft for an operation to Brunswick only for the operation to be cancelled at 17.00 hours. The same day 106 Squadron acted as Pathfinders to a 617 Squadron operation to another explosives factory at Angouleme in France. The target was located on H2S radar and accurately illuminated for the duration of 617 Squadrons' successful bombing of the target. The 106 Squadron aircraft circled while watching enormous fires and explosions. The squadron then went into the attack themselves, dropping almost fifteen tons of incendiaries onto the already burning buildings. Photographs taken at the time along with subsequent reconnaissance daylight photography revealed the almost total destruction of every single primary building.

21st March. Nineteen Lancasters were detailed for operations which were later cancelled.

22nd March. Bomber Command detailed over 800 aircraft for another attack on Frankfurt. Another opportunity to destroy the many war material producing factories. There was three to five-tenths cloud over the target, but the Pathfinder markers were very much in evidence. As the raid progressed the bombing became accurate and concentrated which led to the smoke from the fires rising to a height of three miles and visible from 200 miles distant. This was all evidence of a very successful raid. Eighteen 106 Squadron Lancasters took part in the operation, the operation was again split into waves with five of 106 Squadrons Lancasters detailed to support the Pathfinders. Seventeen of the Lancasters made successful attacks on the target and returned safely home. One aircraft was lost, that of P/O Rosser, presumed attacked and shot down by a fighter, P/O Rosser and all of the crew were killed. On this raid the Squadron dropped its highest tonnage of bombs on a single target, a total 99.2 tons.

23rd March. There was a general stand down for the squadron, but this did not stop the planners offering six Lancasters for cooperation once again with 617 Squadron. The main target was the Signa Aero Engine factories near Lyons. The 106 Squadron Lancasters were given the task of marking the target for 617 Squadron and demolishing the powerhouse of the factories after the main attack had finished. The target was covered in a thick haze which required more than anticipated flares to be dropped by 106 Squadron to illuminate the target for the 617 Squadron main force. This meant that there were no flares available to illuminate 106 Squadron's specific target of the powerhouse. F/L Gibbs made a low-level effort to mark the target with green markers, but this failed, and as it was not possible to accurately identify the powerhouse, on the instructions of the leader of 617 Squadron the operation was abandoned, with all bombs brought back to base.

The same day, Johnny, Norman's rear gunner, wrote a letter to his parents, which was to be found several years later in a box in the attic of their house by persons unknown. The letter was subsequently sold at auction and part of the first page was printed in the press. It read:

RAF Metheringham.

23rd March 1944.

My dear Mother and Father.

This is just a note I am writing to you

in case anything unfortunate happens

to me while I am operations.

The only regrets I shall

have on my life ending

are those of being parted

from you all, my very dear

family, who I love so very much.

I should like both of you

to know my dears

how very much I have

appreciated my home and

all that you have both given me.

Johnny was only just 20 years of age, and tragically, from the date of the letter, had only another 35 days to live[24].

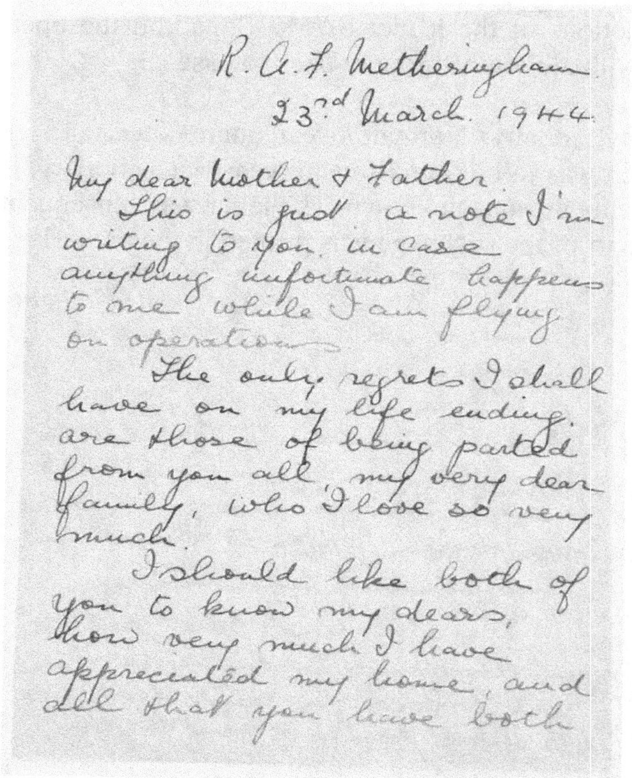

The first page of Norman Johnson's letter to his parents.

---

[24] Aircrew were encouraged to leave a final letter with their personal possessions, so that these could be returned to their loved ones in the not-unlikely event that they were posted missing. This letter might be updated periodically but was intended to provide a measure of comfort to their grieving relatives.

24th March. Bomber Command carried out one final operation against the German capital city of Berlin. 811 aircraft were detailed for this raid which included fourteen Lancasters from 106 Squadron. W/C Piercy led the 106 Squadron contingent, this being his second time in charge since taking command of the squadron. After joining up with the main bomber stream, the force was routed over southern Denmark and the Baltic, to a reference point north-east of Berlin. From there the stream turned to approach the target from the north-east, flying across the city to the south-west. W/C Piercy suffered complete instrument failure just over an hour after his take-off at 18.35 hours and returned to base.

The rest of the squadron were away safely and once at cruising altitude began to experience very unfamiliar winds. Bomber Command had developed a system that was designed to keep crews up to date with the

wind direction and windspeed. All squadrons taking part in the raid would have designated 'wind finder' crews, who would ascertain the

The contents of a suitcase found in the attic of Norman Johnson's parents' home.

true wind speed and direction and transmit this information back to the operation controllers at HQ[25].

This night proved to be extremely difficult for accurate wind information because of a phenomenon unknown at the time, the Jetstream[26]. This Jetstream was blowing from the north, so the effect on the bomber stream was to push it continually south of the planned track. Such powerful winds were something that the wind finders had never experienced before, and they found it difficult to trust the readings from their own instruments. Fearing that their calculations would be derided as simply wrong, many wind finders reduced their reported winds to what they felt were more credible, though still high, speeds. Unfortunately, these induced errors were exacerbated by the controllers of the raid who themselves thought the adjusted readings too high and reduced them further. They then transmitted the new readings to the navigators of the bomber stream as the true wind speed and direction. The result was a bomber stream that became scattered out all-over northern Germany.

As the bomber stream arrived over the target area, they found the ground markers and release point flares to be scattered over a wide area and this led to a scattered attack with little or no concentration. The route home for the bomber stream was to make two dogleg turns to starboard which took them to the north of Magdeburg and south of Hanover. They then

---

[25] The controllers would then make the required adjustments to the figures given to them from all the wind finder aircraft, which were at different positions in the stream, meaning that a degree of difference in their wind speed and direction was expected. This gave a better picture of the expected wind strength and direction at various points along the route, which was intended to assist the other navigators, especially those in less-experienced crews.

[26] Jetstream's are high-altitude winds that drive weather systems. Typically, they are encountered at around 30,000 feet, which was significantly higher than the operational ceiling of the bombers. Occasionally their effects are felt at lower altitudes, resulting in very strong winds at the level of the bomber stream. These could be at speeds of over 100 mph and, if not anticipated, would blow the aircraft off course very quickly and very far. It is likely that, on such occasions, several bombers posted as 'lost without trace' were blown so far off course that they eventually ran out of fuel and crashed into the North Sea or Atlantic Ocean.

made a turn to port, across Holland and out over the North Sea via Egmund.

F/Sgt. Hall along with his crew were on their first operation together. On their first run across Berlin to the target area they found themselves too far to the south of the city, where they came under a heavy flak attack which resulted in the loss of one engine. They repositioned for another run at the target and were, according to the squadron Operations Record Book, the last to deliver their bombs before turning for home. F/Sgt. Hall made the return journey on three engines and eventually managed to bring the Lancaster back to England and land safely at RAF Wing in Buckinghamshire at 02.40 hours. For his perseverance and his flying skills, F/Sgt. Hall received an immediate Distinguished Flying Medal (DFM).

The raid itself was a complete shambles despite post-raid reconnaissance reporting that some fresh damage had been inflicted upon Berlin, resulting in de-housing of around 20,000 people. The cost to Bomber Command was the loss of 72 aircraft and 504 aircrew, many of the bombers being shot down by flak batteries as the high winds forced the returning bombers over the heavily defended Ruhr area. Fourteen aircraft fell victim to nightfighters while over the target.

This was the nineteenth attack on Berlin since the previous August and the sixteenth since the November resumption of operations against the city. This would be the last attack on the city by the Royal Air Force heavy bombers; from now on it would be the Mosquitos of 8 Group's Night Striking Force that would continue the operations on Berlin. This they did and only halted operations on the city when the Soviet Red Army arrived in the outskirts of the capital.

25th March. The night following the raid on Berlin, 106 Squadron detailed six Lancaster aircraft to once again assist 617 Squadron in another attempt to destroy the Signa Aero Engine Works at Lyons. With W/C E.K. Piercy leading the squadron they took off from 19.30 hours. Once over the target the weather was an improvement on the previous attack and visibility was much improved. W/C Piercy flew over the target and dropped his flares, then waited for 20 minutes before being called in by W/C Leonard Cheshire, the CO of 617 Squadron, to bomb on the red spot fires. After dropping his own flares, F/L Gibbs of 106 Squadron circled for just over 30 minutes and then came in to drop his full load of incendiaries at 23.45 hours from 6,000 feet. As the illumination of the target was deemed accurate there was no need for F/L Anderson from 106 Squadron to deploy his flares, but he did drop his incendiary load at 23.52 hours and then turned for home. Some very good aiming point photos were taken. However, at Woodhall Spa, questions were being asked regarding the accuracy of the 617 Squadron red spot fires dropped by W/C Cheshire, along with F/L Shannon and F/L McCarthy. This raised doubts as to whether the bomber crews had hit correctly placed markers.

The last aircraft to bomb was at 00.06 hours, one hour after the commencement of the raid, at this time the target was completely obscured by smoke and the Signa factory could not be seen. It was not possible to tell if it had been hit. Cheshire reported fires covering an area of one square mile. The post-raid report stated that the bombing had been concentrated but to the south-west of the Signa factory, in other words, the factory was still standing and operational.

26th March. 705 aircraft were dispatched for an operation on Essen. For Bomber Command Essen was an important centre for war production, and any delay in production from these factories would help in bringing the war to an earlier conclusion. It was to be a *Parramatta* attack, meaning ground markers were laid for the bombers to aim at. 106 Squadron provided seventeen Lancasters for this attack with F/L Gibbs, F/L Ginder, and F/L Lee from 106 Squadron as the senior pilots on duty. All seventeen Lancasters were airborne through an eighteen-minute time slot from 17.42 hours. There were no 106 Squadron early returns, and they all arrived over the target at the allotted time.

There was ten-tenths cloud cover over the target which made the freshly laid *Parramatta* ground markers difficult to locate. Some of the aircraft managed to see cascading red TIs, or indeed, the glow of them, and used these as a reference point to aim their bomb loads, the others had to rely on a positional fix from H2S radar. All 106 aircraft dropped their bombs between 22.00 and 22.17 hours. There were spoof sky marker flares, which were seen by many of the crews, laid down by the Germans to draw the bombers away from the intended target but this proved to be unsuccessful. All of 106 Squadrons Lancasters returned safely, and the crews reported differing results, some observed no fires at all, and some the glow of many fires. They all thought the attack was scattered with one or two very large explosions. In fact, the attack was quite the opposite. Analysis found that the target had suffered heavily from accurate bombing, more than 1,700 houses were destroyed along with many industrial buildings and factories which suffered considerable damage. The cost to Bomber Command for this attack was nine aircraft lost along with 63 airmen, which was much lower than expected.

27th March. 106 Squadron was stood down from operations. Flying training for the Squadron with two nighttime cross-country exercises.

28th March. 106 Squadron was detailed to supply seventeen Lancasters for an operation over Germany, but it was however cancelled.

29th March. A third attempt was made at eliminating the target of the Signa Aero Engine Works at Lyons. 106 Squadron this time detailed four Lancasters which were led by W/C Piercy. They all departed Metheringham at 19.40 hours, each carrying 20 flares. As they arrived over the target area they were greeted with clear skies and clear visibility judged at up to eight miles distant. F/L Ginder of 106 Squadron was the first to drop his flares on the target, he first dropped three flares at 22.56 hours. The delivery of the flares by three of the 106 Squadron Lancasters was to be co-ordinated to ensure a constant illumination of the target, W/C Piercy dropped three flares at 23.05 hours, six flares at 23.13 hours, six more at 23.20 hours and finally four at 23.26 hours. As the fourth Lancaster of 106 Squadron flown by F/O Hinkley arrived over the target, 617 Squadron's leader, W/C Leonard Cheshire radioed that he was more than satisfied with the illumination of the target and that F/O Hinkley should retain his flares. 617 Squadron then went into the attack and delivered their bombs directly onto the marker flares laid down by 106 Squadron. All 106 Squadron aircraft returned safely, and the squadron commander was informed the following day that the bombing had been successful and that sixteen of the 22 key buildings at the Signa Aero Engine Works had been destroyed.

30th March. This the chosen date for an attack on Nuremberg, an attack that would prove to be a disaster in planning and a catastrophe for the participating crews of Bomber Command. Air Vice Marshall Cochrane of 5 Group put forward his preferred plan of a direct route to the target. This involved a 200-mile straight course from Belgium, across Germany, and then to a point which was 50 miles to the north of Nuremberg, from where the final approach to the target would be made. There was some agreement with his plan from the other Group Commanders even though the plan contained no diversion tactics and no spoof operations to draw the fighters away.

Both Air Vice Marshal Bennett of 8 Group and Air Vice Marshal Carr of 4 Group were totally against the plan and let their feelings of an impending disaster known but they were outvoted. The weather forecast made during the planning was that there would be dense cloud at the cruising altitude which would conceal the bomber stream. This report was completely debunked by a Meteorological Flight Mosquito crew that radioed through a weather report stating that this was not the case, and that clear skies may be expected. Their report was ignored, and no expected cancellation of the operation was forthcoming. 795 aircraft departed in the late evening having been given weather reports of dense cloud at the cruising altitude.

106 Squadron participated with seventeen Lancasters and they were all airborne at around 22.30 hours. F/Ls Ginder, Sprawson and Lee were the senior pilots on duty. As they formed up with the bomber stream on the outward journey it became very clear that the weather conditions were completely different to those briefed to the crews. The Jetstream that had affected the earlier Berlin operation when blowing from the north was now blowing from the south, leaving a sky clear of cloud and bright moonlight at the cruising altitude. In fact, visibility was reported as crystal clear. Instead of being enclosed in total darkness the aircraft in the bomber stream were clearly visible to each other, with dozens of aircraft clearly being seen. As if that was not enough condensation trails formed in the cold night air behind each bomber acting as target guide for the fighters.

For the nightfighters of the *Luftwaffe*, this was a gift from the gods. 245 fighters were reported to be active that night and they needed almost no guiding from the ground controller to locate the bomber stream. Bomber crews on their return spoke of seeing upwards of 50 bombers destroyed by fighters on their way to the target, the actual figure was more than 80 aircraft destroyed before the target had even been reached.

The wind strength and direction given to the navigators of the bomber stream was completely inaccurate and many were blown up to 50 miles north of their intended track and so turned on to their final heading from a position that was different from where they believed. This resulted in more than 100 aircraft bombing Schweinfurt in error. With the horrendous losses on route, and the erroneous bombing of Schweinfurt, the number of aircraft reaching the target area of Nuremberg was substantially reduced and very little significant damage was inflicted on the target.

106 Squadron had two early returns due to engine failures. Over Charleroi in Belgium, F/O Penman and his crew flying Lancaster ND332, came under attack from two-nightfighters, and the aircraft was extensively damaged. The rear turret also became unserviceable as did the mid upper turret when the engine itself that supplied the power to these turrets failed. F/O Penman ordered the bombs jettisoned and after managing to shake off the nightfighters turned for home. They managed to get the Lancaster back to Manston aerodrome on the Kent coast, and on landing, the undercarriage collapsed on touch down. All the crew survived this incident and thought themselves extremely lucky to have done so, but unfortunately it would not be very long before their luck ran out.

Three crews from 106 Squadron were missing. F/Sgt. Hall DFM's Lancaster JB566 was attacked by fighters on their way to the target and exploded near to Berghausen, north-west of Frankfurt. F/Sgt. Hall, along with four of his crew, were killed, the two other crew members managing to escape by parachute. P/O Starkey flying Lancaster ND535, *Queen of Sheba*, was also attacked and shot down, this victory being claimed by the German nightfighter ace, Oblt. Martin Becker. ND535 crashed eight miles north-west of Giessen, north of Frankfurt, and blew up when it hit the ground, throwing the pilot, P/O Starkey, and the bomb aimer F/Sgt. Paris, clear. Miraculously both survived and were captured, though the other five members of the crew were killed. P/O Moxey RAAF, flying Lancaster NA585, had found the target, delivered his bomb load, and was on his return journey but unwittingly drifted to the north of his track over Belgium. The aircraft was spotted by a nightfighter and attacked, and it was shot down south-west of Namar. P/O Moxey was killed along with all his crew.

On this one operation Bomber Command lost 95 aircraft along with 665 aircrew, nearly all of whom were killed. Bomber Command lost more aircrew on this one night, than Fighter Command had during the whole of the Battle of Britain. This was the worst operation in the history of Bomber Command. Had the German defences been able to inflict a similar toll on many other nights during the long and bloody campaign, history might well have been different.

31st March. Weather misty, no flying today.

During the month of March, 106 Squadron had taken part in operations on thirteen nights and flown 156 sorties, losing four aircraft along with 28 aircrew. This was the highest number of sorties in a single month flown by the squadron since May 1942, when they had re-equipped with Lancasters. Something for the squadron to cheer about was announced with the results of the February bombing statistics, which stated that 106 Squadron had won the 5 Group bombing competition for the third month running.

Without doubt, this long six-month winter campaign was the most arduous faced by any of Bomber Command aircrews throughout the entire war. Although the moral of the crews was never questioned, it must have been obvious that battle fatigue was starting to take its toll. The cost in aircrew and aircraft had been much greater than had been planned for, and Harris's plan to destroy Berlin from end to end and break the will of the German people could only be viewed as a failure.

The crews of Bomber Command were now required to engage in an expansion of attacks on targets such as marshalling yards and other railway facilities[27], such as those already carried out in early March at Trappes, and Le Mans. Following these attacks Bomber Command had expanded the list of marshalling yard targets to include Amiens, Aulnoye, Courtrai, Laon, and Vaires. The importance of these targets could not be underestimated, and they had been attacked with good results. It was now time for the onslaught against Germany itself to be put on hold, and from April 14th Bomber Command was taken under the wing of the Supreme Headquarters Allied Expeditionary Force, (SHAEF) under General Eisenhower and they would be subject to the requirements of this organisation until the end of what was to be a momentous Summer.

1st April. There was training for the squadron. Norman's crew might have been stood down from operational flying for the time being, even though the crew were available for operations if required, but they were still involved in the day-to-day training that took place regularly. Today there were high level bombing and H2S radar exercises.

2nd, 3rd and 4th April. The following three days were plagued with heavy rain and consequently no flying training took place other than some limited local flying.

5th April. The next operation was against the aircraft repair factory at Saint Martin du Touch in Toulouse, south-west France. Bomber Command detailed 144 Lancasters with twelve from 106 Squadron. One Mosquito aircraft was also in the bomber group, flown by W/C Leonard Cheshire who was leading the three aircraft from 617 Squadron. They were to mark the target using their new experimental low level precision method.

106 Squadron's aircraft, led by W/C Piercy, were airborne at 20.30 hours in dreadful weather. This improved as the bomber stream crossed over into France and they found themselves flying through clear skies. W/C Piercy experienced some kind of problem with his aircraft and

---

[27] The German forces in France relied heavily on the railway network for the movement of significant numbers of troops, equipment, and supplies. If this could be disrupted to any great extent, the Wehrmacht's reinforcements and ammunition supplies would be degraded.

returned to Metheringham early, landing at 21.45 hours. No details of this return are given in the squadron Operations Record Book other than 'Operation Abandoned'. The weather was then clear all the way to the target area where the factory was visibly identified. W/C Cheshire was the first over the heavily defended target, diving to below 1,000 feet and delivered two red spot fires directly onto the factory. These were delivered with such accuracy that the two other aircraft from 617 Squadron flown by Munro and McCarthy were not required to lay their markers and were instructed by Cheshire to act as beacons for the approaching bombing force.

At this time, it was only 106 and 617 Squadrons that had participated in precision bombing at lower altitude. The main bomber force had no training at all in precision bombing and was used to bombing at much higher altitude where they were a much smaller target for the flak guns. However, the result was that they bombed between 12,000 and 15,000 feet and the target was destroyed. Due to the accuracy of the target marking and low-level bombing very little collateral damage was caused to civilian housing. There was little opposition, and the raid was deemed a complete success. All 106 Squadron aircraft arrived back at Metheringham safely.

It was this operation that convinced Air Marshal Harris that visual target marking from a low level was completely viable and he authorised that, under the appropriate conditions, 5 Group could operate independently of the other Groups. The following three days saw no operations but intensive training every day.

6th April. There were bombing details and H2S radar exercises.

7th April. Intensive day and night training on the 7th. These consisted of H2S radar exercises with night cross country flights for new crews.

8th April. Normans 25th birthday.
Bombing details, air firing and H2S radar exercises, the night exercises were cancelled due to fog.

9th April. Bomber Command detailed 56 Lancasters for a mining operation in the Baltic Sea. Eight Lancasters were from 106 Squadron. In contrast to this main operation, three Lancasters of 106 Squadron were detailed for a task necessitating low-level flying. The Königsberg Seekanal, was the only means of sea communication between the German naval base at Königsberg and the Baltic, which it joins at Pillau. This canal, which is only 54 yards wide, was a vital link in the enemy's waterway traffic system and its disruption, even if only temporary, would have serious consequences. F/O Latham, P/O Milne and F/O Anderson were detailed to mine this canal and, to ensure accuracy, it was necessary to drop the mines from 150 feet. Although the target was nearly 1,000 miles from base, it was successfully located by all three crews, who had to run the gauntlet of fierce and accurate opposition from light flak, and heavy machine guns which were placed on both sides of the canal bank. In addition, there were many searchlights, some beams being exposed horizontally and forming an almost impenetrable dazzle. Despite this formidable opposition, each pilot made a steady run along the canal at 150 feet and the mines were carefully and accurately deposited in their allotted positions. Not until the task was completed did the aircraft take any evasive action, although the gunners had returned the enemy fire with some spirit. All three aircraft were damaged but there were no casualties, and all returned safely. It should be added that F/O Anderson was unable to release one mine but dropped it eventually in an alternative area. The whole operation was completed with skill, resolution and outstanding courage and resulted in many congratulatory messages upon its successful completion. 55 mines were dropped, a total of 38.5 tons of explosive.

10th April. Another operation was detailed involving 106 Squadron, this time against the marshalling yards at Tours. 5 Group detailed 178 Lancasters of which eleven were from 106 Squadron. The weather was fine with good visibility. The red spot fires that had been dropped over the target were unfortunately not very accurately placed and the Master Bomber had to instruct the bomber crews to place their bombs 600 yards to the east of the red spot fires for their bombs to hit the target. The crews bombed either visually or on the instructions of the Master Bomber from a height of 6,000 feet between 01.35 and 01.56 hours. Despite the initial error the bombing was reported as very accurate with much damage caused to the marshalling yards. There was no opposition, and all aircraft returned safely.

11th April. Daytime local flying exercises took place, and an operation was detailed for the third consecutive night. This time the target was the two marshalling yards at Aachen, one in the east of the city and one in the west. This was an all-Lancaster operation with 340 aircraft detailed for the operation, 106 Squadron put up seven Lancasters with S/L Murdoch taking the lead. There were thunderstorms over Lincolnshire as the aircraft from Metheringham became airborne between 20.30 and 21.15 hours. One aircraft, piloted by P/O Durrant, had to return to base early due to a failed engine. The other 106 Squadron aircraft reached the target area to find eight-tenths cloud, but through which the red and green markers were clearly visible. The crews bombed from 17,000 feet between 22.43 and 22.55 hours. Most of the bombing fell into central and southern districts resulting in massive damage. This was the town's heaviest raid of the war. The damage to the railway system was extensive but not complete and a further operation would be necessary to finish the job.

Air Marshal Harris had decided that it was now the time for 5 Group to have its own capability for the low-level marking of targets. He therefore transferred 83 and 97 Squadrons from the Pathfinders at 8 Group, to 5 Group. They were to be joined by 627 Squadron who were equipped with Mosquitos. This caused a great deal of animosity, not only from the chief of 8 Group, Air Vice Marshal Don Bennett, but the crews of 83 and 97 Squadron as well. Even though they had originally been members of 5 Group before transferring to the Pathfinders, they were proud of their status as Pathfinders and were keen not to lose their step up in rank, which was given once joining the Pathfinders. After much consideration the outcome was that they were allowed to retain their ranks along with the coveted Pathfinder badge.

12th April. 106 Squadron had a stand down from operations, which allowed for intensive training both day and night with special emphasis on H2S radar. Bombing and air-firing exercises were also carried out.

13th April. There was more training with radar exercises, high-level bombing, and with air-firing.

14th April. Sixteen Lancasters of 106 Squadron were detailed for an attack on Osnabruck. However, the operation was cancelled 45 minutes before take-off with the crews in their Lancasters getting ready for the operation.

15th April. There was a day of more training, chiefly radar exercises.

16th April. There were more radar exercises day and night.

17th April. Twelve aircraft from 106 Squadron were detailed for an operation which was later cancelled.

Operation 26: Stettin Bay, Swinemunde
18th / 19th April 1944

Aircraft assigned: Lancaster JB612

Crew:
Pilot: F/O F.M. Mifflin
2nd Pilot: P/O. W.G. Fraser
Flight engineer: F/Sgt. N.C. Jackson
Navigator: F/Sgt. F.L. Higgins
Bomb aimer: F/Sgt. M.H. Toft
Wireless operator: F/Sgt. E. Sandelands
Mid upper gunner: Sgt. W Smith
Rear gunner: F/Sgt. N.H. Johnson

Bomb load: 5 x Sea mines
Take off: 21.00 hours.
Time down: 04.20 hours.
Duration of operation: 7 hours 20 minutes.

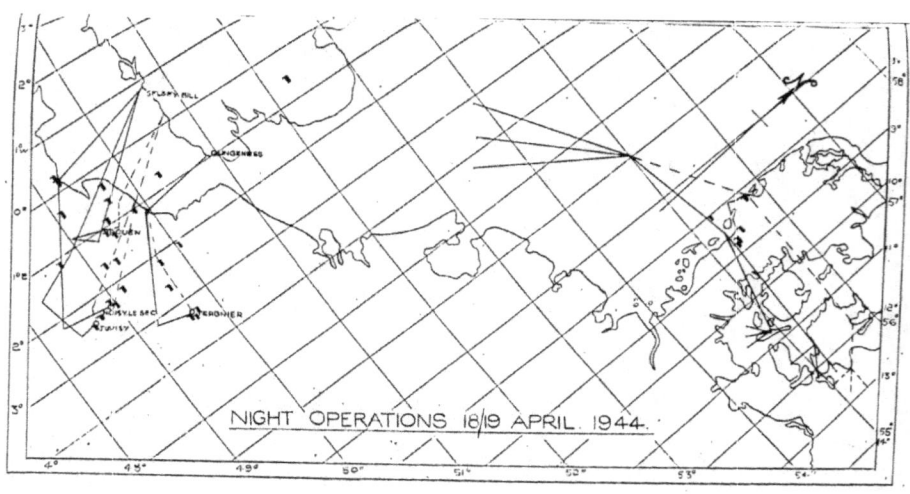

Norman's crew were detailed for an operation of mine laying in Stettin Bay, Swinemunde. This would be a return to operational flying for Miff their pilot after his much-needed rest. On this operation they had a second pilot, P/O W.G. Fraser, on board.

Nine Lancasters from 106 Squadron all got safely airborne and were led by W/C Piercy. As they arrived over Stettin Bay the skies were clear but there was a thick haze which made pinpointing the dropping area for the mines difficult. Some dropped their mines in the Dievenon 'gardening' area, rather than Coperaw See, the aiming point. Normans was amongst the crews to pinpoint the Coperaw See aiming point and Tofty laid their mines at 00.28 hours from 15,000 feet. They were followed by W/C Piercy at 00.32 hours. There were no incidents, and all nine aircraft returned safely.

19th April. More training for the crews, mainly on radar exercises.

An atmospheric image of 106 Squadron Lancasters preparing to depart on a moonlit night. Crews hated moonlight.

Operation 27: La Chapelle Marshalling Yards, 20th / 21st April 1944

Aircraft assigned: Lancaster JB612

Crew:
Pilot: F/O F.M. Mifflin
Flight engineer: F/Sgt. N.C. Jackson
Navigator: F/Sgt. F.L. Higgins
Bomb aimer: F/Sgt. M.H. Toft
Wireless operator: F/Sgt. E. Sandelands
Mid upper gunner: Sgt. W Smith
Rear gunner: F/Sgt. N.H. Johnson

Bomb load: 14 x 1,000lb
Take off: 23.20 hours.
Time down: 03.45 hours.
Duration of operation: 4 hours 25 minutes.

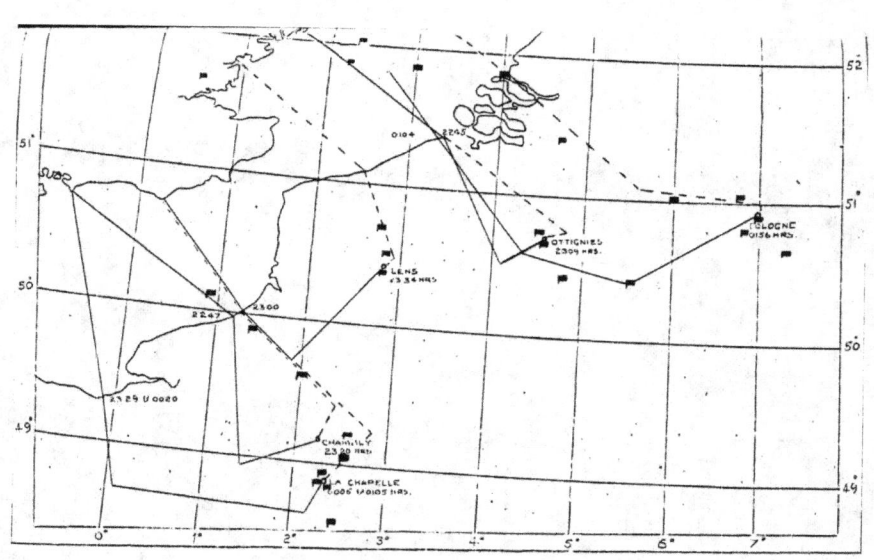

Bomber Command detailed 247 Lancasters and sixteen Mosquitos to bomb the La Chapelle marshalling yards in Paris. The weather en route was good with excellent visibility, and the Mosquitoes laid their red spot fires accurately.

106 Squadron supplied eighteen aircraft which were divided amongst the different waves with five on the first, four on the second, five on the third and four on the fourth wave. All eighteen 106 Squadron aircraft reached the target and made successful attacks between 01.21 and 01.45 hours.

Tofty located the aiming point by the red spot fires that were clearly seen and bombed from 9,000 feet at 01.37 hours. The photographs taken were plotted from between 600 and 2,000 yards from the aiming point. There were no reported incidents, and all aircraft returned safely.

21st April. No flying today.

Operation 28: Brunswick, 22nd / 23rd April 1944

Aircraft assigned: Lancaster JB612

Crew:
Pilot: F/O F.M. Mifflin
Flight engineer: F/Sgt. N.C. Jackson
Navigator: F/Sgt. F.L. Higgins
Bomb aimer: F/Sgt. M.H. Toft
Wireless operator: F/Sgt. E. Sandelands
Mid upper gunner Sgt. W Smith
Rear gunner F/Sgt. N.H. Johnson

Bomb load: 2 x 2,000lb. 140 x 30lb.
Take off: 23.15 hours.
Time down: 05.00 hours.
Duration of operation: 5 hours 45 minutes.

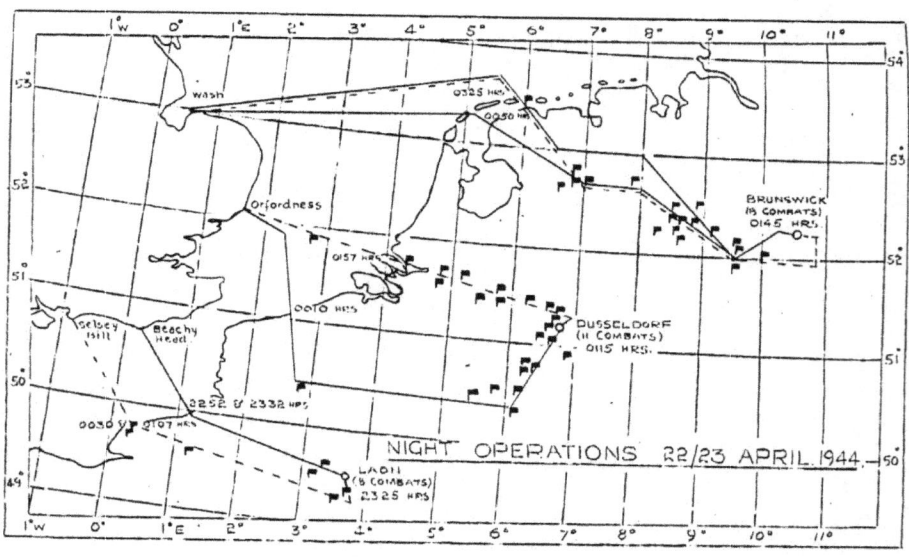

The target for this night, and Norman's 28th op, was back to Germany. The city chosen was Brunswick, or Braunschweig giving it its German name. The code name given to the city by Bomber Command was *Skate*[28], The city of Brunswick was ringed by anti-aircraft guns as it was an important centre for the arms industry.

This was a 5 Group attack, with 248 Lancasters and ten Mosquitoes detailed for the operation. 106 Squadron supplied 20 aircraft, one of which returned early due to technical issues. The weather was good and as the aircraft arrived over the target the red spot fires laid down by the ten Mosquitoes were clearly visible.

As Norman's aircraft approached the target, Miff handed direction of the aircraft over to Tofty. On lining up his bomb run Maurice aimed for a single red spot fire and released his bombs from 20,300 feet at 01.58 hours. Although the visibility was good on the approach to the target Norman's crew reported that visibility over the target was almost nil at 20,000 feet. The bombing was accurate and towards the end of the attack the whole of Brunswick was engulfed in fires and smoke. The raid was deemed successful.

The Squadron Operation Book states that F/Sgt. Cunningham deserved a special mention on this occasion. One of his engines failed before reaching the target and, instead of abandoning the operation, he carried on, completed his operation and made the return journey on three engines. Four aircraft were lost on this raid including one from 106 Squadron. F/L JHS Lee, flying Lancaster JB567, was on his 29th operation. The aircraft was hit by a barrage of heavy flak and attacked by a nightfighter, the combined effect of which brought the aircraft down. F/L Lee along with five of the crew lost their lives, and a 'second dickey' pilot on board, P/O Tucker, was also killed. The flight engineer, F/Sgt. Simes, along with the bomb aimer, F/O Beven, managed to bail out and survived to be taken prisoner. The defence over the target was reported as 'moderate to heavy flak', and a few fighters in evidence.

---

[28] It was recognised that the identity of targets should be disguised for security reasons. AVM Robert Saundby, deputy to Harris, was tasked with assigning code names to each German city target. As he was an avid fisherman, he used the names of fish for each of these.

Although they were blissfully unaware of the fact, this was to be the last occasion on which Norman and his crew took JB612 ZN-U ("Uncle") on an operation. JB612 was one of the 106 Sqn contingent tasked with attacking an ammunition depot at Salbris in France on 7th / 8th May 1944. She came down at St-Viatre, just south of Salbris, and exploded on impact, killing P/O H.K. Rose and all but one of the crew. The sole survivor was the bomb aimer, Sgt. J.F. Smith, who evaded capture. The site of the crash was marked by a propeller from JB612.

23rd April. It was another day of no flying for the crews apart from one new crew who completed a cross-country exercise.

Operation 29: Munich, 24th / 25th April 1944

Aircraft assigned: Lancaster JB664

Crew:
Pilot: F/O F.M. Mifflin
Flight engineer: F/Sgt. N.C. Jackson
Navigator   F/Sgt. F.L. Higgins
Bomb aimer: F/Sgt. M.H. Toft
Wireless operator   F/Sgt. E. Sandelands
Mid upper gunner   Sgt. W Smith
Rear gunner   F/Sgt. N.H. Johnson

Bomb load: 232 x 30lb.
Take off: 21.00 hours.
Time down: 06.35 hours.
Duration of operation: 9 hours 35 minutes.

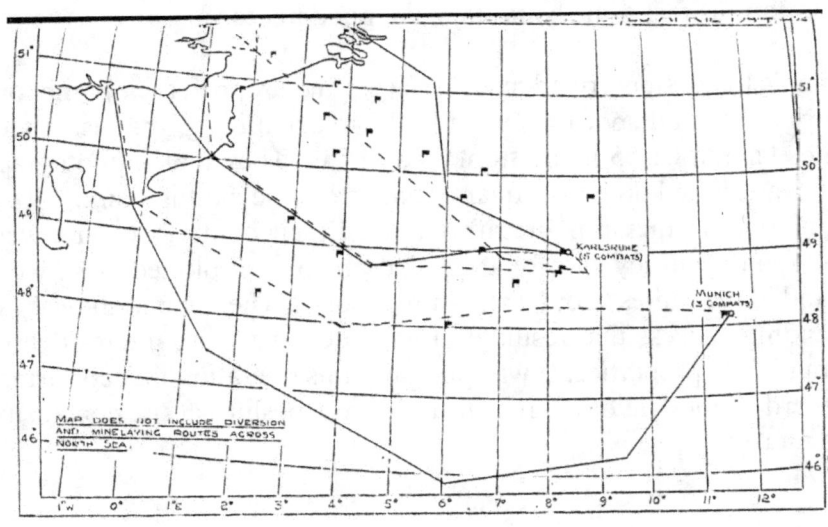

Munich had been on the receiving end of many raids of varying intensity in the past but had invariably escaped lightly compared with other cities. 24th April, however, was the night that the city received its severest punishment to-date. This was a comparatively small force consisting of 260 Lancasters and Mosquitoes all from 5 Group, along with some help from 617 Squadron.

106 Squadron, led by W/C Piercy and S/L de Belleroche, detailed seventeen Lancasters for this operation with eleven in the first wave, and six in the second. There was one early return, F/L E. Sprawson's Lancaster ME668 suffered an engine failure, despite the best efforts of his flight engineer Sgt. K. Anderson to keep it running. All the other aircraft continued to the target routing over southern France. The route to the target contained some elements of deception on the part of Bomber Command. 617 Squadron Lancasters carried out a feint by dropping flares and TIs over Milan, suggesting that Italy was the destination of the bomber stream. In the meantime, Mosquitoes from 627 Squadron were on a more direct route to Munich to drop window aluminium strips two and a half minutes ahead of the Pathfinder flare laying force. This was intended to confuse the German fighter controllers. At 01.40 hours, Leonard Cheshire dived through the searchlights, whilst receiving the attention of some 200 light flak guns. At a height of 1,500 feet, he delivered his markers and then flew across the rooftops as fast as he could to make good his escape.

Norman's Lancaster arrived over the target and dropped their bomb load directly on the red spot fires west of the marshalling yards just fifteen minutes later at 01.55 hours from 20,500 feet. They took a photograph which was plotted one and a quarter mile from the aiming point. All the remaining 106 Squadron aircraft delivered their bomb loads and were on the return journey shortly after 02.00 hours, all plotted at between one and three miles from the aiming point. The operation was an outstanding success that resulted in huge destruction to the residential and municipal properties. It was probably this operation that confirmed the award of the Victoria Cross to Leonard Cheshire at the conclusion of his tour.

25th April. Training was carried out day and night which included cross country exercises for new crews.

On the 26th of April, following the successful raid on Munich, an operation was detailed for 216 Lancasters and Mosquitoes to attack Schweinfurt. The city was home to the major ball bearing producing factories in the German Reich. The US 8th Air Force had a bad day out there on 14th October 1943, a day which became known as Black Thursday. The route to the target was well defended all the way by fighters and flak guns and the Americans suffered heavily. After their escort fighters turned back at the German border, the bomber stream fought a running battle against the Luftwaffe. As well as the fighters they faced heavy flak and had to fight their way to the target and then back again across central Europe.

Out of 291 aircraft, 60 were shot down which resulted in some 600 USAAF airmen lost over enemy territory. Of the bombers that returned, seventeen crashed in England or were scrapped and 121 needed repairs, and many of these aircraft brought back wounded or dead crewmen. Following this raid USAAF leaders suspended strikes against targets beyond the range of their fighter escort, until the advent of the Merlin-powered P51 Mustang in early 1944, which could eventually reach Berlin.

The following day, 26th April 1944, Norman received a message to say that he was now a father to a baby boy, Brian. He and the rest of the crew were jubilant at the news and were looking forward to celebrating the birth on their return from Schweinfurt. It would, however, be another thirteen months before Norman got to see his son for the first time, and his wife again.

This was to be Norman's thirtieth and last operation of his tour[29]. However, having got one ahead of the rest of the crew by volunteering for the operation to Clermont-Ferrand in Central France, he had agreed

---

[29] Although it was not a hard and fast rule, Bomber Command aircrew could expect to be stood down from operational duties after completing 30 ops. Following this they were given an alternative posting, usually to a training unit, for a period of six months before returning for a second 'tour', usually of twenty ops.

with his crew that, following this operation, he would complete one more trip to see them through their own tour of 30 operations. He had not discussed this with Alma, who believed that this would be his last operation for a while and expected him home for some well-deserved leave. As Norman saw it, the next trip should count as the first operation of his second tour, which he anticipated would probably be with a Pathfinders squadron. Norman considered that the Pathfinders was the posting you got if you were lucky, and if you were unlucky, you would wind up at a Training Unit[30].

JB612, their trusted Lancaster code name U for Uncle, which they had flown on fifteen of their last sixteen operations had undergone extensive servicing work including work on the elevators and their controls. A flight check was required that afternoon with the full crew on board along with the two ground engineers responsible for the work, they were on board the Lancaster to make sure everything was working correctly. The moment that JB612 lifted into the air it was obvious to Fred Mifflin and Norman that all was not well with the aircraft. JB612 was almost unflyable, the crew, as Sandy Sandelands wrote in a future letter, thought they were going to be killed that afternoon, it was only the skill of Fred Mifflin working the ailerons and rudders, and Norman working the throttles and elevator trim tabs that they managed to fly the aircraft around the circuit and back into land. The ground engineers were deathly white he wrote, almost physically ill on the aircraft. Before climbing out of the aircraft they thanked Fred and Norman for saving their lives, Norman said, I think you have a bit more work to do on our aircraft before we take you up again, with that they were out of the aircraft and off. JB612 was not serviceable, and a new replacement Lancaster, ME669, O for Oboe, was made ready for the crew.

---

[30] Training units had, by definition, inexperienced crews who were learning to fly unfamiliar aircraft, in poor weather, and at night. To increase the risk, they were allocated older, and usually battle-worn, aircraft. It was no sinecure.

Operation 30: Schweinfurt, 26th April 1944

Aircraft assigned: Lancaster ME669

Crew:
Pilot: F/O F.M. Mifflin
Flight engineer: F/Sgt. N.C. Jackson
Navigator   F/Sgt. F.L. Higgins
Bomb aimer: F/Sgt. M.H. Toft
Wireless operator   F/Sgt. E. Sandelands
Mid upper gunner   Sgt. W Smith
Rear gunner   F/Sgt. N.H. Johnson

Bomb load: 1 x 4,000lb. 132 x 30lb.
Take off: 21.35 hours.

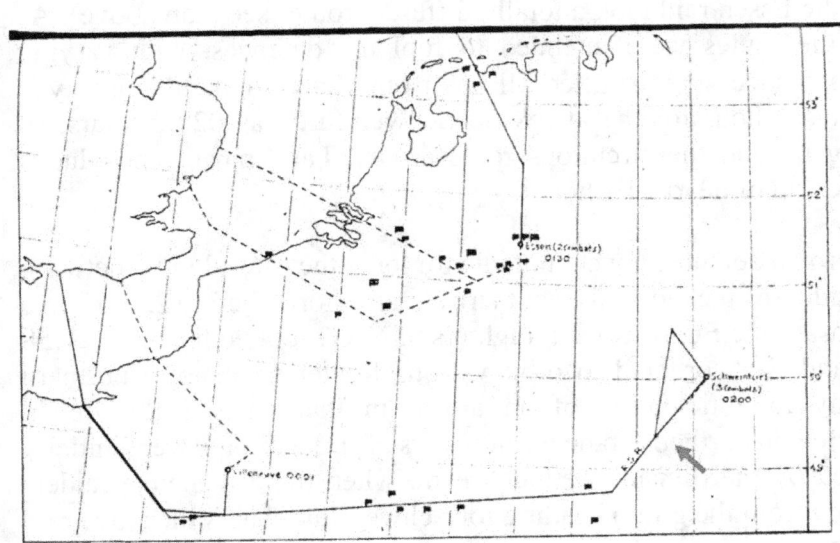

The raid route maps from the Night Raids Report, 26th / 27th April 1944. Unfortunately, the original image from The National Archives is of poor quality. The position of the ME669 crash site is indicated by the red arrow.

Three separate raids had been mounted, with 215 Lancasters and 11 Mosquitos attacking Schweinfurt, 493 bombers, a mixed bag of Lancasters, Halifaxes, and Mosquitos, targeting Essen, and 217 aircraft, mostly Halifaxes, being sent against Villeneuve-St-Georges. Schweinfurt was to bear the brunt of the losses, with 21 Lancasters and close to 150 aircrew failing to return. Meanwhile, seven aircraft were lost against Essen, and a single Halifax failed to make it back from Villeneuve-St-Georges. That night 106 Squadron detailed sixteen Lancasters for the Schweinfurt raid, of which five would not return. The squadron records state that this was the worst night for losses that the unit had experienced.

The route to the target once airborne was south from Metheringham, crossing the English south coast over Portsmouth, and from there to Le Havre. After crossing the French coast, they carried on down to the southwest of Paris before making a left turn, then they had a long straight run towards eastern France just north of Strasbourg. Crossing the Rhine into Germany they made a further left turn and started the run in to Schweinfurt. This route combined the streams attacking Schweinfurt and Villeneuve until they were south of the latter target, whilst the Essen raid took a totally different route (see map above). As usual, the routes were intended to fool the defences, with varying degrees of success. Miff lifted ME669 from Metheringham's runway at 21.35hrs. H-hour for the attack on Schweinfurt was 02:00 hours, so forming up and the circuitous route around Paris meant an arduous outward trip of nearly 4½ hours.

The German defences[31] were not idle for long; the coastal radar network of I. Jagdkorps picked up the southern stream shortly before 22:00 hours as it crossed the English coast. Fighters of NJG3 took to the air at 21:58 hours and were ordered to orbit various fighter beacons in northern Germany in anticipation of an attack in that part of the Reich. Meanwhile in northern France, controllers of II. Jagdkorps were initially confused by the division of the stream, when the Villeneuve raiders separated from the group heading for Schweinfurt. The Villeneuve raid

---

[31] Details of nightfighter activity are taken from Nachtjagd Combat Archive 1944 Part 2, by Theo Boiten, Red Kite, UK, 2020.

encountered little fighter opposition, with two combats occurring; a third suspected fighter attack turned out to be a 'friendly fire' combat between two confused Halifax gunners. The sole Halifax lost was brought down by flak.

Once the defence controllers realised what was going on, they deployed their fighters straight away. Initial contact with the stream was made by fighters from the Luftwaffe airfields at Laon-Athies and Juvincourt, scrambled between 23:20 and 23:45 hours. The first loss from the Schweinfurt raid, a 101 Squadron Lancaster, occurred at 00:24 hours.

106 Squadron lost its first two crews of the night at 00:50 hours. JB601, 'Victory', was flown by S/L Murdoch, 'B' Flight's commander, with whom Norman and Tofty had attacked Frankfurt on 18th March. Murdoch had a 'second dickie' pilot, Sgt. Bradley, who was the only man to survive. JB601 became the 26th victim of Hptm. Helmut Bergmann, flying his Bf.110 from Juvincourt. Bergmann noted in his combat report:

> *Y-reports guided me into the bomber stream near St. Dizier*
>
> *My radio operator gave me a running commentary of SN-2[32] readings. Towards 00:47 hours I spotted the first enemy aircraft (4-mot, twin fin) ahead and about 400 metres above. Enemy height 4800 metres. At 00:48 hours I attacked from below at 100 metres range. The aircraft caught fire at once in the starboard wing with a bright flame. At 00:50 hours I observed the crash fire.*

Bergmann claimed further victims at 00:57 and 01:01 hours, marking an extremely busy quarter of an hour.

---

[32] SN-2 was the 'Lichtenstein' airborne interception radar carried by Luftwaffe nightfighters.

At the same time, another noted ace, Hptm. Martin Drewes attacked P/O W.G. Fraser's ND850. Fraser had flown as 'second dickie' with Norman's crew on the Swinemunde raid of 18th April. The aircraft caught fire, and the pilot and three others managed to parachute to safety, managing to avoid capture. ND850 was Drewes's 24th victim overall, and his second of the night.

P/O Harper died with four of his crew in JB562, which crashed southeast of Heidelberg, shot down at 02:12 hours by Lt. Otto Keller.

Amongst the fighters taking to the air was a Do217 flown by the highly decorated Hptm. Walter Bornschein of the *Führer Kürierstaffel*, Hitler's courier and liaison flight. Bornschein, who was a former bomber pilot, was equally adept when it came to night-fighting, and at 02:18 hours engaged ND853 which had just bombed the target. The Lancaster, flown by P/O Bishop, was hit, and eventually exploded and crashed, killing Bishop and all but his navigator and bomb aimer, who were captured. In a last gesture of heroic defiance, Bishop's gunners managed to hit Bornschein's Do217, which crashed in flames with the loss of its three-man crew.

There was, of course, a fifth empty dispersal on the morning of 27th April, that of ME669.
Sadly, for all the cost in men and machines, the raid on Schweinfurt was not a success. The low-level marking, by Mosquitos, was inaccurate, whilst unexpectedly strong headwinds, of 45 mph, had delayed the backers-up and main force Lancasters. Fierce harassment by nightfighters also interfered with the attack and much of the bombing fell outside Schweinfurt. Of the 226 aircraft despatched to Schweinfurt, 215 bombed the primary target, but only 27 bombed within the target area, and 196 within three miles.

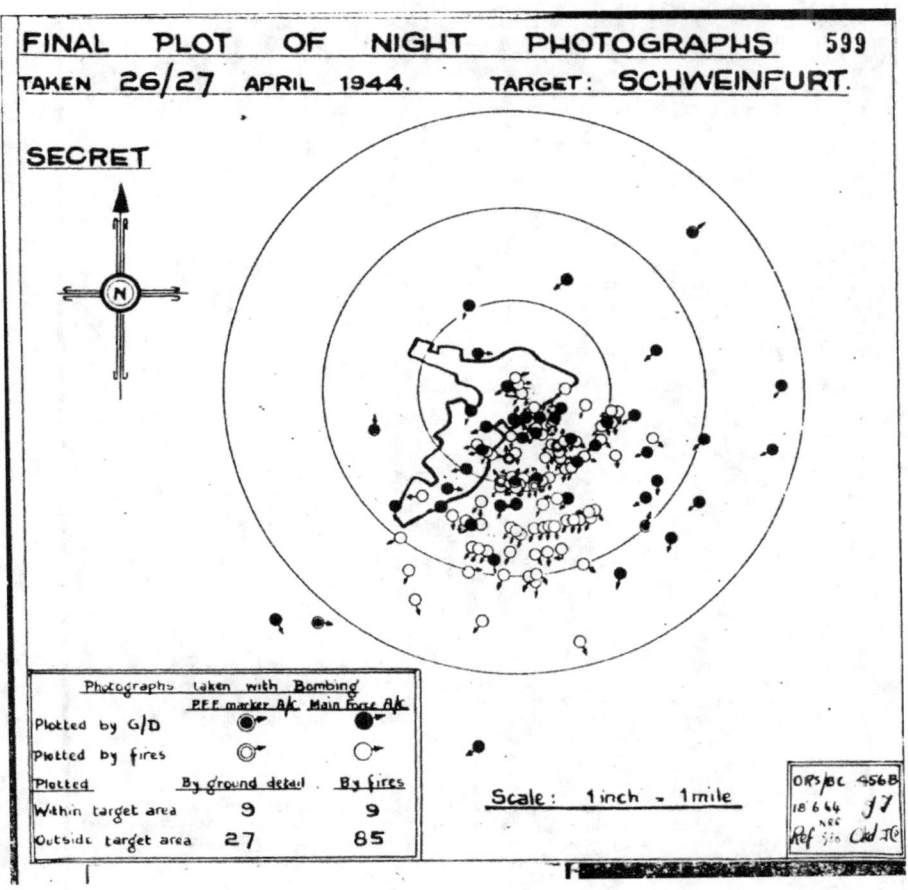

Bomb plot for Schweinfurt on 26th / 27th April 1944, from the Night Raid Reports (TNA via Steve C. Smith)

SCHWEINFURT

ATTACK

A datum point at 4956N 0949E was to be marked with yellow T.I. at H-4. 9237 0925E., half the force (carrying 30 lb. incendiaries) and the marking were to proceed direct to the target, the other half approaching downwind to north 20 minutes after the first force had attacked. The first force pass over the target, turn to port when ordered or at H+15 (whichever was), and approach the target downwind. By this time, the A/P would have been with a red spot fire, backed up by 24 more. But if this red spot was ctly positioned, a new A/P would be marked with a green spot fire, backed red spot fires. If the green was hard to see among the reds, the Master was to order the markers to drop more green spot fires or cascading green the A/P. If cloud prevented visual marking, the A/P was to be marked with green T.I. cascading from 10,000 ft. H = 0200 (when the first force pass over the target).

3.

```
No. of aircraft despatched ............................... 226
No. of aircraft reporting attack on primary area ......... 215 (95.1%)
No. of aircraft reporting attack on alternative area ..... 2  (0.9%)
No. of abortive sorties .................................. 9  (4.0%)
No. of aircraft missing .................................. 21 (9.3%)
```

WEATHER EXPERIENCED

No cloud. Moderate visibility. New moon, setting at 0130 hours.

PHOTOGRAPHIC STATISTICS

```
No. of aircraft plotted in target area (ground detail ... 9)
                                       (fire tracks ..... 9) ...... 18

  "   "   "      "  off   "   "        (ground detail ...27)
                                       (fire tracks .....35) ......112

  "   "   "      estimated to have bombed in target area .......... 27

  "   "   "      "     "     "     "    within 3 miles of A/P ...191
```

TIME OF ATTACK

Owing to a head wind of 45 m.p.h., the flares were late and scattered. The spot fires fell S. of the River, and were followed by others still further mark. The Master Bomber made every effort to redeem the situation, by sting aircraft to over shoot the green marking; but he was poorly received, and bock became concentrated S. of the target area.

RECONNAISSANCE

Despite the displacement of the attack, useful damage was caused in the S.W. einfurt, involving the marshalling yards and 4 of the ball-bearing factories. th ball-bearing plant, in the centre of the town, was also hit. Several of residential damage occurred in the built-up area.

DEFENCES

Ground Defences 40-60 searchlights operated ineffectively. Heavy flak was at 13-21,000 ft., with meagre light flak to 6-8,000 ft. Marker aircraft d undamaged between 400 ft. and 5,000 ft. over the target. More accurate tion was met en route between Troyes and Strasbourg.

Fighters Fighter opposition was stronger than the figure of only 4 attacks suggest. Most of the combats took place on the long easterly leg into the which was identified in time for the fighters to arrive there before the

/second force .....

Extract from the Night Raid Reports series, held in The National Archives. The digital original is poor, but legible (TNA via Steve C. Smith).

second force. They probably claimed 14 victims, making a total of 13 attacks; a large figure for a force of 226 aircraft. One FW.190 was destroyed near St.Dizi on the way out.

CASUALTIES

23. 21 aircraft (9.3%) were lost. 7 fell to flak, 3 between Troyes and Stra 2 at Karlsruhe and 2 at Schweinfurt. 3 are known to have been destroyed in com 6 on the long easterly leg, one just after leaving the target and one near Pari 6 more probably went down near the target. There were no landing or taxying ac

VILLENEUVE ST. GEORGE

PLAN OF ATTACK

24. **Method of attack** OBOE groundmarking on both A/Ps, under the directions Master Bomber. The S. A/P was to be marked first, and the N. 30 minutes later. each instance, 4 Mosquitos were to drop yellow, green and red T.I. and red spot Illuminators were to drop flares and bombs at the T.I. The Master Bomber and hi deputy were to direct the bombing and drop other markers if necessary. If the had dropped no T.I. by zero hour, the Master Bomber was to release white T.I. wh The main force were to be directed by the Master Bomber.

25. **Timing**   Zero hour : S. A/P : 0005
                              N. A/P : 0035

    Duration of Attack : S. A/P : 2359–0015
                         N. A/P : 0029–0045

```
4 Mosq.                    @ H-6, -4, -2, and -1
Master Bomber  )
Deputy         )           @ H-5
Illuminators        6  @  H-5
                    2  @  H+2
Main Force         29  @  H to H+4
                   32  @  H+4 to H+7
                   29  @  H+7 to H+10
```

The same timing was to be followed for both A/Ps.

SORTIES

26. No. of aircraft despatched 217
     No. of aircraft reporting attack on target 202
     No. of abortive sorties 15
     No. of aircraft missing 1

WEATHER EXPERIENCED

27. Cloudless over target and whole route. New moon.

NARRATIVE OF ATTACK

28. The markers dropped by the Mosquitos fell N.E. of the S. A/P, and the Ma Bomber instructed main force crews to wait until flares had been dropped, wherev he dropped accurate white T.I. The bombing was well concentrated round these the second attack, the Master Bomber could not be heard, probably because of ja and the bombing was divided between the 2 sets of gr ndmarkers.

DAY RECONNAISSANCE

29. The main weight of the attack fell on the southern end of the yards. Ext damage was caused to wagon construction shops, carriage workshops, rolling stoc railroad tracks. One direct hit was scored on a train at the end of a bridge. damage was caused to residential property S.W. of the target.

/ENEMY DEFENCES .....

'MISSING': The 106 Squadron Operations Record Book notes that 'Nothing was heard from this aircraft after take-off.' It was an all-too-common occurrence.

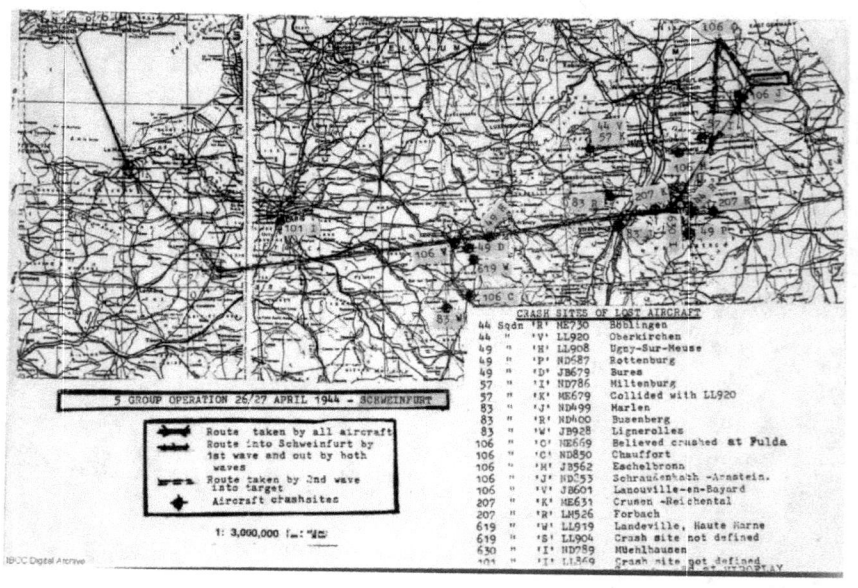

Schweinfurt route and crash sites.

Part Three: 'The Most Conspicuous Bravery'

Norman and his crew could see many combats taking place in the night sky, with Lancaster after Lancaster falling from the sky or just exploding on this long run towards the Rhine. There were fighters everywhere. They had never seen so many combats taking place at any one time, more Lancasters were going down in flames along with what looked like some of the fighters that had been hit during their attacks. On the final turn up to Schweinfurt the crew were just waiting, with a growing sense of inevitability, to be engaged.

Due to unexpected strong headwinds the bomber stream, along with the Pathfinder target markers, were delayed in reaching the target. The bomber force was enduring the headwinds along with the constant harassment of enemy fighters all the way to the target, but they pressed on.

As Norman's aircraft approached the target, the visibility was good, but there was a thick haze. The aiming point was identified by the green TIs and flares. Tofty aimed at these markers and released his bombs just before 02.30 hours from 20,000 feet.

After hearing the call from Maurice, "Bombs gone!", Miff held the Lancaster straight and level for some eleven interminable seconds, to get the vital target photograph. Then Sandy saw on H2S Fishpond that they were being tracked by a fighter. "Miff, Miff!" he called, "We are being tracked by a fighter, it's at eight hundred yards now and closing!" Then he warned 'Johnny' Johnson in the rear turret, that he thought it was a Junkers 88. Johnny had already spotted it as had 'Smudge' Smith in the mid upper turret. Both gunners had been on the highest of alerts ever since the turn at the southwest of Paris, Johnny shouted into his intercom, "Dive, dive starboard, starboard, corkscrew, skipper, it's a Focke-Wulf 190, and it's coming straight at me!"

Both gunners opened fire on the fighter as Miff took evasive action, turning the Lancaster to the starboard, but before he could dive, the Lancaster was racked with 20mm high explosive cannon fire. As the cannon fire hit and tore through the starboard wing some of the exploding shrapnel came through the starboard side of cockpit and hit Norman, who was standing alongside Miff in the cockpit.

Norman sustained shrapnel wounds to the back of his head, his right shoulder, and right leg, and was thrown to the floor. As he fell, he hit his head with a glancing blow on the throttle console. As Miff levelled the aircraft, Norman stood back up and immediately started checking the aircraft for damage. The high explosive cannon shells had done their job, ripping open the inner fuel tank on the upper surface of the starboard wing and starting a fire. The fuel tank had been ruptured just forward of the centre line of the wing and behind the inner starboard engine, the flames from the fire were travelling back and over the control surfaces of the trailing edge of the wing. Norman knew that if this fire could not be controlled, the aircraft would be lost. He also knew that the fire could not be controlled from within the cockpit, and as it was a fuel fire on top of the wing, putting the Lancaster into a dive would not extinguish the fire.

Norman told Miff that the starboard inner fuel tank had been ruptured and there was a fire on top of the starboard wing. The pilot asked, "Is there anything to be done, Jacko?"

Norman replied that there was nothing within the cockpit that could be done, but that he could deal with it. "I have a plan, Skipper," he said, "And with your permission, I would like to try. We should reduce the power on the inboard starboard engine to idle and then feather the propeller, adjust the throttle settings on the other engines to maintain level flight. Then I'm going to climb out of the aircraft and down onto the wing with a fire extinguisher and do my best to put the fire out."

Miff looked up at Norman incredulously, but then nodded his approval and said, "Okay Jacko, over to you." Such was the confidence that the members of the crew had in each other.

After Miff had reduced the power on the starboard inner engine Norman feathered the propeller. The reason for this was to minimise the airflow from the propeller back over the wing, whilst the engine could be returned to normal operation when required. He and Miff then adjusted the RPM of the other engines as necessary. Without the weight of the bomb load the Lancaster could maintain altitude on three engines and would lose very little speed. Norman disconnected his oxygen mask from the main oxygen supply along with his intercom, he then attached one of the small portable ten-minute oxygen cylinders, which he pushed into the top left-hand side of his flying jacket. Norman was not wearing a Mae West life jacket, this being common practice among crews who would remove them when not flying over water. He clipped on his chest parachute and Fred Mifflin passed Norman the handheld cockpit fire extinguisher from the left side of the pilot's seat, which he pushed into the top right-hand side of his flying jacket.

Norman then called for Sandy to pass forward the handheld fire extinguisher from his position, as Norman moved back towards the wireless operator's position Sandy passed the extinguisher forward and Norman pushed it into the top right-hand side of his jacket as well. He then asked Sandy to pass him the aircraft axe which was kept in the casualty station area close to the wireless operator's position. The axe had an ice pick on one side and a standard axe blade on the other. Norman then returned to the cockpit.

Pops came out from behind his curtain, the light from within the navigator's section reflecting on Norman's face, Pops looked straight at Norman and told him that he had been injured and was bleeding from underneath his flying helmet. Norman thought this was from the blow on the throttle levers console. He wiped the blood away with the back of his glove and said it was not an issue. Miff told Pops that he was assisting Norman in his plan to save the aircraft, but to get ready to evacuate the aircraft, if necessary, Pops returned to his station and pulled the curtain back across, to update their exact position. With the axe and the two fire extinguishers, Norman was almost ready to go.

The Pyrene portable fire extinguisher carried by the Lancaster had a cylinder body of twelve inches in length which contained a high velocity spray. The extinguisher operated like a bicycle pump, a double action, pulling the centre rod outwards by its T-shaped top would operate the spray and pushing it back in would operate the spray, giving a constant flow of liquid, The Carbon Tetrachloride liquid was very effective at fighting fuel and electrical fires.

Miff gave the order for all the crew to be on standby to bail out of the aircraft. Norman changed the portable oxygen bottle for a fresh one, pulled down his goggles, and with the axe in his left hand, reached up above his head with his right and jettisoned the ditching escape hatch in the centre of the cockpit canopy Perspex roof. Then, facing towards the navigator's position, he lowered his right hand and took hold of the ripcord of his parachute and pulled.

The parachute spilled into the rear cockpit. With that single action, he had reduced his chances of survival to an absolute minimum. Rather than being kept safely stowed in his chest pack from where it might be safely deployed in mid-air it was now to be used as an accessory in his journey down onto the wing and to the air intake on the leading edge. This made it extremely vulnerable to becoming snagged, torn, or set on fire, rendering it useless as his only means of salvation.

Norman called for Sandy, who was now moving forward into the cockpit area, and Pops, who came out again from behind his curtain, to hold onto the rigging lines and pay them out as he climbed out and down onto the wing.

"Keep them just tight enough until I'm at the air intake on the leading edge of the starboard wing and then hold them tight," he instructed the two men.

"What's your plan, Jacko?" both men wanted to know.

"Look, I haven't got time to explain the whole plan, but I am going out onto the wing to deal with that fire. That's my job, I have the skipper's permission. Believe me, it's the only way to save the aircraft and get you back home."

Sandy and Pops thought it was suicide and did not want him to try but accepted this decision without further question. They started to gather up the parachute knowing they had to hold onto the parachute which they thought he had somehow deployed accidentally.

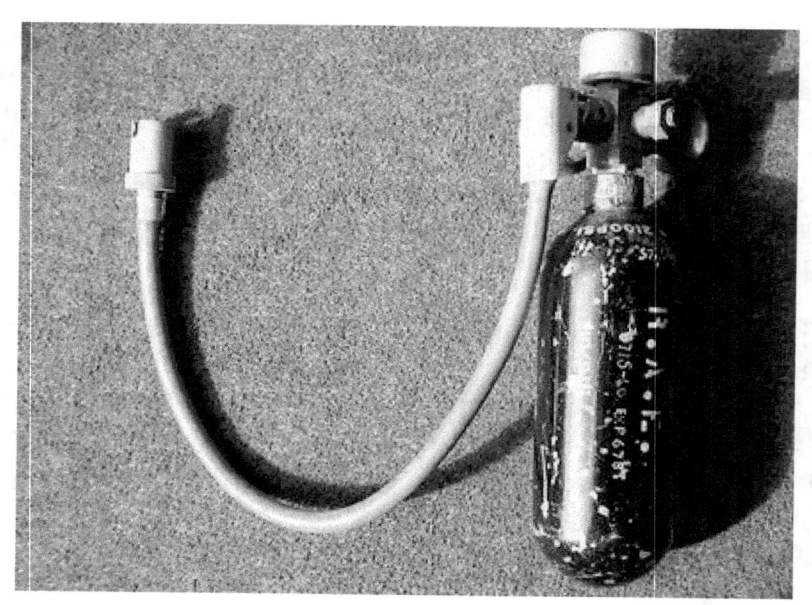

Portable oxygen bottle with hose.

Pyrene fire extinguisher and mounting bracket.

Lancaster emergency axe

Tofty climbed up into the cockpit from his position in the nose. He was not sure himself what was going on but said he would assist where possible. Norman reached up to the escape hatch, placed a foot on the navigators table, pulled himself up, and climbed out of the escape hatch so that his back was against the slipstream. As Norman moved out of the cockpit, he kept his body as flat as possible on the top of the Lancaster fuselage to give him the best chance of not being swept backwards by the slipstream which was rushing past him at close to 200 miles per hour. Anchoring himself by hooking his feet into the escape hatch, he worked his way as far back along the fuselage as he could.

He then eased himself down and to his left and held the broad-edged blade of the axe in his left hand, with his feet still hooked inside the cockpit canopy hatch, Norman forced the ice pick into the fuselage just below the rear of the cockpit canopy Perspex and in front of the line of rivets that secured the 0.7mm aluminium skin of the Lancaster to the main frame. With the ice pick blade of the axe placed in this position, it was directly in front of one of the spars of the mainframe. Even in the dark Norman knew instinctively where this line of rivets would be. Using the axe head as a hand hold for his left hand on the side of the aircraft, and with the two crew members carefully paying out the rigging lines, but keeping them as taught as they judged necessary, Norman swung his legs out of the escape hatch, around and downwards towards the wing. As he did so, he grabbed the axe with his right hand then, with the crew still holding his parachute rigging chords, placed his feet onto the top front edge of the starboard wing, but they immediately slipped off due to the damp ice cold surface of the wing, he was now stretched out along the side of the fuselage, but only just above the wing and not far from his goal of the leading edge air intake.

He released his right hand's grip on the axe and threw his right arm down and backwards over the leading edge of the starboard wing. Next, he let go of the axe with his left hand as well, threw his left arm down and over the leading edge of the starboard wing. His crewmates in the cockpit let out some more of the parachute rigging lines as he dropped onto the wing, he then, with his head and shoulders held down over the leading edge, and his arms wrapped over and just under the leading edge, eased a bit at a time to his right towards the air intake which was about another two feet to his right hand side. As he reached the air intake, he pulled back his right arm and slid his hand into the air intake, he then did the same with his left, and let his head and shoulders move back along the wing, he was now laying, stretched out, on the starboard wing directly next to the fire.

Getting a good grip with his right hand, and with the crew now holding the parachute rigging lines tight, with his left hand he took the first fire extinguisher from the right-hand side of his jacket. However, as he pulled it out it snagged on one of the parachute cords attached to his parachute chest pack, he lost his grip on it, and it flew away into the night. Reaching into his jacket for the second extinguisher, he got a good grip, pulled it from his jacket and pushed the extinguisher nozzle-first under his right arm and trapped it there. He turned the T-shaped top of the pump handle a quarter of a turn to the left to release the safety lock, pulled the handle out and started pumping the handle with his left hand. The Carbon Tetrachloride liquid poured onto the top of the wing and into the fire.

All was going well with the fire starting to be controlled, but then, the oxygen from the small portable oxygen cylinder inside Norman's jacket started to become difficult to breathe as its supply was running out. 'Damn,' Norman thought, 'That was a quick ten minutes!' Removing his left hand from the fire extinguisher, Norman turned his head away from the slipstream and unclipped his oxygen mask on one side to breathe whatever air was available at that height. He then returned to pumping the fire extinguisher with his left hand. The fire now seemed to be coming under control but at that moment, just as success seemed possible, a nightfighter came in for another attack and fired once again on the Lancaster.

The crew inside the cockpit were unaware of this second attack and so took no evasive action. They thought that the inner fuel tank on the starboard wing had just exploded, 'Smudge' Smith, the mid upper gunner, said that he felt this attack must have been from below the aircraft as it was unseen by him, and he was correct.

The German records for this second attack state that the Lancaster was attacked and subsequently shot down one and a half miles west of Kirchensall in the area of Württemberg, the combat taking place at 5,800 meters, just over 19,000 feet, 300 meters below the aircraft at 02.45 hours. The Luftwaffe pilot was an accredited ace, Feldwebel Gunther Bahr of 3. /NJG6, who was flying a Messerschmitt Bf110 G4, equipped with the upward firing 20mm cannon which fired high explosive cannon shells[33]. Bahr claimed Lancaster ME669 as his fifteenth victim of the war; he would go on to claim 37 victories in total for which he was awarded the Knights Cross. He survived the war and died on 29th April 2009.

The starboard inner wing fuel tank under the top half of Norman's body erupted and he was engulfed in flames. He received two more wounds in his right leg as the exploding cannon shells burst into shrapnel and two large pieces tore through his thigh along with more smaller shrapnel into his right side and underside of his right arm. Norman threw his left hand up and grabbed the air intake to hold on with both hands. The flames spread and erupted inside the air intake, though he was at least afforded some protection from the fire by his thick leather flying jacket, flying helmet, goggles and gloves, this was unfortunately about to change; as Norman lifted his head away from the flames the slipstream filled the inside of his flying helmet, and the fastening strap under Norman's chin gave way. The slipstream sent his helmet, goggles and oxygen mask flying backwards but they were still attached to the oxygen bottle inside Norman's flying jacket. His gloves had now been completely burnt away. Norman later said that with the flames from the fire in the air intake being fanned by the 200 miles per hour slipstream, it was the same as holding your hands into the flames of several blow torches. He was now suffering severe burns to both his face and his hands, and his parachute chords were now being damaged by their proximity to the flames. With his hands being attacked by the fire in the air intake, Norman could no longer maintain his grip. The slipstream lifted him off the wing and he was thrown backwards, suddenly coming

---

[33] This was called by the Germans *Schrage Musik*, which translates literally as 'slanted music', the German term for Jazz.

Gunther Bahr during the war (left) and in later life (right).

Gunther Bahr (centre) with his crew, in front of their Messerschmitt Bf110 night fighter.

to a halt as his parachute was still being held inside the cockpit. He was being dragged above and behind the Lancaster.

Inside the cockpit the crew realised that there was no way they could drag Norman back inside the cockpit but thought he had been killed, or that with the damage to his parachute he might not be able to survive a descent. However, if the 'chute was not too badly damaged it might still deploy and that was probably his only chance of surviving. They managed to feed the rest of the parachute out of the cockpit escape hatch as best they could, though the parachute suffered more damage as it was being pulled out of the cockpit by Norman's weight. As the last of the parachute was fed through the hatch, Norman disappeared into the night.

Inside the Lancaster, Miff gave the order to bail out. Sandy was the first to reach the side door towards the rear of the aircraft. Despite his slight size and weight, he pulled the door inwards as if it was made of cardboard. But rather than escape the burning aircraft as quickly as he could, Sandy waited for Smudge to evacuate first, followed by Pops. Sandy thought that Johnny would have evacuated the aircraft from his rear turret which was the normal escape route for the rear gunner, Tofty and Miff, would use the emergency escape hatch in the floor of the bomb aimer's compartment, access to which was forward of and below the flight engineer's position. Believing that no one else would be coming to the rear door, Sandy then, and only then, threw himself out of the burning Lancaster and into the night[34].

In fact, as he eventually fell away from the Lancaster, Norman was very much alive, albeit suffering greatly. His parachute canopy opened but it was only partially inflated as it was damaged in several places. The rigging lines had been damaged by the fire and were smouldering. Norman tried as best he could to douse the smouldering cords, but his hands were so badly burnt he could do little other than hope that the cold night air rushing through the cords would cool them down and stop the burning, and that the parachute would hold together which it did, just.

---

[34] This detailed account was as given to the author by Frank Higgins.

Norman's flying helmet, goggles and oxygen mask were flapping above him as he descended but did not interfere with the parachute. He was finding it hard to breath, now that the thin air at this altitude was no longer being forced into his lungs by the 200 miles per hour slipstream. However, he knew that his breathing would improve as he descended into the denser air below.

He could do little to slow his rapid descent, and landed heavily next to a wooded area, breaking one ankle and badly twisting the other.
Norman lay there until first light. He had broken one ankle, with the other badly twisted, along with several shrapnel wounds over his body. His face was very badly burnt which had caused his right eye to close completely. His hands were also severely burnt, with all layers of skin and some of the flesh completely gone, so that they were useless. He was, as the reports said, in a pitiful state.

"Terror Flieger!"

At first light Norman managed to work the oxygen bottle out of his flying jacket using his left elbow, and with his teeth pulling on the oxygen line. It dropped to the ground. He could not unclip his parachute, or what was left of it due to the condition of his hands.

He had landed on a raised area and could see a village on the outskirts of a much larger town some way off in what looked like a valley. With thoughts of escape pushed out of his mind, he got into the crawl position, lifted his hands and feet off the ground, and started to crawl forward on his elbows and knees in the direction of the village with his parachute dragging behind him. He was making very slow progress but continued, having to rest every 100 yards or so due to the physical effort and pain. Eventually after about two hours he reached the outskirts of the village. It was still early and there seemed to be no one around, so he crawled towards the smallest cottage where he thought he had the best chance of being treated with some form of compassion. On arriving at the door, he lifted his right arm and banged on the door with his elbow. After just a few seconds an upstairs window opened, a man looked out, and asked quite politely, "Wer ist das?[35]"

Norman looked up at the man and said, "R.A.F", but the words came out as a whisper. The man in the window, apparently unable to hear Norman's reply, repeated, "Wer ist das?"

Norman cleared his throat and as loud as he could say, "R.A.F!" The man's voice now changed, and he shouted out of the window, "Terror Flieger! Churchill Gangster!" and then pulled the window shut.

After around thirty seconds, Norman could hear the door locks being opened from the inside and as the door opened, flinched, because he expected to be kicked or beaten. Standing in the doorway were two women, who appeared to be the wife and the daughter of the man in the window. They helped Norman into the cottage, unclipped his parachute, and placed him onto a settee, they then started to help with Norman's

---

[35] "Who is that?"

wounds as best they could. The man then appeared, spoke angrily in German and left the cottage. Norman said he was lying there like a lord, being looked after by these two women as they tried their best to help with the burns on his hands and face when the front door flew open. In came the man along with a policeman and a man dressed in black who Norman thought may have been Gestapo. The man in black then ordered that Norman be lifted to his feet despite the two women protesting in German, seemingly upset by this treatment. Supported by the policeman, Norman was marched towards the door of the cottage, and as he reached the threshold, he turned and thanked the two women for their help. Both were crying and still protesting.

Norman was marched down to the police station, trying to walk with one ankle broken and the other badly twisted. Even though he was supported by the policeman, it took him about half an hour as progress was slow, and his body was wracked with unimaginable pain. Arriving at the police station Norman was placed into a handcart and paraded through the streets to what Norman thought was some sort of confinement centre. En route he was jeered at by the local population, and some threw stones at him despite his pitiful state, Norman always said he perfectly understood this as bomber crews were not exactly welcomed[36].

At this centre Norman was placed on a trolley, he received some basic first aid consisting of his hands and face being bandaged, no treatment to his leg, ankles. or body wounds was given at all. Two other members of his crew, Frank Higgins and Maurice Toft, who had bailed out of the Lancaster, were also in this building having been picked up that morning. They saw the figure on the trolley whose head, they said, was completely bandaged, but with a little bit of nose sticking out, along with both hands completely bandaged. They also saw the RAF blue uniform and immediately thought it was Miff. On closer inspection they realised it was Norman and could not believe that he had survived, or indeed, considering his condition whether he would survive his injuries.

---

[36] In the summer of 1944, Hitler decreed that captured allied aircrew should be treated as war criminals and summarily executed. Whilst this was not routinely carried out, there were many instances of airmen being shot, lynched, beaten to death, or sent to concentration camps such as Buchenwald.

They lent over Norman and said, "Norman, its Frank and Maurice. How are you feeling?"

His reply was in a whisper through the bandages, "Bloody marvellous... did all the crew get out?" They replied that, yes, they believed so. Norman then asked, where are we, Frank Higgins said that they were in some sort of jail or holding centre, but not sure which town, possibly Neuenstein. Maurice told him there were some Luftwaffe personnel in the building, one of whom spoke to them in English and said that they were being taken to Frankfurt.

Norman, along with the other two crew members, were transferred from this holding centre to the Dulag Luft transit camp near Frankfurt, where prisoners of war were interrogated for information[37]. Back at home in England Alma received a telegram which at first, she thought was from Norman, regarding the completion of his 30 operations, and that he would be coming home for some leave. It was instead the dreaded proforma telegram, saying that her husband was 'Missing in action believed killed.' With her son only a few days old she was being informed that she could now be a widow. Alma refused to believe that Norman was dead and said she would wait for confirmation that he was still alive. That was all she could do, hold on to that belief.

Alma's faith was rewarded a few days later, when a further message that Norman had survived and was a prisoner of war was delivered by the local policeman who had been cycling around and around trying to find her. Alma had not been at home but visiting the local children's clinic. The policeman entered the clinic to find Alma standing in the reception area with her lifelong friend Nelly Hall. When he told her that they had received information that her husband was alive and a prisoner of war she shouted, "I knew it, I knew he was still alive!" and, with tears running down her face, she threw her arms around the policeman and thanked him. Nelly Hall, whilst also very pleased with the news, thought

---

[37] Norman's citation states that on this trip he bore the intense pain and discomfort of the journey with magnificent fortitude.

the policeman was rather good looking and so took the opportunity to throw her arms around him as well.

Meanwhile in Germany, because of his injuries Norman had been transferred almost immediately, to the Hohemark Hospital, which was close to the Dulag Luft transit camp. There the doctors tended to his various wounds. They placed fresh burns dressings on his hands and face. The shrapnel wounds in Norman's leg and body had started to show signs of infection and so needed to be dealt with straight away. The worst of the shrapnel wounds were in Norman's right thigh; the shrapnel had passed straight through his leg missing the bone. Norman later referred to these as '...just flesh wounds.'

Tofty and Pops were both transferred from Dulag Luft to Stalag 357 Kopernikus prisoner of war camp at Thorn, known as Torun in Poland. The camp was around 180 miles northwest of Warsaw. They were joined there by Sandy and 'Smudge' Smith, but there was still no news of the whereabouts of Miff or Johnny, the rear gunner.

After a few days as Norman was laying on his bed a doctor who spoke good English came into the room, he said that Norman had a very important visitor, Norman thought it must be a member of the crew, possibly Miff. Through the door came what Norman took to be a Luftwaffe officer in full dress uniform.

In perfect English he said, "Good morning, sergeant, I would like to identify myself, I am Feldwebel Gunther Barr, Feldwebel is the Luftwaffe rank of Sergeant, I am a member of the Luftwaffe."

Norman said, "Good morning, my name is Sergeant Jackson, I am a member of the Royal Air Force, I trust you are not here to invite me to dinner in your mess, if so, I must decline the invitation as my uniform is currently being repaired."

"Very good," said the Luftwaffe Sergeant, "I like the British sense of humour, I would like to apologise for your many injuries, but this is war, and we in the Luftwaffe are just trying to defend our country."

Norman replied, "Really? I thought you were trying to take over the world."

"Not all Germans are Nazis, Sergeant Jackson," he replied.

"No," Norman said, "I can believe that of some Germans that I have met." He was thinking of the two women in the cottage that had helped him. "I would say that the doctors and nurses in this hospital, who are doing their best for me, are just good Germans, but you, standing there in that uniform, well at least you are on the same side aren't you?" With that, the Luftwaffe sergeant threw his right arm out in front of him and saluted, turned and left the room. When the doctor returned, Norman asked him why the Luftwaffe Officer had visited him. The doctor replied that it was the man who had shot down Norman's aircraft and as he was in the area thought he would pay a visit. Norman thought this unlikely, and wondered how he could have known that he was from ME669. Then he thought the Feldwebel would have known that all captured aircrew were taken to the Dulag Luft transit camp for interrogation, which was close by. Maybe his Luftwaffe colleagues had told him that there was only one member of the crew still in the vicinity, at the hospital,

Norman thought little of it under the circumstances but did remember the Luftwaffe man's name, Gunther Barr, as it resembled his adoptive name of Gunter, and his surname was like a bar in a pub[38].

Early one morning, with fresh dressings on his burnt hands and his face, a plaster cast on his right lower leg, a splinted and bandaged left ankle, and dressings on seventeen different shrapnel wounds, Norman was carried on a stretcher to an ambulance and placed on a shelf in the back. There were some other patients in the ambulance along with two nurses. He was then driven close to 200 miles to the Reservelazarett IX C (a) hospital in the town of Obermassfeld near Leipzig, Reservelazarett IX

---

[38] It was many years later, after Norman's death, when the author was researching the official German records of the attack on Norman's aircraft that he came across the name of the Luftwaffe pilot who had shot down ME669. The German documents identified the fighter pilot as Feldwebel Gunther Barr.

C (a) was where the most seriously wounded British prisoners of war were accommodated.

They stopped a few times along the route and some of the patients left, Norman presumed to an alternative medical centre of some kind. He remembered arriving at Obermassfeld sometime in the late afternoon or early evening. The hospital was a three-storey stone building, which came under the administration of the Stalag IX C prisoner of war camp, which was close by. The hospital was itself a prisoner of war camp with German guards to stop the patients from escaping, and German civilian administration.

Norman was carried into the hospital, and placed in a ward which had seven beds including the one he was in. All the patients had varying degrees of injuries. He was then attended by a doctor who spoke and sounded English. When Norman asked the doctor about this, he replied, "I am English. This Hospital is staffed by captured British, Canadian and New Zealand doctors, nurses and medical staff, although we must work under the watchful eyes of the Germans.

A postwar photograph of Reservelazarett IX-C at Obermassfeld
(Roger O'Brien via pegasusarchive.org)

Norman's numerous injuries were assessed; the burns on his hands were so severe that the doctor asked how they had come about. "Well," said Norman, happy to be talking to a fellow countryman, "I am a flight engineer in Bomber Command, I climbed out onto the wing of my burning Lancaster with a fire extinguisher. I had to deal with a fire involving the fuel tanks after we had been attacked by a nightfighter. That was my job, to keep the Lancaster flying and for the crew to make it safely home."

"My God!" exclaimed the doctor, "You did what?!" He then turned to a nurse and asked, "Do we have a psychiatric ward here nurse? If so, I have a patient for them."

The doctor then said that they had a surgeon at the hospital and that he will get him to examine Norman's hands because they need specialist help. The following day he was examined by the surgeon, who was with the Royal Army Medical Corps, along with a Canadian colleague who was also a surgeon. They told Norman that they would have to take several skin grafts taken from his legs and placed onto his hands.

"Whatever you think is best is OK with me," said Norman. "Do you have all of the required instruments here for that kind of surgery?"

The surgeon replied, "No, we do not. That is why the skin grafting will be carried out using razor blades." They said that the burns to his face were not deep enough to require skin grafting and would be better treated in the normal way. The surgeons did their best to rebuild Norman's hands but told him that because of the damage to the tendons, and muscles, they would always have a skeletal appearance and may well be of limited use[39].

They continued the treatment to the shrapnel wounds in his right leg and removed several pieces of shrapnel from his body. They decided to leave the shrapnel in the back of his head as they felt it would work its

---

[39] The author recalls Norman's hands having that skeletal appearance and being a totally different colour to the rest of his body. The colour difference started from a circle line on each wrist, it was as if he was wearing a pair of silicone, tight fitting, almost translucent gloves.

way to the surface over the coming years and could be removed then. Over the first couple of months both ankles healed, and the cast and dressings were removed. The treatment on Normans hands continued over several months. Once the skin grafts had healed, work started on exercising both hands to build up the damaged muscles. The hospital, which Norman said was always understaffed, was considerably augmented in October of that year by the arrival of an entire ambulance team of the British First Airborne Division who had been captured at Arnhem. There were then many more medical staff able to assist the overworked doctors and nurses in attending to each patient. Norman stayed at the hospital receiving what he described as 'excellent treatment' for ten months.

In early February 1945 Norman was presented with a Royal Air Force uniform, including shoes, socks, and underwear. He had no idea where it had come from. A German told him to get dressed as he was being transferred. The uniform was much too large for him, so after putting on the underwear he put back on his pyjamas and then the uniform over the top. Not only would this fill out the oversized uniform but would also give him extra layers on insulation against the cold if, as he suspected, he was being transferred to a prisoner of war camp.

Norman was collected by the authorities and was to be transferred by a truck to Stalag IX C prisoner of war camp in Mühlhausen near Bad Sulza. As he left the hospital, he had two armed guards with him who escorted him to the back of the truck. They gestured for him to climb up into the back of the truck. As he did so he noticed an overcoat, of the type worn by removal men, laying across the bench seat. He slid the coat to one side and sat down. The guards were at the back of the truck and talking to another man, whom Norman presumed was the driver, who was showing the guards some paperwork. He was obviously not happy with some part of the situation, so turned away from the guards and walked back towards the hospital. The two guards started to follow him and Norman saw his chance. He grabbed the overcoat climbed out of the back of the truck ran down the opposite side of the truck from the guards, without being seen. Then he turned down a side road to his left, ran and then turned again into another road on his right. Running on, he kept changing direction, trying to make it as difficult for the guards to work out where he had gone. He kept checking behind him to see if he was being chased, but as yet there was no sign of any pursuers. Seeing a bicycle leaning up against a building, he pulled the overcoat on over his uniform, got onto the bicycle and was off. At first he pedalled fast, to get some distance between him and whoever owned the bike, but then slowed down, thinking that would help him blend in and not to look like he was in a hurry.

Norman was at large for two days, sleeping rough at night. On the third day he was challenged by a local policeman. It did not take long for the policeman to realise that Norman was an escaped prisoner of war, and he was taken into custody. He had managed to get to cover a distance of some seventy miles and was just ten miles short of Nuremburg, which he thought was not a bad effort. Norman was held at the police station, and after processing he was once again placed into a truck and driven back to Stalag IX-C itself, and this time the guards did not leave his side. The camp was 25 kilometres northeast of Weimer in a broad valley set aside a fast-flowing river. It consisted of a series of wooden huts, with windows that were barred or covered with heavy gauge netting. The camp, which was triangular, was surrounded by two, ten-foot-high barbed wire fences some 200 yards long on one side and around 150 yards on the other with a much shorter fence at the apex of the camp. There was an area of ground in between the fences of around six feet in width; this area was covered in coiled barbed wire around waist high.

On each corner stood a watch tower, equipped with machine guns which the guards kept aimed at the prisoners. Security in this camp was, as ever, of the utmost importance to the Germans. The camp was crowded with prisoners of war from what seemed like all the services, including many different nationalities, who were housed in their own areas of the camp. The sleeping quarters were basic, and Norman had no pillow on his wooden slatted bunk and so slept every night with his right arm folded backwards and tucked under his head. The bunk had very few wooden slats; Norman remembered they had about eight per bunk instead of the thirty or so that should have been there. The missing slats had been burnt in the hut stove when other fuel ran out, the beds stripped down to the minimum number of slats required to support a mattress.

The food was not nutritional and fell well short of the Geneva Convention requirement which stated that prisoners of war should receive the same rations as a frontline soldier. Each day the ration was a watery soup served at midday, sometimes added with a supplement of potatoes or rice along with either swede, cabbage or carrot as a means of flavouring. The evening meal would generally be some form of tinned meat substitute served with brown bread made from potatoes with some form of grease, and a mug of tea. The tea was a mug of hot water with some leaves thrown in, usually mint or some sort of nettle. The only time the prisoners received sufficient food was when the Red Cross parcels arrived.

At night the guards would patrol outside the barbed wire fences, which were floodlit from suspended electric lamps. The guard towers were occupied 24 hours a day, seven days a week. This existence carried on from day to day. The prisoners could walk around during the day for exercise, gather in groups to chat or just stay in their huts and read whatever books or reading material that they had.

Towards the end of March 1945 there was a lot of talk in the camp of the advancing Allies who it was reported were only a short distance to the west from the main town of Mühlhausen. This information came from new prisoners of war arriving at the camp. Norman started to think that escape was now possible, believing that the Allied lines would not take long to reach. He mentioned this to other prisoners who were thinking the same, but most considered that it might be safer to stay put and wait for the Allies to liberate the camp. There was also the reality that the guards were constantly watching them. Then on 29th March 1945, all prisoners able to walk were ordered to collect their few belongings. Norman took his blanket as he had no topcoat, and the men were then lined up outside the camp in groups of around 200 to 300. They were then forcibly marched eastwards away from the advancing Allies. The POWs assumed that breaking the whole camp contingent into smaller groups was to ensure that the guards escorting them could keep control.

Norman thought his chances of escape were now higher than ever. He decided to wait for dark, which would be his best chance of not being spotted by the guards. On the first night they were ordered to sleep in some factory buildings and were constantly watched. The POWs talked amongst themselves, and none could understand the point of this march, thinking that the Germans knew that, sooner or later, the Allies would catch up with them. Norman said that he intended, if he got the chance, to try for an escape and make his way back towards the Allied lines. He told the group that if any of them wanted to join him they would be more than welcome. A few said that they would consider this idea but felt the chances of being spotted by the guards were quite high, and the Germans would not hesitate to shoot any who tried to break away.

They started marching again the following morning having had next to nothing to eat. Norman realised that as there was so little food, it would not be long before the men, who were already quite weak from hunger, would start to drop by the roadside. They could expect little compassion from the guards if that happened. As evening approached on the second day and darkness fell, the column turned a long corner with woods on either side, he decided this was his moment. Norman told the POWs close to him that he was now going to take his chance to escape and if they wanted to try then they should follow him. He managed to slip out of the column and into the woods, he made his way deep into the trees and then turned back to look if anyone else had followed, but he was on his own.

Norman turned west, in the direction that they had come from. His intention was to make his way back towards the advancing Allied troops. Intensely cold, he slept little, despite his best efforts. His blanket did, however, provide at least some warmth. He drank from ditches that were filled with water from the recent rains, but there was still no food. Norman travelled by day and night; in the morning he put the sun at his back to give him a westward heading and then tried to follow the direction of the sun in the afternoon as it moved to its setting position. Norman's aim was to cover as much distance as possible before what little strength he had gave out. The thought that with every step he must be getting closer to the allied lines drove him on. A few mornings later, he was crawling through some thick undergrowth when he heard voices. He stopped, crouched lower, and listened. 'My God,' he thought, 'They are speaking English!' Peering through the tangled roots and branches, he saw a vehicle about twenty yards away; it was a Jeep and was clearly marked as a US Army vehicle.

The voices seemed to be between Norman and the Jeep, but he could not see anyone. He decided to take a chance and shouted from the undergrowth, "Good morning gentlemen. My name is Flight Sergeant Norman Jackson, I am a member of Royal Air Force Bomber Command and an escaped prisoner of war."

An American voice shouted back for him to show himself with his hands held high, which he did. He was then ordered to walk towards a group of three men who had their weapons pointed at him. Sensibly, he did exactly as he was told. He had encountered advance scouts of the advancing US Sixth Armoured Division.

After a thorough body search, he was asked some questions, including whether he had escaped from the prison that the American troops had seen late yesterday afternoon.

"If that was Stalag IX C, then yes, but I didn't escape from the prison camp itself. We were forced to march eastwards away from you chaps a few days ago. I escaped from the marching column. I thought I could get back behind the Allied lines and decided to take a chance."

"Well, you have succeeded in your quest," said one of the Americans, "You look like you could be hungry, here you go," he said, and passed over a packet of food which Norman tried to eat but found quite tasteless. He was then given a seat in the Jeep.

"We will give you a lift," one of the GIs said, "We are on our way back now." Norman was driven back to the American lines, which was a journey of around three to four hours. The Americans told him it was around 60 miles.

"Where are all the German soldiers?" Norman asked.

"We don't see that many now," replied one of the GIs, "They are either marching away from us or surrendering, the sensible ones, according to them that is, surrender to us rather than the Russians, which is who they will meet if they keep heading eastwards."

When Norman reached the American lines, he was given a more thorough interrogation, after which he was told that he would be given some food. He sat at a table and a plate of food was placed in front of him. It was like nothing he had seen for the past year, and he just stared at it. Then he picked up the knife and fork, but as he did so an arm came in front of him and swept the plate to one side. A very well-spoken English voice said, "No, Sergeant, you will suffer a great deal if you eat that."

The voice belonged to an English doctor who later, with a smile on his face, told Norman that he was on loan to this American division, but for how long, he was not sure. He was expecting to be transferred any day now back to England. "They keep referring to me as their posh Limey Medic, or their posh Limey Doc, and want to keep me here as long as they can," he said. Norman told the doctor that he had been given a packet of food by one of his rescuers and he seemed to have digested that okay. 'K-rations probably," said the Doctor. "They are easier to digest than normal food but certainly have an odd taste."

Following medical checks, Norman was introduced to small amounts of what he thought was mashed potato. This was then followed by a gradual move to a more balanced diet to allow his stomach to accept normal food without making him ill. His body weight was now under nine stone, down from his usual eleven.

Norman was then transferred back up the line for repatriation. He arrived back in the UK on the 8$^{th\ of}$ May 1945, which was VE Day. He was brought home as part of *Operation Exodus*, which ran from the beginning of April to the end of May 1945. This was the repatriation of prisoners of war by the Royal Air Force using various types of aircraft including converted Lancasters. With a reduced crew, they could carry up to 24 POWs at a time and arrived at airfields in southern England. Under *Operation* Exodus, the Royal Air Force carried out approximately 3,500 flights and brought home 75,000 men.

Part Four: Aftermath

Return of a Modest Hero

Before reporting back to 106 Squadron at Metheringham, Norman was permitted first to journey to Twickenham to see his wife and son. Alma had been informed that he would be coming home but had no idea when he would be repatriated until she heard a knock at the door. When she opened the door, she did not immediately recognise the man standing there, he was in uniform but very thin and gaunt looking. Hello Alma, Norman said, it only took a moment for Alma to realise that this was her husband, and they fell into each other's arms. Alma said that she cried for around an hour. This was also Norman's first sight of his son Brian, who was now just over one year of age.

On returning to his squadron at Metheringham, Norman was promoted to Warrant Officer along with the other surviving members of the crew except for Frank Higgins, who had earlier applied for a commission. This had now come through and Pops was now a Flying Officer. The crew had all been repatriated before Norman, except for Miff and Johnny Johnson. There was still no news of either man. The other four members of the crew reported that Miff was last seen getting ready to bail out of the aircraft, he had left his pilot's seat, and was last seen half standing in the cockpit, presumably starting to move towards the entrance to the bomb aimer's compartment with its escape hatch in the floor. None knew the whereabouts or movements of Johhny Johnson, whose most obvious escape route had been to don his parachute, rotate the rear turret, and simply fall out backwards. No one could see a reason why Miff and Johnny should not have taken to their parachutes, though it was possible that they had been caught and killed on the ground by the local population.

Knowing Miff as he did, Norman thought it possible that if Johnny had been injured in one of the attacks, and unable to escape the aircraft, the pilot would not have abandoned him. He would either have tried to help him or to bring the aircraft down to a landing somewhere if possible.

It would be another two years before their whereabouts became known. Investigating Officers of the Royal Air Force Missing Research and

Enquiry Service, (MRES)[40], visited Wuerttemberg and exhumed from Kirchenstall cemetery two bodies that had been buried in the same grave and marked as unknown. The investigators were told that they were found in a crashed aircraft but were unidentifiable. The Officers exhumed the bodies and identified them as Frederick Manuel Mifflin age 21, and F/Sgt. Norman Hugh Johnson age 20, and they were re-interred in separate graves, but side by side, in Bad Tolz (Durnbach) Military Cemetery.

The surviving crew members were debriefed after their return to England, as was the case with all escapers, evaders, and POWs. Norman's crewmates told the story of his attempt to save the aircraft, despite him having little or no chance of regaining the safety of the cockpit or indeed of making a safe descent with a spilled and damaged parachute. When he was questioned on his return, Norman's only comment on the matter was that it was his job to keep the aircraft flying and the crew safe, and that should be an end to it. "I was just doing my duty," he said, "I want to hear no more about it."

On his questionnaire form (Appendix 6) Frank Higgins wrote:

'I wish to bring notice of the heroic action of F/Sgt. Jackson F/E flying in my aircraft the night we were shot down. When he discovered that a small fire had broken out on the trailing edge of the stbd. main plane after an attack by a fighter, he immediately fixed his chute, took hold of an extinguisher and climbed on to the roof of the a/c and commenced making his way to the seat of the fire in an attempt to put it out. He was assisted by the pilot, F/O MIFFLIN. He reached the fire but due to the bad burns he received he was unable to maintain his hold on the a/c or extinguisher. At the same time his chute was inadvertently pulled, and he was blown off. I saw him later when he was brought into the Luftwaffe jail where I was held, in a very badly burnt condition.'

---

[40] The MRES was set up in 1944 to trace 42,000 Royal Air Force aircrew who were listed as missing believed killed.

Group Captain Leonard Cheshire VC (left) and Norman outside Buckingham Palace at their investiture.

A few months later Norman received a call to inform him that he had been awarded the Victoria Cross. His immediate retort was, "What the bloody hell for?"

Norman's investiture, by King George VI, took place at Buckingham Palace on 26th October 1945. Alongside Norman was Group Captain Leonard Cheshire who was also to receive the Victoria Cross. Leonard Cheshire insisted that Norman should receive the Victoria Cross first, saying, "He stuck his neck out much more than I ever did," but protocol would not allow this as a Group Captain outranks a Warrant Officer. However, Leonard Cheshire insisted that they approach the King together to receive their awards.[41]

The final paragraph of Norman's award citation states that:

'This airman's attempt to extinguish the fire and save the aircraft and crew from falling into enemy hands was an act of outstanding gallantry. To venture outside, when travelling at 200 miles an hour, at a great height and in intense cold, was an almost incredible feat. Had he succeeded in subduing the flames, there was little or no prospect of his regaining the cockpit. The spilling of his parachute and the risk of grave damage to its canopy reduced his chances of survival to a minimum. By his ready willingness to face these dangers he set an example of self-sacrifice which will ever be remembered.'

---

[41] The author had the pleasure over the years of meeting Leonard Cheshire on some three occasions and each time Cheshire reminded him of this story. The author notes, 'I found Leonard Cheshire a remarkable person, very softly spoken, but it seemed that every sentence he spoke would be one of the most important sentences you would ever hear.'

ME669: After the Attack

ME669 crashed less than a half a mile to the west of Kirchensall in Southern Bavaria. Following the discovery of the bodies of Flying Officer Fred Manuel Mifflin, and Flight Sergeant Norman Hugh Johnson and their subsequent identification and re-internment in Bad Tolz (Durnbach) Military Cemetery, nothing more was known about the sequence of events that led up to the crash following the attack by the German nightfighters. This all changed in 2019 with the discovery of eyewitness accounts regarding the crash and the events leading up to the demise of ME669. A German film company produced a programme about this aircraft crash, and it was from this programme that the evidence of that night came to light. The video is narrated by a gentleman who talks of many eyewitness accounts of the crash in the early hours of the 27th of April 1944. The translation of the eyewitness documents reveals very similar experiences on the night of the 27th of April 1944 to that gained previously from the surviving members of the crew. The film concentrates on three separate eyewitness statements which have been translated.

The first eyewitness was a lady who, at the time the film was made, was 93 years of age, and 18 years old in April 1944. She describes the aircraft, on fire and flying straight and level over the forest. She then saw two crewmen escape the burning aircraft by parachute, then the aircraft turned and headed in her direction, towards the edge of the forest, and the open fields at a much lower altitude. The aircraft then turned again and flew in a circle and headed for a large open space with a slight uphill rising. It then disappeared from her view, but there was a large explosion. The eyewitness then had to shelter in a nearby house as she thought that ammunition on board the aircraft had started to detonate in the fire and was flying in all directions.

Herr Klaus Wuemberger, of Neuenstein, Kirchensall, stated that he had been told by 91-year-old Herr Friedrich Strecker:

"The British bomber came over the Kochor valley towards us, one of the engines was out, thereupon crew members should already have parachuted from the aircraft over the Kochertal. Only the pilot and one other crew member remained in the aircraft. As the aircraft approached their area the dead engine started again. At the height of the Stolzeneck he turned the aircraft but could no longer avoid the crash or landing. He hit the ground near Gottenhoff and the aircraft exploded. The pilot and one other crew member were killed. The impact on the earth pushed an engine into the aircraft under which the pilot was trapped. Two English airmen were buried together in Kirchensall Cemetery."

Herr Strecker then went on to state that '...some of the crew parachuted out of the aircraft over Ailringen an der Jagst. The following morning two Englishmen were found in the garden of Dr. Ing. Med. Frohmair in Neuenstein, Gottenhof Mainhardsall, where they had landed.'

These two crew members were Flight Sergeant Maurice Toft, the bomb aimer, and Flight Sergeant Frank Higgins, the navigator.

Irmgrad Claus, 91 years of age stated:

'One person parachuted on the approach from the Kochertal over the Goltenhof. He landed in the woods at Rappenholz at Mainhardsall and hung in a tree where his parachute was found. The bomber crashed in a field near Kirchensall, and I saw it turn in a circle over the field before hitting the ground. The bomber came from the attack on Schweinfurt. I myself was 16 years of age in 1944. With my two brothers I visited the place of the crash. The site was closed off by the German military so that you could only see the plane from afar. I do not know anything else.'

The crewman that parachuted into the forest was Flight Sergeant Ernest Sandelands, the wireless operator.

There is a map showing the flight path of ME669 over Neuenstein where two crewmen were seen to parachute out of the aircraft. It then flew on over Grosshirschbach towards the east of Haberhof, where it turned to the right and descended towards the open fields to the west of Kirchensall. It circled again before attempting to make a crash landing.

The area of ME669's crash site. The thin red line shows the track of ME669 as it descended.

The aircraft making a right turn, flying on and then circling over the fields before the crash landing shows that the aircraft was still under the control of Flying Officer Fred Mifflin, which tends to corroborate Norman's opinion that Miff stayed with the aircraft to try for a forced landing. This could quite possibly have been because the rear gunner, Flight Sergeant Norman Johnson, was badly injured and unable to vacate the aircraft. Miff could have left the aircraft at any time as the escape hatch was no more than a few feet from his pilot's position, assuming he could have set the controls with the autopilot for straight and level flight and parachuted safely from the aircraft. It seems that he chose to stay with the aircraft and conduct yet another act of outstanding gallantry on board the aircraft that night, seemingly sacrificing his own young life, just 21 years of age, to save that of his even younger rear gunner and friend, Flight Sergeant Norman Johnson aged 20.

If this information had been known at the time of the discovery of the two men's bodies in 1947, there would surely have been a case for highlighting the heroism of Flying Officer Fred Mifflin. The bravery, courage, and dedication to duty, of these young men that served as aircrew in Bomber Command is nothing short of breathtaking.

Uwe Benkel is the leader of the Working Group for the Missing, which searches for and excavates downed aircraft from the Second World War and attempts to identify the lost crews within. The group has found and identified over 140 aircraft. Uwe Benkel has been searching the crash site of ME669 and located the parts of the aircraft below.

 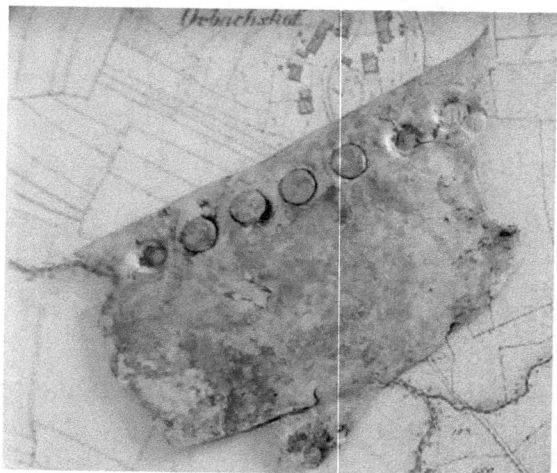

(Left) Uwe Benkel. (Right and below) Various unidentified parts of ME669.

Following On

On leaving the Royal Air Force Norman's first priorities were employment and a home for Alma and him to bring up their planned large family. The condition of Norman's hands ruled out a return to his pre-war career as a fitter turner and so he had to consider another career.

After a lot of consideration and listening as well as talking to a lot of people, he decided that he would like to become a sales representative. He applied for and was offered a position with the company J.V.R Brandy as a representative and enjoyed the freedom of travelling from client to client. These clients generally owned, or managed, hotels, restaurants or public houses. Norman was there to open new accounts. He was very successful at this, and his success did not go unnoticed by other groups within the Distillers Company Ltd., of which J.V.R Brandy was part. He was approached by John Haig Whisky and an attractive offer was put forward, and after consideration he joined that company. Norman stayed with this company for the rest of his working life. At first much of his time was with prospective clients to show them the benefits of opening an account with John Haig Whisky. The company would tell the prospective clients that they are sending their top man, Norman Cyril Jackson VC. The clients, who in the early days, were mostly ex-servicemen themselves, were delighted to meet Norman, and John Haig Whisky thereby enrolled many new clients. Norman would then go on to service these accounts over the following years.[42]

On the home front Norman, in late 1946, purchased a large plot of land in Hampton Hill directly opposite Fulwell Golf Course. He then proceeded to build a four-bedroomed detached property with the help of an overdraft from Barclays Bank, the manager nervously cycling along to the site to judge progress whenever large cheques were cashed.

---

[42] This information was given to the author by Mr. Leslie Batt, who was one of the Directors of The Distillers Company Ltd. and a colleague of Norman. The author remembers as a child, frequent visits to his home to discuss business with Norman, usually conducted over a glass of whisky, John Haig of course.

Norman and Alma went on to have seven children, four boys and three girls, Brian Norman, the eldest, born on the day of the Schweinfurt operation, and then after the war followed by Pauline Rose, Brenda Lilian, Peter Geoffrey, David Michael, Ian, and finally Shirley Anne.

Norman and Alma adored their family and did everything they possibly could to give all their children a great start in life. The children remember a childhood filled with laughter and adventure. They were always taught the importance of manners in life by their parents along with many profound lessons in life itself, such as looking to understand before trying to be understood. The author was asked on many occasions by school teachers to bring his father's medals into school so that they could be shown to the class and then followed by an inspirational story, Norman would always agree to this as it was for the school, but as his son put the medals into his pocket, and feeling ten feet tall, would always say, "Remember David, no showing off."

Norman spent as much time as possible following the war with his brother Geoffrey and his wife. She was German-born and carried a degree of animosity towards Norman as he was a member of Bomber Command during the war. Charitably, Norman considered that this was understandable. This all came to an end with the tragic death of Geoffrey during the Mau-Mau uprising in Kenya. Norman and Alma never heard from Geoffrey's wife again, despite several attempts to contact and comfort her. The loss of his brother hit Norman quite hard, but he knew that, with the life that Geoffrey had chosen, there was always a risk that this would happen, as had been the case with his own service in the war.

Norman carried out a lot of work with The Bomber Command Association, along with helping the Royal Air Force Benevolent Fund in any way he could. This usually entailed attending events to give a talk, along with the signing of whatever was put in front of him. There were also Lancaster bomber prints which were signed and then sold for the charity. These prints being delivered to the family home several hundred at a time, and Norman spent hours signing them until needing to rest his hands. After a short break he would get back to signing them, saying that this was important as they were for the Royal Air Force

Benevolent Fund and the quicker, he could finish them the quicker the fund would receive money.

Unless it was impossible, Norman would never miss an event to which he was invited to in connection with Bomber Command. He valued spending time with, as he put it, 'these great men.' Talking to others who understood about their experiences while flying on operations during the war was so important to all of them. Their traumatic experiences during the war were exacerbated afterwards by the lack of appreciation from government, not just for their own service, but that of their comrades who paid the ultimate price in such large numbers.

Norman saw his attendance of these events, whether the RAF Benevolent Fund, or the Bomber Command Association, as his duty. Even when, in 1994, he was very ill and in the last few weeks of his life, he agreed to a visit to Metheringham to show his respects for the fallen of 106 Squadron. Sadly, this was to be one of the rare appointments that he would not keep. Norman passed away at home on the 26th of March 1994, aged 74. He rests in Twickenham Cemetery in Southeast London.

Norman in later life, at the wedding of his daughter Shirley Anne..

End Note

Norman was interviewed many times over the years regarding his action on the night of 26th / 27th April 1944 but would prefer to talk about the other members of Bomber Command. In particular, he highlighted the unsung heroes of the ground crews who worked outside on the aircraft tirelessly in all weathers in just a pair of overalls with a leather sleeveless jacket on top. Of his own action he would say that it was all a long time ago and all they had to do was refer to his citation. When I asked if he had ever read his citation, Norman's answer was, "Of course not, why should I read that? That's of no interest to me."

Of the aircrew who were all volunteers, he used to say that they were wonderful men, and all tried nothing more than to do their duty despite knowing that their chances of survival were little more than 1 in 2.

125,000 men volunteered for aircrew in Bomber Command during World War Two, 55,573 men lost their lives on operations, a further 8,403 were wounded in action, many succumbing to their wounds, and 9,838 became prisoners of war. This was an overall casualty rate of almost 60%, the highest loss rate of any of the armed services, and yet, following the end of the war, they were not included in the Victory Parade through London nor, as I have said, did they receive a medal for their service.

I leave it to the readers of this book to decide whether they consider that fair treatment of young men who volunteered not only to risk but also give their lives in the service of their nation against an evil that had to be vanquished.

'When you go home
Tell them of us and say
For your tomorrow
We gave our today'

The Kohima Epitaph

The grave of Frederick Manuel Mifflin DFC.

The grave of Norman Hugh Johnson.

Morality of the Bombing Campaign

The bombing of Dresden even today, stands out as one of the most controversial actions by the allies during World War Two. The air attacks on the city occurred between 13th and 15th February 1945. The first attack, carried out by Bomber Command in two waves on the night of 13th / 14th February 1945 saw 805 bombers drop 2,700 tons of explosive and incendiaries. On the ground, hundreds of small fires combined to create such powerful winds that in turn produced a powerful firestorm which decimated the German city. Victims on the ground who survived the direct effects of bombs and falling buildings were suffocated in their underground shelters when the conflagration used up all the oxygen in the air.

The US 8th Air Force then carried out daylight raids on 14th and 15th February, but it was the firestorm of the first night that was responsible for most of the death and destruction. The carnage was seized upon by Joseph Goebbels, the German propaganda minister, as an opportunity to show the supposed brutality of the allies. He greatly inflated the number of deaths caused by the raid to underline this point. The initial, highly partisan, estimate of the number of deaths claimed that the bombing of Dresden was uniquely cruel. This belief was underlined in David Irving's book, published in 1963, *The Destruction of Dresden*. Irving claimed that this raid was the single largest massacre in European history, and estimated the number of deaths directly caused by the raid was between 150,000 to 250,000 civilians killed. This figure was accepted at the time without any dispute. However, when he further went on to assert that Dresden was the 'Hiroshima of Germany' his remarks quickly drew criticism, not only for the lack of evidence in his claims, but also because he had earned notoriety, and a criminal conviction, as a Holocaust denier.

In 2004, and in part to prevent Nazi apologists from exploiting widespread speculation about the death toll caused by the raid, the City of Dresden set up its own historical commission to produce more precise data. This included data from military, forensic and archaeological research. The results from this historical commission were published in a report on 17th March 2010, which concluded that the number of deaths from the raid was between 22,700 and 25,000. Although still regrettable, this number of civilian deaths were certainly not unusual in the context of 'total war' and certainly did not mark Dresden out as unique. The 'Battle of Hamburg', a series of six bombing raids on the city between 24th July and 3rd August 1943, resulted in approximately 40,000 civilian deaths; the Nazi bombing of the city of Warsaw caused the deaths of 25,000 civilians; the Blitz on England took the lives of 43,000 civilians, whilst the non-nuclear bombing of Tokyo killed at least 80,000 and maybe as high as 100,000 civilians. The estimated toll from the atomic bombs dropped on Japan was, 70,000 to 125,000 civilians killed in Hiroshima, whilst in the second nuclear attack, on Nagasaki, 60,000 to 80,000 civilians were killed.

The attack on Dresden was part of a pre-planned mini-campaign, *Operation Thunderclap,* coming just four weeks after 19,000 US troops were killed in Germany's last-ditch offensive of the Battle of the Bulge, and three weeks after the discovery of the Nazi atrocities at Auschwitz. It had been part of the allies' endgame plan to disrupt German reinforcements and the movement of troops and supplies between the eastern and western fronts, this timed to cause the greatest disruption and close out the war. The method was to devastate communications and transport hubs, if necessary, by making movement next to impossible through rubble and disrupted civilian traffic.

The Russian government put pressure on the British government to bomb their chosen target of Dresden, along with its neighbouring Saxon cities of Chemnitz and Leipzig, to stop the German army from attempting another last-ditch effort through that city to stop their advance on Berlin. There were reports that the Germans might well be able to hold out until November 1945, if they could prevent the Soviets from taking Silesia, with fears of a Nazi redoubt being established in or around Dresden, or of the Russian advance faltering, any assistance given to the Soviets on the Eastern front could only lead to shortening the war. The raid was also an effort to force surrender, with the intention of terrorising not only the local population but the Germans nationwide, and it certainly did have that effect. Dresden was not chosen by Bomber Command as a target, but by the government. Following criticism of the raid because of the falsely inflated number of deaths, Churchill, who had initially taken part in the planning of *Operation Thunderclap*, was at pains to distance himself from the resulting apocalypse. Shamefully, the government placed the blame solely at the door of Bomber Command and Air Marshal Sir Arthur Harris, and that is where it has remained in the imagination of so many.

From the outbreak of the war in Europe, when the Germans launched unprovoked invasions across Europe, right up until D-Day it was only the bombers of Bomber Command along with the US 8th Air Force that could take the fight to Nazi Germany in the European theatre. Meanwhile millions of civilians were suffering hellish brutality under the occupying forces. As the German Armaments Minister Albert Speer noted, '...the air war became a second front.' It was a front that absorbed men and machines which otherwise could have been used on the Eastern Front against Russia, and in coastal defences in northern France. The bombing campaign was not about killing as many German civilians as possible, which would have cost much and achieved nothing. The Second World War was not a battle between two armies on a foreign field, in which whoever won the battle won the day; this was total war, a war for survival of the free world, and a war for the survival of democracy.

Total war involves all in the belligerent countries, not just the armed forces, but civilians as well. It is the civilians who work in the factories that produce the aeroplanes, ships, tanks, guns, ammunition, uniforms and boots, all necessary to wage that war, and therefore civilians become a large part of the war effort of the country. If the factories have no workers, then they cannot produce the armaments in order to conduct a war, if the civilians have no housing close to the factories due to continuous area bombing then working in those factories becomes almost impossible.

Every bombing operation was a further step in defeating a powerful and evil enemy which still had a powerful war machine in operation and was quite capable of carrying on the war long enough to develop and use the more powerful weapons which they were working on, namely guided rockets and the atomic bomb.

The bombing campaign's aims were to destroy Germany's capacity to produce weapons, disrupt the transport networks along with the oil, steel and coal supplies, to destroy the German air force, and break civilian morale.

The official military objective of the strategic bombing of Germany are indicated in several directives formulated by the Allied Joint Chiefs of Staff. The Casablanca conference in January 1943 noted that the objective of the bombing offensive was the progressive destruction and dislocation of the German military, industrial and economic system, and the undermining of the morale of the German people to a point where their capacity for armed resistance was fatally weakened. This was amended in June 1943 with the *Pointblank* directive emphasizing the importance of destroying the German fighter aircraft production in readiness for the D-Day Normandy Landings planned for the summer of 1944. Air superiority had to be achieved before the Allies could contemplate a land invasion of northern Europe or their planned armada would be destroyed. This was further amended by the Quebec conference of August 1943 which reaffirmed the objectives of both Casablanca and Pointblank but omitted the objective of German civilian morale.

There are many accounts of the bombing campaign and countless documentaries, many portraying a negative view of it. Modern day commentators on the bombing of Germany by the Royal Air Force, with the benefit of hindsight and the ability to judge from a perspective in which they are safe and comfortable, appear to show little awareness of the brutal realities faced by the Allies between 1939 and 1945.

They preach that 'carpet bombing' was wrong, but they suggest no alternative way in which the German nation might have been prevented from continuing the war that their leaders had started. In the view of the author, there simply was no other alternative. Against an enemy whose master plan included not just eliminating all opposition but systematically liquidating whole races of people it considered inferior, we had to take the strongest measures. Doing nothing was certainly not an option.

It was not until the spring of 1944 that radar-equipped Lancasters were capable of bombing at night with considerable accuracy. Before then, the only alternative was to bomb from a much lower altitude to hit the desired target, which would have left the bombers as much easier targets for the flak guns and the losses would have been so great that Bomber Command may well have ceased to exist.

Following the end of the war there was not even a Bomber Command Medal to signify the service of a veteran, as there was for just about every other service that was engaged in the war.

Eventually recognition came on 26th February 2013, more than 67 years after the war, when following a campaign for recognition, a small bronze clasp was sent to all surviving members of Bomber Command for them to wear. Many surviving veterans thought of this as an insult.

Many veterans were reticent to discuss the time they spent on bombers, not only because of modesty, but maybe, as Norman told the author, because those who they were talking to have no real understanding of what it could have possibly been like to serve as a member of a Bomber crew. How could someone who had not been there know what it was like to face the prospect of death every day and night that they took to the air, whether on operations or during training? Only their fellow crew members, who had shared the same experiences, understood what it was really like to be a volunteer and go to war in a bomber. This explains why, for these men, squadron reunions were so important for the rest of their lives.

As these veterans reached the later part of their lives many of them would begin to speak quite openly for the first time regarding their young lives in Bomber Command, and most, if not all, were extremely hurt by the callous treatment that they received from successive governments regarding the lack of recognition of their heroic contribution to victory.

It is sad that recognition, in the form of a national memorial in Green Park, London, which had to be funded through public donations, the largest of which was from Lord Michael Ashcroft, and the granting of the Bomber Command clasp, came too late for most of the veterans, including Norman.

The Bomber Command Memorial was unveiled by Her Majesty Queen Elizabeth the Second on 28th June 2012.

Norman's medal group.

The Bomber Command Clasp, worn on the 1939 to 1945 Star.

The magnificent, and long overdue, Bomber Command Memorial in Green Park, London.

Norman being presented with a silver engraved Lancaster Bomber at AVRO works. 8th March 1946. Norman's skeletal hands are clearly visible. Third from left, in the light suit, is Sandy Sandelands.

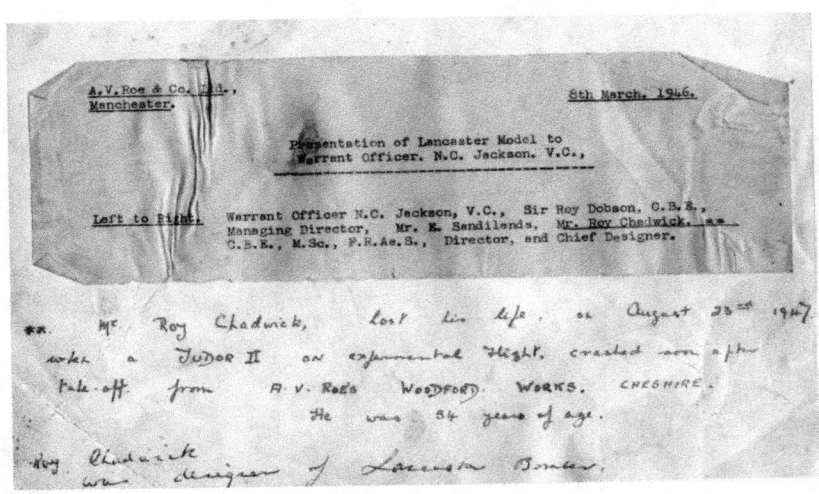

Original description of those present.

The Silver Lancaster model today. Only five were ever presented.

Norman and Alma with six of their children at home in the late 1950's, Shirley Anne, their seventh child, was not born until 1961. Left to right, Pauline. Ian. Brian. David. Peter. Brenda. Alma and Norman at rear.

Shirley Anne aged around four years.

Shirley Anne today.

Norman outside the family home with the Lancaster window.

The Lancaster window, Note the artist had given the aircraft incorrect identification letters for 106 Squadron, NZ, instead of ZN. This quite amused Norman.

Norman Cyril Jackson in Flight Engineer's position in Lancaster many years after the war.

The author's nephew Sean emulating his grandfather, of whom he is very proud.

Appendix 1: Operations Record of F/Sgt. Norman Cyril Jackson

Op	T/O Date	Target	Pilot	Total Sorties	Losses	Loss Rate
1	22/08/1943	Leverkusen	Fred Mifflin	462	5	1.08%
2	27/08/1943	Nuremberg	Fred Mifflin	674	33	4.90%
3	30/08/1943	Mönchengladbach / Rheydt	Fred Mifflin	660	25	3.79%
4	03/09/1943	Berlin	Fred Mifflin	320	22	6.88%
5	05/09/1943	Mannheim / Ludwigshafen	Fred Mifflin	605	34	5.62%
6	01/10/1943	Hagen	Fred Mifflin	251	2	0.80%
7	02/10/1943	Munich	Fred Mifflin	296	8	2.70%
8	07/10/1943	Stuttgart	Fred Mifflin	343	4	1.17%
9	20/10/1943	Leipzig (Bergen Alkrinar alt)	Fred Mifflin	358	16	4.47%
10	10/11/1943	Modane	Fred Mifflin	313	0	0.00%
11	18/11/1943	Berlin	Fred Mifflin	444	9	2.03%
12	22/11/1943	Berlin	Fred Mifflin	764	26	3.40%
13	26/11/1943	Berlin	Fred Mifflin	450	42	9.33%
14	02/12/1943	Berlin	Fred Mifflin	458	40	8.73%
15	20/01/1944	Berlin	Fred Mifflin	769	37	4.81%
16	21/01/1944	Magdeburg	Fred Mifflin	648	57	8.80%
17	27/01/1944	Berlin	Fred Mifflin	530	33	6.23%
18	29/01/1944	Berlin	Fred Mifflin	677	46	6.79%
19	30/01/1944	Berlin	Fred Mifflin	534	33	6.18%
20	15/02/1944	Berlin	Fred Mifflin	891	43	4.83%
21	19/02/1944	Leipzig	Fred Mifflin	823	78	9.48%
22	20/02/1944	Stuttgart	Fred Mifflin	598	9	1.51%
23	01/03/1944	Stuttgart	Fred Mifflin	557	4	0.72%
24	16/03/1944	Clermont-Ferrand	P/O O'Leary	21	0	0.00%
25	18/03/1944	Frankfurt	S/L Murdoch	846	22	2.60%
26	18/04/1944	Swinemunde	Fred Mifflin	168	3	1.79%
27	20/04/1944	La Chapelle	Fred Mifflin	269	6	2.23%
28	22/04/1944	Brunswick	Fred Mifflin	265	4	1.51%
29	24/04/1944	Munich	Fred Mifflin	260	9	3.46%
30	26/04/1944	Schweinfurt	Fred Mifflin	216	21	9.72%
				14470	671	4.64%

Appendix 2: Citation for W/O Norman Cyril Jackson, VC.

Numb. 37324　　　　　　　　　　　　　　　　5233

FOURTH SUPPLEMENT
TO
The London Gazette
Of TUESDAY, the 23rd of OCTOBER, 1945
Published by Authority

Registered as a newspaper

FRIDAY, 26 OCTOBER, 1945

Air Ministry, 26th October, 1945.

The KING has been graciously pleased to confer the VICTORIA CROSS on the undermentioned airman in recognition of most conspicuous bravery:—

905192 Sergeant (now Warrant Officer) Norman Cyril JACKSON, R.A.F.V.R., 106 Squadron.

This airman was the flight engineer in a Lancaster detailed to attack Schweinfurt on the night of 26th April, 1944. Bombs were dropped successfully and the aircraft was climbing out of the target area. Suddenly it was attacked by a fighter at about 20,000 feet. The captain took evading action at once, but the enemy secured many hits. A fire started near a petrol tank on the upper surface of the starboard wing, between the fuselage and the inner engine.

Sergeant Jackson was thrown to the floor during the engagement. Wounds which he received from shell splinters in the right leg and shoulder were probably sustained at that time. Recovering himself, he remarked that he could deal with the fire on the wing and obtained his captain's permission to try to put out the flames.

Pushing a hand fire-extinguisher into the top of his life-saving jacket and clipping on his parachute pack, Sergeant Jackson jettisoned the escape hatch above the pilot's head. He then started to climb out of the cockpit and back along the top of the fuselage to the starboard wing. Before he could leave the fuselage his parachute pack opened and the whole canopy and rigging lines spilled into the cockpit.

Undeterred, Sergeant Jackson continued. The pilot, bomb aimer and navigator gathered the parachute together and held on to the rigging lines, paying them out as the airman crawled aft. Eventually he slipped and, falling from the fuselage to the starboard wing, grasped an air intake on the leading edge of the wing. He succeeded in clinging on but lost the extinguisher, which was blown away.

By this time, the fire had spread rapidly and Sergeant Jackson was involved. His face, hands and clothing were severely burnt. Unable to retain his hold, he was swept through the flames and over the trailing edge of the wing, dragging his parachute behind. When last seen it was only partly inflated and was burning in a number of places.

Realising that the fire could not be controlled, the captain gave the order to abandon aircraft. Four of the remaining members of the crew landed safely. The captain and rear gunner have not been accounted for.

Sergeant Jackson was unable to control his descent and landed heavily. He sustained a broken ankle, his right eye was closed through burns and his hands were useless. These injuries, together with the wounds received earlier, reduced him to a pitiable state. At daybreak he crawled to the nearest village, where he was taken prisoner. He bore the intense pain and discomfort of the journey to Dulag Luft with magnificent fortitude. After 10 months in hospital he made a good recovery, though his hands require further treatment and are only of limited use.

This airman's attempt to extingush the fire and save the aircraft and crew from falling into enemy hands was an act of outstanding gallantry. To venture outside, when travelling at 200 miles an hour, at a great height and in intense cold, was an almost incredible feat. Had he succeeded in subduing the flames, there was little or no prospect of his regaining the cockpit. The spilling of his parachute and the risk of grave damage to its canopy reduced his chances of survival to a minimum. By his ready willingness to face these dangers he set an example of self-sacrifice which will ever be remembered.

Appendix 3: Citation for F/Sgt. Frank Higgins

SUPPLEMENT TO THE LONDON GAZETTE, 27 JUNE, 1944   3043

Clifford Owen RUSSELL (138804), R.A.F.V.R., 51 Sqn.
Raymond Terence SALVONI (155196), R.A.F.V.R., 640 Sqn.
Gordon George TAYLOR (160015), R.A.F.V.R., 619 Sqn.
Reginald Martin WELLER (155190), R.A.F.V.R., 640 Sqn.
Lionel WILK (78451), R.A.F.V.R., 141 Sqn.
Thomas WILKIE (130871), R.A.F.V.R., 619 Sqn.

Pilot Officers.

Eric Keith ALLEY (168814), R.A.F.V.R., 619 Sqn.
Donald ANDREW (172881), R.A.F.V.R., 49 Sqn.
Kenneth Harold BLACKHAM (171194), R.A.F.V.R., 49 Sqn.
Sydney James BUTLER (170462), R.A.F.V.R., 10 Sqn.
Ronald Mervin CHESSWASS (169390), R.A.F.V.R., 78 Sqn.
Frederick George HAYLER (171167), R.A.F.V.R., 9 Sqn.
Albert John HORTON (170875), R.A.F.V.R., 115 Sqn.
Ronald Gilbert JACKSON (169974), R.A.F.V.R., 149 Sqn.
Francis William McLELLAND (160622), R.A.F.V.R., 51 Sqn.
Peter James MOYES (160518), R.A.F.V.R., 156 sqn.
Jack Richard SANDS (172710), R.A.F.V.R., 78 Sqn.
Paul Edward THOMPSON (172099), R.A.F.V.R., 50 Sqn.
George Alfred TURNBULL (53934), R.A.F., 61 Sqn.

Warrant Officer.

Alfred WHITEHOUSE (1214028), R.A.F.V.R., 83 Sqn.

Distinguished Flying Medal.

Flight Sergeants.

1388773 Colin Lionel ALLIKPE, R.A.F.V.R., 51 Sqn.
1130413 Robert APPLEYARD, R.A.F.V.R., 106 Sqn.
644725 Herbert BAILEY, R.A.F., 149 Sqn.
1319049 William Henry BARKER, R.A.F.V.R., 44 Sqn.
1475553 Albert Leslie BARTLETT (now Pilot Officer), R.A.F.V.R., 50 Sqn.
936181 Cyril BENTHAM, R.A.F.V.R., 156 Sqn.
1604400 Eric Norman BICKLEY, R.A.F.V.R., 101 Sqn.
1549867 Norman Hugh BOYD, R.A.F.V.R., 138 Sqn.
1281461 Cecil Arthur BRYANT, R.A.F.V.R., 138 Sqn.
1131118 James William CLARK, R.A.F.V.R., 166 Sqn.
1544112 Harry Cunningham CLAYTON, R.A.F.V.R., 77 Sqn.
1125510 John CLYDE, R.A.F.V.R., 10 Sqn.
1601399 William George DAY, R.A.F.V.R., 76 Sqn.
1392217 Kenneth Albert DRURY, R.A.F.V.R., 100 Sqn.
1334200 Jack GOLDING, R.A.F.V.R., 35 Sqn.
1311296 Arthur Joseph GURR, R.A.F.V.R., 44 Sqn.
1520847 Frank Lewis HIGGINS, R.A.F.V.R., 106 Sqn.
1312464 Benjamin William HILL, R.A.F.V.R., 101 Sqn.
1145051 Norman Joseph HORSLEY, R.A.F.V.R., 50 Sqn.
1267383 Patrick Anthony HUGHES, R.A.F.V.R., 51 Sqn.
1077301 Abraham Samuel JACKSON, R.A.F.V.R., 77 Sqn.
1396487 Basil Lawrence Ivor JOHNSON, R.A.F.V.R., 156 Sqn.
1005045 George KING, R.A.F.V.R., 35 Sqn.
1415475 George Alfred LEONARD, R.A.F.V.R., 97 Sqn.
1601860 Frederick James LITTLEJOHNS, R.A.F.V.R., 51 Sqn.
1354270 Robert Graham LOMAS, R.A.F.V.R., 9 Sqn.
1130601 Frank LOMAX, R.A.F.V.R., 9 Sqn.
1489909 Harry MARSHALL, R.A.F.V.R., 429 Sqn.
1294748 Leonard Edward Garry MIDDLETON, R.A.F.V.R., 432 (R.C.A.F.) Sqn.
656706 John MILROY, R.A.F.V.R., 51 Sqn.
1483331 Frank MYCOR, R.A.F.V.R., 106 Sqn.
7394753 Dennis Gilbert PARTOS, R.A.F.V.R., 97 Sqn.
990308 Douglas PINCKARD, R.A.F.V.R., 106 Sqn.
1382584 Victor Fulton PITCHER, R.A.F.V.R., 49 Sqn.
1076493 James RYAN, R.A.F.V.R., 9 Sqn.
1549822 Joseph Clement Augustine RONGERS, R.A.F.V.R., 50 Sqn.
1488306 Albert SIMPSON, R.A.F.V.R., 7 Sqn.

1129452 Alfred David Forester SPRUCE, R.A.F.V.R., 50 Sqn.
1326420 William TWORT, R.A.F.V.R., 51 Sqn.
1583038 Dennis Arthur WEST, R.A.F.V.R., 429 Sqn.
1435609 Peter WILD, R.A.F.V.R., 103 Sqn.

Sergeants.

1200823 Victor Henry BLACKWELL, R.A.F.V.R., 106 Sqn.
984297 David CHALMERS, R.A.F.V.R., 44 Sqn.
1604593 Wallace Arthur CLARKE, R.A.F.V.R., 51 Sqn.
1685085 Samuel Lawrence COLE, R.A.F.V.R., 166 Sqn.
1142884 Francis Gerard DOWLING, R.A.F.V.R., 207 Sqn.
1117103 Richard Malcolm GALLOWAY, R.A.F.V.R., 207 Sqn.
1289051 William Gerald Edward GRIFFITHS, R.A.F.V.R., 640 Sqn.
921981 Michael Harry Gardner KING, R.A.F.V.R., 619 Sqn.
532050 James MURRAY, R.A.F., 101 Sqn.
1214044 George Frederick PHILLIPSON, R.A.F.V.R., 10 Sqn.
983597 Evan OWEN, R.A.F.V.R., 103 Sqn.
1361514 John RUSSELL, R.A.F.V.R., 51 Sqn.
1603926 John Gordon SERVICE, R.A.F.V.R., 51 Sqn.
539478 John Holyoake TURNER, R.A.F., 9 Sqn.

ROYAL AUSTRALIAN AIR FORCE.

Distinguished Flying Cross.

Acting Flight Lieutenants.

Daniel Thomas CONWAY (Aus.415402), 467 (R.A.A.F.) Sqn.
Vivian Ernest Richard PIPER (Aus.406538), 105 (R.A.A.F.) Sqn.
Alexander Edward VOWELS (Aus.405780), 463 (R.A.A.F.) Sqn.
Frank Brian May WILSON (Aus.404361), 463 (R.A.A.F.) Sqn.

Flying Officers.

William Harry BROOKES (Aus.407989), 463 (R.A.A.F.) Sqn.
Peter Harrison SWAN (Aus.400498), 139 Sqn.

Pilot Officers.

Richard Townshend BOULYBEE (Aus.415223), 619 Sqn.
Charles Alfred HAIGH (Aus.421972), 61 Sqn.
Henry Russell MAHON (Aus.413675), 463 (R.A.A.F.) Sqn.

Warrant Officers.

Bernard Thomas James HUCKS (Aus.409707), 619 Sqn.
Charles George TURNBULL (Aus.414279), 619 Sqn.

Distinguished Flying Medal.

Flight Sergeant.

Aus.422122 Lester John BURROWS, 460 (R.A.A.F.) Sqn.

ROYAL CANADIAN AIR FORCE.

Bar to Distinguished Flying Cross.

Pilot Officer Edgar Thompson JONES, D.F.C. (Can/J.19171), 103 Sqn.

Distinguished Flying Cross.

Acting Squadron Leader.

Douglas Julian SALE, D.S.O. (Can/J.9929), 35 Sqn.

Flight Lieutenant.

George Lachlan COURT (Can/J.5304), 405 (R.C.A.F.) Sqn.

Acting Flight Lieutenants.

Bruce Ervin BETCHER (Can/J20078), 419 (R.C.A.F.) Sqn.
Norman Beverley MORRISON (Can/J.13721), 619 Sqn.
Erwin Earl OSLER, D.F.M. (Can/J.16724), 635 Sqn.
William Douglas RENTON (Can/J 22484), 405 (R.C.A.F.) Sqn.
John Cameron TURNBULL (Can/J 27370), 424 (R.C.A.F.) Sqn.
Kenneth Herbert WHITTINGTON (Can/J.19155), 102 Sqn.

HIGGINS, Frank Lewis.   1320847 Flight Sergeant, No.106 Sqn.
L.G. 27/6/1944.   Sorties 23, Flying hours 159.40.   Navigator.   Air2/8780.

Flight Sergeant Higgins as Navigator has carried out 23 successful operational sorties against some of the most heavily defended targets in enemy territory including Munich and Berlin (11 times). This N.C.O.'s navigation has always been most accurate and he has consistently produced good logs of his work during these sorties. At all times he has displayed the greatest keenness and enthusiasm for operational flying and fully deserves the award of the D.F.M.

15th March, 1944.

Appendix 4: POW Questionnaire – Norman Jackson

25.10.45

PART I.

TOP SECRET
M.I.9/Gen/
MIS-X

GENERAL QUESTIONNAIRE FOR BRITISH/AMERICAN EX-PRISONERS OF WAR.

1. No. 905192   RANK F/Sgt   SURNAME JACKSON
   CHRISTIAN NAMES Norman Cyril
   DECORATIONS V.C.

2. SHIP (R.N., U.S.N. or MERCHANT NAVY)
   UNIT (ARMY)
   SQUADRON (R.A.F. or A.A.F.) 106 Sqd

3. DIVISION (ARMY), COMMAND (R.A.F. or A.A.F.) R.A.F. Bomber

4. DATE OF BIRTH 8/4/19

5. DATE OF ENLISTMENT 10/10/39

6. CIVILIAN TRADE OR PROFESSION
   (OR EXAMINATIONS PASSED WHILE P/W)

7. PRIVATE ADDRESS 28 Ianw Copse, 2nd
   Twickenham, Middlesex

8. PLACE AND DATE OF ORIGINAL CAPTURE

9. WERE YOU WOUNDED WHEN CAPTURED? Yes

10. MAIN CAMPS OR HOSPITALS IN WHICH IMPRISONED.

Camp No.	Location	From	Till
Hospital/28F	Meiningen	2/5/44	30/8/45
Luft 3	Nurenberg	20/2/44	14/4/45
Stalag 7A	Moosburg	15/4/45	6/5/45

11. WERE YOU IN A WORKING CAMP?

Location	From	Till	Nature of Work

12. DID YOU SUFFER FROM ANY SERIOUS ILLNESSES WHILE A P/W?

Nature of Illness	Cause	Duration

(b) DID YOU RECEIVE ADEQUATE MEDICAL TREATMENT? Yes

TOP SECRET
M.I.9/Gen/
MIS-X

GENERAL QUESTIONNAIRE. PART II. TOP SECRET.

1. No. 905142   RANK F/Sgt   SURNAME JACKSON
   CHRISTIAN NAMES NORMAN CYRIL

2. LECTURES before Capture:
   (a) Were you lectured in your unit on how to behave in the event of capture? (State where, when and by whom).
   YES   106 SQD
   SQD COMMANDER

   (b) Were you lectured on escape and evasion? (State where, when and by whom).

3. INTERROGATION after capture:
   Were you specially interrogated by the enemy? (State where, when and methods employed by enemy).

4. ESCAPES attempted:
   Did you make any attempted or partly successful escapes? (Give details of each attempt separately, stating where, when, method employed, names of your companions, where and when recaptured and by whom. Were you physically fit? What happened to your companions?)

   ESCAPED FROM MARION MARSH
   ESCAPED FROM NEWMARK 8/10/08
   RECAPTURED 10 MILES FROM
   NUREMBURG 10/10/08. CAPTURED BY CIVIL
   POLICE. NO COMPANIONS I WAS FIT

5. SABOTAGE:
   Did you do any sabotage or destruction of enemy factory plant, war material, communications, etc., when employed on working-parties or during escape? (Give details, places and dates.)

6. COLLABORATION with enemy:
   Do you know of any British or American personnel who collaborated with the enemy or in any way helped the enemy against other Allied Prisoners of War? (Give details, names of person(s) concerned, camp(s), dates and nature of collaboration or help given to enemy).

7. WAR CRIMES:
   If you have any information or evidence of bad treatment by the enemy to yourself or to others, or knowledge of any enemy violation of Geneva Convention you should ask for a copy of "Form Q" on which to make your statement.
   (NOTE: Form Q is a separate form inviting information on "War Crimes" and describes the kinds of offences coming under this title.)

GENERAL QUESTIONNAIRE. PART II. TOP SECRET.
(*continued*)

TOP SECRET
M.I.9 Gen/
MIS-X

8. Have you any other matter of any kind you wish to bring to notice?

_____
_____
_____
_____
_____

SECURITY UNDERTAKING.

I fully realise that all information relating to the matters covered by the questions in Part II. are of a highly secret and official nature.

I have had explained to me and fully understand that under Defence Regulations or U.S.A.R. 380-5 I am forbidden to publish or communicate any information concerning these matters.

Date 7/5/45   Signature [signature]

Appendix 5: POW Questionnaire – Maurice Toft

GENERAL QUESTIONNAIRE. PART II. TOP SECRET.

TOP SECRET
M.I.9/Gen/
MIS-X

1. No. .... RANK .... SURNAME Toft

   CHRISTIAN NAMES Spencer Henry

2. LECTURES before Capture:
   (a) Were you lectured in your unit on how to behave in the event of capture? Yes
   (State where, when and by whom).
   ..... by Intelligence Officer F/Lt. Matthews (I.O.)
   ..... many escapees at sqdn.

   (b) Were you lectured on escape and evasion? (State where, when and by whom).
   ..... as above .....

3. INTERROGATION after capture:
   Were you specially interrogated by the enemy? (State where, when and methods employed by enemy).
   ..... No interrogation beyond a prolonged
   ..... persuade me to fill in a so called
   ..... Red form

4. ESCAPES attempted:
   Did you make any attempted or partly successful escapes? (Give details of each attempt separately, stating where, when, method employed, names of your companions, where and when recaptured and by whom. Were you physically fit? What happened to your companions?)
   No.

5. SABOTAGE:
   Did you do any sabotage or destruction of enemy factory plant, war material, communications, etc., when employed on working-parties or during escape? (Give details, places and dates.)
   No.

6. COLLABORATION with enemy:
   Do you know of any British or American personnel who collaborated with the enemy or in any way helped the enemy against other Allied Prisoners of War? (Give details, names of person(s) concerned, camp(s), dates and nature of collaboration or help given to enemy).
   No.

7. WAR CRIMES:
   If you have any information or evidence of bad treatment by the enemy to yourself or to others, or knowledge of any enemy violation of Geneva Convention you should ask for a copy of " Form Q " on which to make your statement.
   (NOTE: Form Q is a separate form inviting information on " *War Crimes* " and describes the kinds of offences coming under this title.)

GENERAL QUESTIONNAIRE. PART II. TOP SECRET.
(*continued*)

TOP SECRET
M.I.9 Gen/
MIS-X

8. Have you any other matter of any kind you wish to bring to notice?

SECURITY UNDERTAKING.

I fully realise that all information relating to the matters covered by the questions in Part II. are of a highly secret and official nature.

I have had explained to me and fully understand that under Defence Regulations or U.S.A.R. 380-5 I am forbidden to publish or communicate any information concerning these matters.

Date 11 of May 1945.   Signature

Appendix 6: POW Questionnaire – Frank Higgins

PART I.   M.I.9/Gen/
MIS-X

GENERAL QUESTIONNAIRE FOR BRITISH/AMERICAN EX-PRISONERS OF WAR.

1. No. 176171 RANK F/O SURNAME Higgins
   CHRISTIAN NAMES Frank Lewis
   DECORATIONS D.F.C.

2. SHIP (R.N., U.S.N. or MERCHANT NAVY)
   UNIT (ARMY)
   SQUADRON (R.A.F. or A.A.F.) 106 Sqdn

3. DIVISION (ARMY), COMMAND (R.A.F. or A.A.F.)

4. DATE OF BIRTH 26.6.22

5. DATE OF ENLISTMENT 16.6.41

6. CIVILIAN TRADE OR PROFESSION Seedsman
   (OR EXAMINATIONS PASSED WHILE P/W)

7. PRIVATE ADDRESS 87 King St Saffron
   Walden

8. PLACE AND DATE OF ORIGINAL CAPTURE Nr Stettin 23.8.44

9. WERE YOU WOUNDED WHEN CAPTURED? No

10. MAIN CAMPS OR HOSPITALS IN WHICH IMPRISONED.

Camp No.	Location	From	Till
Stalag Luft 4	Hydekrug E. Prussia		
357	Thorn Poland		
	Fallingbostel Hanover		

11. WERE YOU IN A WORKING CAMP? No

Location	From	Till	Nature of Work

12. DID YOU SUFFER FROM ANY SERIOUS ILLNESSES WHILE A P/W? No

Nature of Illness	Cause	Duration

(b) DID YOU RECEIVE ADEQUATE MEDICAL TREATMENT? Yes

GENERAL QUESTIONNAIRE. PART II. TOP SECRET.

1. No. 176171   RANK F/O   SURNAME HIGGINS

   CHRISTIAN NAMES FRANK LEWIS

2. LECTURES before Capture:
   (a) Were you lectured in your unit on how to behave in the event of capture? (State where, when and by whom).
   N OTU JUNE 44 UNKNOWN LECTURER

   (b) Were you lectured on escape and evasion? (State where, when and by whom).
   Yes N OTU JUNE 44

3. INTERROGATION after capture:
   Were you specially interrogated by the enemy? (State where, when and methods employed by enemy).
   No.

4. ESCAPES attempted:
   Did you make any attempted or partly successful escapes? (Give details of each attempt separately, stating where, when, method employed, names of your companions, where and when recaptured and by whom. Were you physically fit? What happened to your companions?)

5. SABOTAGE:
   Did you do any sabotage or destruction of enemy factory plant, war material, communications, etc., when employed on working-parties or during escape? (Give details, places and dates.)

6. COLLABORATION with enemy:
   Do you know of any British or American personnel who collaborated with the enemy or in any way helped the enemy against other Allied Prisoners of War? (Give details, names of person(s) concerned, camp(s), dates and nature of collaboration or help given to enemy).

7. WAR CRIMES:
   If you have any information or evidence of bad treatment by the enemy to yourself or to others, or knowledge of any enemy violation of Geneva Convention you should ask for a copy of "Form Q" on which to make your statement.

GENERAL QUESTIONNAIRE. PART II. TOP SECRET

(*continued*)

MIS-X

8. Have you any other matter of any kind you wish to bring to notice?

I wish to bring notice of the heroic action of [illegible]

[illegible]

[illegible]

[illegible]

[illegible]

[illegible]

Date 25-4-45 Signature [illegible]

his way to the rear of the fire in an attempt to [illegible]

[illegible]

the fire but due to the heat [illegible]

[illegible]

[illegible]

[illegible] he was blown off. [illegible]

[illegible]

in a very [illegible] burned condition.

[illegible]

Appendix 7: POW Questionnaire - Ernest Sandelands

CBF
B 13/7/45
TOP SECRET
PART I.
M.I.9. Gen/69777
MIS-X

GENERAL QUESTIONNAIRE FOR BRITISH/AMERICAN EX-PRISONERS OF WAR

1. No. 1060417 RANK F/SGT. SURNAME SANDELANDS.
   CHRISTIAN NAMES ERNEST.
   DECORATIONS NIL.

2. SHIP (R.N., U.S.N. or MERCHANT NAVY)
   UNIT (ARMY)
   SQUADRON (R.A.F. or A.A.F.) 106 SQUADRON R.A.F.

3. DIVISION (ARMY), COMMAND (R.A.F. or A.A.F.) 5 Group Bomber

4. DATE OF BIRTH JANUARY 10TH 1916.

5. DATE OF ENLISTMENT JULY 22nd 1940.

6. CIVILIAN TRADE OR PROFESSION TROLLEY BUS DRIVER.
   (OR EXAMINATIONS PASSED WHILE P/W)

7. PRIVATE ADDRESS C/o 200 WIGAN ROAD. HINDLEY. WIGAN. LANCASHIRE. ENGLAND.

8. PLACE AND DATE OF ORIGINAL CAPTURE APRIL 30TH/1944. STUTTGART.

9. WERE YOU WOUNDED WHEN CAPTURED? BURNS & EXTERNAL INJURIES.

10. MAIN CAMPS OR HOSPITALS IN WHICH IMPRISONED.

Camp No.	Location	From	Till
DULAG LUFT.	FRANKFURT-ON-MAINE	1/5/44	17/5/44
STALAG LUFT 6	HEYDEKRUG.	21/5/44	JULY/44
STALAG 357 (POLAND)	(POLAND) THORN	JULY/44	SEPTEMBER/44
" 357	FALLINGBOSTEL	SEPTEMBER/44	APRIL/45
ON THE MARCH TO LUBECK AREA.		APRIL 8TH	MAY 2nd

11. WERE YOU IN A WORKING CAMP?
    Location From Till Nature of Work
    NIL.

12. DID YOU SUFFER FROM ANY SERIOUS ILLNESSES WHILE A P/W?
    Nature of Illness Cause Duration

    (b) DID YOU RECEIVE ADEQUATE MEDICAL TREATMENT?

GENERAL QUESTIONNAIRE. PART II. TOP SECRET.

TOP SECRET
M.I.9/Gen/
MIS-X

1. No. *1060417* RANK *F/SGT.* SURNAME *SANDELANDS*
   CHRISTIAN NAMES *ERNEST*

2. LECTURES before Capture:
   (a) Were you lectured in your unit on how to behave in the event of capture? (State where, when and by whom).
   YES – ON O.T.U, CONVERSION UNIT & SQUADRON. BY INTELLIGENCE OFFICERS.

   (b) Were you lectured on escape and evasion? (State where, when and by whom).
   YES. AS ABOVE.

3. INTERROGATION after capture:
   Were you specially interrogated by the enemy? (State where, when and methods employed by enemy).
   YES. DULAG LUFT, APRIL 30TH TO MAY 8TH. SOLITARY CONFINEMENT. SUPER HEATED CELL WITHOUT FRESH AIR. (COLD CELL AT NIGHT) NOT ALLOWED TO WASH OR SHAVE. NO MEDICAL TREATMENT FOR 8 DAYS. POOR FOOD RATIONS — LIES — ETC.

4. ESCAPES attempted:
   Did you make any attempted or partly successful escapes? (Give details of each attempt separately, stating where, when, method employed, names of your companions, where and when recaptured and by whom. Were you physically fit? What happened to your companions?)
   NIL.

5. SABOTAGE:
   Did you do any sabotage or destruction of enemy factory plant, war material, communications, etc., when employed on working-parties or during escape? (Give details, places and dates.)
   NIL

6. COLLABORATION with enemy:
   Do you know of any British or American personnel who collaborated with the enemy or in any way helped the enemy against other Allied Prisoners of War? (Give details, names of person(s) concerned, camp(s), dates and nature of collaboration or help given to enemy).
   NIL.

7. WAR CRIMES:
   If you have any information or evidence of bad treatment by the enemy to yourself or to others, or knowledge of any enemy violation of Geneva Convention you should ask for a copy of " Form Q ", on which to make your statement.
   (NOTE : Form Q is a separate form inviting information on " War Crimes " and describes the kinds of offences coming under this title.)

GENERAL QUESTIONNAIRE. PART II. TOP SECRET.
(continued)

TOP SECRET
M.I.9 Gen/
MIS-X

8. Have you any other matter of any kind you wish to bring to notice?

INSUFFICIENT TREATMENT TO MY F/ENGINEERS INJURIES & BURNS. INSUFFICIENT FOOD. STARVATION DIET IN STALAG 357 FALLINGBOSTEL. REPRISALS (MATTRESSES, TABLES, FORMS, TAKEN AWAY. JANUARY/45. STALAG 357 FALLINGBOSTEL) FORCED MARCHES. WITHOUT MEDICAL OFFICERS. (EXCEPTING A FEW MEDICAL ORDERLIES) APRIL 8TH/45 TO MAY 2ND/45. NO MAIL, OR PERSONNAL PARCELS. LITTLE RED X Food) UNTIL CROSSING OF ELBE. ON MARCH.

SECURITY UNDERTAKING.

I fully realise that all information relating to the matters covered by the questions in Part II. are of a highly secret and official nature.

I have had explained to me and fully understand that under Defence Regulations or U.S.A.R. 380-5 I am forbidden to publish or communicate any information concerning these matters.

Date MAY 6TH 1945.   Signature F/Sgt. E. Sandilands.

Appendix 8: POW Questionnaire – Walter Smith

TOP SECRET
M.I.9/Gen/
MIS X **141885**

PART I.   PZ 30/8/45

GENERAL QUESTIONNAIRE FOR BRITISH/AMERICAN EX-PRISONERS OF WAR.

1. No. _1576279_ RANK _F/SGT_ SURNAME _SMITH_
   CHRISTIAN NAMES _WALTER_
   DECORATIONS _1939 — 43 STAR_

2. SHIP (R.N., U.S.N. or MERCHANT NAVY) _____
   UNIT (ARMY) _____
   SQUADRON (R.A.F. or A.A.F.) _106 Squadron_

3. DIVISION (ARMY), COMMAND (R.A.F. or A.A.F.) _____

4. DATE OF BIRTH _18/8/21_

5. DATE OF ENLISTMENT _1/10/41_

6. CIVILIAN TRADE OR PROFESSION _Electric Welder_
   (OR EXAMINATIONS PASSED WHILE P/W)

7. PRIVATE ADDRESS _13, Thornleigh, Savilstown, Dewsbury, Yorkshire, England_

8. PLACE AND DATE OF ORIGINAL CAPTURE _Near Stuttgart 30/4/44_

9. WERE YOU WOUNDED WHEN CAPTURED? _No_

10. MAIN CAMPS OR HOSPITALS IN WHICH IMPRISONED.

Camp No.	Location	From	Till
Luft. 3	Heydekrug	May 44	July 44
Stalag 357	Thorn, Poland	July 44	Aug. 44
Stalag 357	Fallingbostel	Aug. 44	April 45

11. WERE YOU IN A WORKING CAMP?

Location	From	Till	Nature of Work

12. DID YOU SUFFER FROM ANY SERIOUS ILLNESSES WHILE A P/W?

Nature of Illness	Cause	Duration

(b) DID YOU RECEIVE ADEQUATE MEDICAL TREATMENT?

Appendix 9: 'Johnny' Johnson's Letters Home

1398602 AC.2. Johnson
Hut 53 Room 2.
R.A.F. Station
Upavon Wilts
19.8.42.

Dear Mother & Dad,

Thank you for your which arrived this morning, & at the same time 10/- from the office, very nice indeed don't you think.

I'm afraid I'm developing into a regular old pot-hunter. Yesterday was sports day here, & I won the 1 mile & 3 mile, & got 7/6 in savings stamps for each & also 6/- same for best performance of the day.

I'm coming home on Friday evening, triumphant with my trophies, expect me home any time after about 7 p.m.

Yesterday was very successful taken all round, the sports started at about 10.30 am till dinner time & then continued in the afternoon & the day was finished off with a dance which ended at about 1 a.m, with half the people tight on N.A.A.F.I. beer.

I shall look forward to seeing Christopher, I hope he's tender

Will close now, hoping to see you on Friday evening, love to you all, your affectionate son

Hugh.

1398602 AC2 Johnson
R.A.F. Upavon.
26.10.42.

My dear Pam,

First of all, I must wish you many happy returns of your birthday the 28th. & I hope the small Postal Order will come in useful. I'm afraid I couldn't think what you would like & of course I didn't have much chance to go hunting around shops, but I'll bet you'll know what to buy with the cash. This may reach you a little early, as I'm leaving this morning at 8.15 a.m. for Weston Super Mare, as probably Mother has already told you, & then on Tuesday morning as long I've got through my medical exam, I go to London. Oh! that reminds me, tell Mother that I may be home on Tuesday for a couple of days, but I can't promise anything definite. I hope I can get home because I'll be able to have some of your birthday cake on Wednesday.

Well Pam dear, I must close now, & in case I can't get home, have a good time on Wednesday. Love to Mother & Dad & yourself, your loving brother Hugh

WARD II (A.)
R.A.F. HOSPITAL RAUCEBY.
NR. SLEAFORD.
LINCS.
7. 8. 43.

My dear Mother & Dad,
    Thank you your last letter, & also Mother for the note which Dad brought from you. Of course, it goes almost without saying so, how pleased I was to see you Dad, & I'm glad that you got back O.K.
    Incidently Mother, the bombardier's name is Toft, not Croft. I haven't seen him yet, but he very kindly sent me some cigarettes & chocolate from he & his wife, & a very

nice letter indeed, in which he told me that he'd been on the phone to you. I also received a letter from the Wireless Op.—Sandy. He told me in his letter that he hadn't told his wife about the crash, but that she asked him in the morning, why he'd been saying in his sleep — "Where's Johnny, Frank, for Christ's sake where's Johnny." This is because, presumably they went to the tail of the aircraft to look for me, but there wasn't any tail there.

Somehow it had, when it broke off, finished up about 50 yds. in front of the nose. This all sounds rather dramatic I know, but Biff who came to see me yesterday, told me, the same thing about the tail, & said that being rather shaken, they couldn't make out where I was for the moment. Anyway it's nice to know that they all thought of me when they'd got out. Biff couldn't say whether I'll be able to stick with the crew or not, but I know that, & he'll do his best to keep me with him. He doesn't know yet whether any blame will be attached to him, but said that everyone seems to be regarding it as a very bad bit luck, more than anything. He told me however, that the Group Captain visited him in sick quarters on the station & was very nice, saying that he wasn't to blame.

I didn't know that Jack had been in a crash, & I think that it's rather hard luck if he has got a fractured skull.

I almost forgot to thank you for the envelopes, & they have put me O.K. with regard to all writing material, so please don't send any more, thank you just the same for the kind thought. I shall however appreciate the fruit very much indeed.

I have now been moved out of the surash ward, but I'm still just as comfortable.

Well I must close now, with much love to you all
your affectionate son,
Hugh.

P.S. Mother, have you registered?

R.A.F. METHERINGHAM
LINCOLN
19.11.43

My dear Mother & Dad,
 Thank you so much for your letter & I shall look out for the handkerchiefs which you are sending.

Maurice also heard from his wife that she had met you in Kingston.

Miff can not send you his camera at

present, because he left it at South Shields with his friends up there. He says however that he will send for it, so I'll let you know later when it is coming.

With regard to the snap of the crew, it was taken before we had an Engineer & mid upper gunner.

5.

Also it was taken by Toft's camera, & he has the film.

I hoped you enjoyed having Bill Clark for the night, inspite of the making of the bed.

Thank you for taking my hat to be dyed, I am sure it'll look nice. Thank you also for taking my trousseau & slippers, & seeing about my tie.

I'm glad Pam had a letter from Cliff, but I'm sorry to hear that he may not be home until April.

Pleased to hear that Pam danced so well the other night. Also glad you enjoyed the dance so much

5.

Incidentally, I was initiated last night, Thursday night, by going on my first raid, which was on Berlin. Wasn't too bad at all, apart from the intense cold.

Must close now, with much love to you all, your affectionate son,
Hugh.

1398602. Sgt. Johnson.
Sgts' Mess
R.A.F Metheringham
Lincoln.
28.11.43

My dear Mother & Dad,
   Thank you so much for your letter, & you were correct. I forgot to post that one to you, & then there was no collection on Sunday, so it did not go until Monday. I'm afraid I have not been able

to write to you for a few days, because on Wed & Thursday, we were at another station, having some new secret gun stuff fitted on the kite, & I of course had no writing materials with me. We came back here on Friday about lunch time, & that evening we paid another visit to Berlin, which was the third time

3.

for me. On returning from our said visit, we were diverted to Yorkshire, & did not get back until last night. So you can see that I've been pretty busy these last few days, & this has been my first opportunity to write.

Phew! what an explanation.

Yes, the electric suit does keep me warm, apart from my hands which generally get a little cold. The main trouble is, condensation in the oxygen mask & microphone, is liable to freeze & often does, especially the mike, & then you can't speak to anyone.

I shall certainly look out for Walt

Disney's, "Dav in th Air."
I've heard from other sources
that it is very good.

By the way, please excuse
change in paper, but I've
just started a new pad.

I'm glad you all enjoyed
your dancing lesson, & how
many are you going to
take or haven't you decided?

That was very kind of
Mrs Collin to send her
love, please thank her & give

her my kindest regards.

Thank you also for sending Babs's love, & will you also in your next letter, send me her address, I've mislaid it.

Dad, I hope you enjoyed your birthday cake, which mother made. I'm much afraid that your present will have to wait until I'm on leave, as there are so few shops around here, & it's dreadful to try & get into Lincoln.

At the moment, I'm

waiting to see if the rain will stop so that I can go & see if my parcel has arrived yet. Well while I'm waiting I'll write to Pam & enclose it with this if you don't mind.

Having written it, I've decided that it will be too much in one envelope, so I'm sending it seperately.

By the way, will you please find something for me to give to Pam for

Christmas, because as I said earlier in this epistle, it is very difficult to do any shopping around here. There are only the local villages, which of course have nothing, & it is impossible to get Lincoln in time for shopping. What a lot of weak excuses.

To-day – Monday, parcel has arrived for which many thanks. I'll give my verdict on cake later when I've tasted it.

Cheerio, much love to you both, your affectionate son Hugh

Sgts' Mess.
R.A.F. Metheringham.
Lincoln.
18.4.44

My dear Mother & Dad,
    I arrived back quite safely yesterday after, not too bad a journey. Betty met me on Tuesday at Huntingdon, & I stayed at her camp, leaving there at lunch time yesterday.
    I'm still feeling a little tired after the

2
NOT CONCENTRATING!

rather hectic, ~~and sad~~ but most pleasant leave.

Having arrived in Lincoln, I decided to spend the evening there, so I proceeded to the Gt. Northern where I met Frank, & also F/Lt. Rayhauld, the one who used to box at school. I also met his wife who had just arrived to stay a few days. He of course only came back recently from Italy.

Please thank Cliff for my keys he had returned, by registered, I collected them to-day.

Well as usual, having just returned there is very little to write about, so I'll bring this epistle to a close.

Thank you again my dears for your Easter present, it was very kind indeed of you.

I hope Pam is enjoying the rest of her holiday.

Much love to you all, yours affectionately

Hugh.

P.S. Duff is now fit.

Appendix 10: Letter to Cliff Johnson from Ernest Sandelands.

c/o. 200. Wigan Road
Hindley
Wigan. Lancashire
Nov. 1st / 1945.

Dear Cliff,

It was a delight to read your letter, this morning, and I never expected such pleasing news. that you are so close to us. - and, apparently, "in the pink".

It seems so long since Nottingham days. - and. then there are times, very many times when - to me - we are still, all together - awaiting the next Op. Sharing the same joys - the same laughs; the same sorrows. "Flying off the handle" - and clapping each other at the each and everyone, successes.

2

How it all comes back. when one sits around with those silent thoughts. I remember so well when you came down to the Squadron. The good time we had together! The "scrap" we had in the Nissen hut at night! (A regular occurrence with our crew!) - and, I remember too, your last night with us. (Remember. Cliff? "Johnny" had "gone out" that night with F/Lt. Ginger. "Black" Nuremberg.) You were sleeping at the top end of the hut. You never saw the anxious looks that Frank and myself exchanged. across the room. It was getting around 8.30 a.m. - and no "Johnny."
    Then "Johnny" came.
(But. let me go. on Cliff! my heart is master of my pen - and

5

I must "talk" it out.)
Often I go over that last "op"
- over every minute from breakfast
to briefing - from briefing to
take-off and take off to –
all that followed.
We took "Uncle" on test that
afternoon of April 25th/44. It
was only by a miracle then
that we lived. The fitters had
"booked" with the elevators. Kiff
& Jackie kept her flying - and
we landed - a little white - and
with two fitters, who came with
us - looking deathly.
We took "OBOE" to Schweinfurt.
My last fleeting smile with
Johnny at the Rear entrance
will ever remain with me.
It was "Thumbs Up" to the
last.
I have "seen him" many times since.

Cliff. I shall always see him. For I shall always want to.

Sorry Cliff. I hope you don't mind.

I have been home now since August 1st. just awaiting a posting to Resettlement and Demobbing. But these last weeks. we (Lilian & myself) have been chasing around like someone mad. We have had the good fortune - and it is good fortune these days! - to get the tenancy of a house. in this locality. We never had much furniture of our own. or carpets & fittings. (After Dorothy's death - Lilian had her world "knocked out" of her.) However. We had the Utility Dockets etc. come through the other day – and what a job we have had trying to spin them out. There is very little encouragement. with todays stocks – and prices. to "set up" house anywhere. With luck – we hope to "be in" within a fortnight.

That is the state that your letter has caught us in –! Plaster. and Paint – all over the place." But, we've always time to "pack up" for a meeting with you Cliff – and I am leaving to you to write making a date that suits you best. We are at home all the time – yet! and your hours may not be so arranged. If you find yourself this way. at all. come right over to this address. There's a welcome always. So. Cliff reply

and give us the day. when
we could see you. I'll be along
with Lilian. She wants to see
Liverpool. for some shopping.
    Personally. I don't see
why we should shop. Cliff...!!!
    So. Thanks again. for remembering
I have not forgotten Mrs Johnson
I'll be down. don't worry. Cliff.
(If Walter Smith had taken any
notice of me - we would have
been down 2 months ago).
    Cheerio Cliff.
        Sincerely
        Ernest Sunderlands.

Appendix 11: Air Ministry Letter to Johnny's Father.

DH

Tel. No.
SLOANE 3467 Ext............. .....

AIR MINISTRY,
2, SEVILLE STREET,
LONDON, S.W.I.

P.416458/44/S.14.Cas.C.7.

1st May, 1948.

Dear Mr. Johnson,

    I am very sorry to renew your grief in the sad loss of your son Flight Sergeant N.H. Johnson, but I feel sure you will wish to know that a report has now been received from the Royal Air Force Missing Research and Enquiry Service operating in Germany who have been investigating the fate of his aircraft and crew.

    The Search Officers' report reveals that the aircraft crashed in the early hours of the morning of the 27th April, 1944, approximately one mile west of Kirchensall and that the two members of the crew who lost their lives, were buried by the Germans as "unknown" in a Communal Grave in Wuerttemberg.

    Exhumation was undertaken and you will be glad to know it was possible to establish the individual identity of your son and Flying Officer Mifflin, D.F.C., who will later be reverently re-interred in a British Military Cemetery.

    This policy of reburial has been agreed upon by His Majesty's and the Commonwealth Governments because it is felt that our fallen in Germany should not be left in isolated cemeteries, but should be reverently re-interred in British Military Cemeteries specially selected for the beauty and peace of their surroundings and where the graves will be maintained for all time by the Imperial War Graves Commission.

    You will be informed when this takes place and the Commission will consult you later regarding the inscription

/upon

H. Johnson, Esq.,
   71, Gloucester Road,
      Hampton,
         Middlesex.

upon the headstone they will erect to his memory.

I do sincerely hope the information I have now been able to give will afford you some consolation in the great loss you have sustained.

Yours sincerely,

Burch

Appendix 12: Letter from Miff to Johnny's Father.

Mr Mason

277 Stanhope Rd.,
South Shields.

RCAF   March 26/44

Dear Mr. Johnson:-

Rec'd your letter re-directed from Raueby, a couple of days ago and was very glad to hear from you again.

I bet that it has been good having all the boys back home again. Guess they painted the town pretty thoroughly.

Re-watch. I'm darn sorry if I put you to any inconvenience. I should have known from the price of the watch that you got for me that you had gotten it through friends. Anyhow I didn't promise to get her one so it doesn't make any difference.

323

2.

Yes I saw Johnny just after he came back off leave. He's looking fine and has done a couple of trips recently.

Thanks a lot for the invitation to stay with you people and I'd love to see you all again. However I had promised these people that I would come here and so my bed was made. Nevertheless I may see you in the near future.

Give my kindest regards to the family and I trust that you are all well.

Love & best wishes to you all,

Appendix 13: 1943 Christmas Card from Miff.

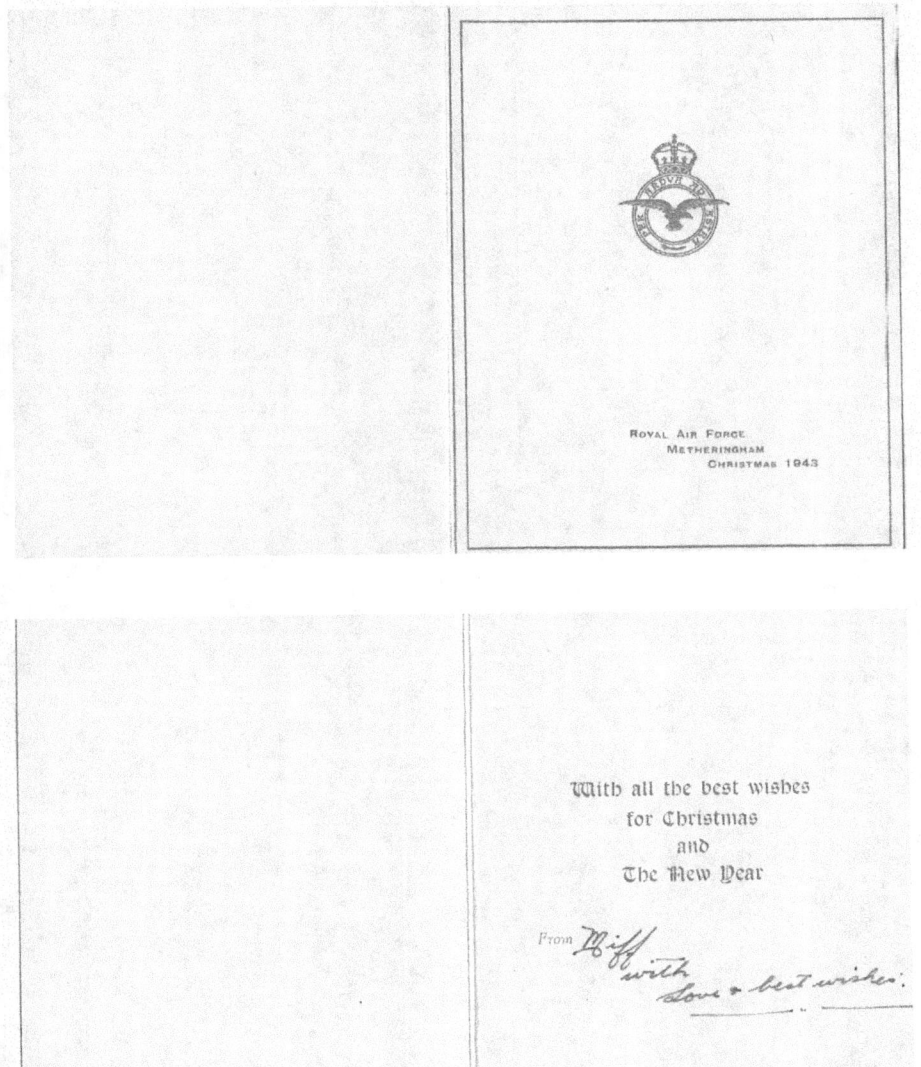

About The Author

David Jackson was born in Hampton Hill Middlesex and now lives with his partner Penelope in West Sussex. He was educated at a private school and went on to study history at university. David runs his own electrical company along with having dabbled over the years in property development with Penelope who is a fitness instructor.

David is a qualified pilot and has always had a passion for any form of aviation history. For many years he had planned to write this book, and it was only when asked to give a talk to a Royal Air Force group about his father, that in preparing for the talk the manuscript started to take form, and he started to believe that he could write the book.

Norman Jackson was always a great inspiration in David's life and gave encouragement in adopting a positive attitude towards any issues that life throws at us, saying, "We do not have problems, only solutions," and that statement David uses to this day. The solution to fulfilling a lifetime passion to write this book was to get on and do it.

David and Penelope are both keen sailors and a good deal of this book was written while on their yacht *Lady Penelope* in the Greek Islands. This gave David the time for the necessary in-depth research, not only trying to get every detail correct, but endeavouring to create an emotional connection between the reader of this book and the courageous young men of Bomber Command.

These men, of whom Norman Jackson considered himself but one amongst many, should never be forgotten and deserve their nation's appreciation, honour and respect.

David Michael Jackson.

Spring 2025

www.ingramcontent.com/pod-product-compliance
Lightning Source LLC
Chambersburg PA
CBHW070750230426
43665CB00017B/2320